Design by Accident
For a New History of Design

Alexandra Midal

Design by Accident

For a New History of Design

Sternberg Press

Preface

Design history and its interlocutors—practitioners, educators, manifesto makers—have long had an identity crisis. Searching for not only a home but an origin story, design history has hovered somewhere within the human sciences, never sitting comfortably—and rightly so—in the shadow of so-called sister disciplines such as art history. Written by historians of architecture and instrumentalized, as the author of this book highlights, "as a prism through which social change could be explored, rather than an independent field of study in itself," design history has been fashioned in the hands of others as a tool for their use rather than shaping its own identities and destinies. The field has come into being, as the title of this text invokes, somewhat unintentionally.

Enter Alexandra Midal.

I had long known her name and admired her work by the time I first encountered in person the full force of Alexandra Midal's genre-bending and expansive mind. A few years ago, when I worked at the Museum of Modern Art, in New York, we collaborated (alongside Paola Antonelli) on an ambitious (and some might say foolhardy) eight-hour-long public program. In advance of the 2017 exhibition "Items: Is Fashion Modern?," the impetus was to find a compelling way to investigate the historical lacuna around fashion design in the near ninety-year history of collecting and exhibiting at that institution. Alexandra suggested her abecedarium format, a veritable durational speed date between audience and speakers in which twenty-six presenters each took on a pinpoint-specific topic. The end result was somewhere between a circus performance, a Happening, and a scholarly symposium. It was a hit. Its success rested, to a great extent, in the audacious leap into the void Alexandra led us on—curators, institution, and audience—taking on a subject whose edges were hard to discern, and dissecting it with such judicious and surgical precision that its dismembered whole might be critically considered, clarified, and reconstituted anew. As with fashion's histories in the abecedarium, so too with design's histories in this book.

Design by Accident is a genealogical odyssey that masterfully—and critically, and lovingly—interweaves stories and ideas, casting back and forth between center, periphery, the long forgotten, and the never recognized to establish design as a field with discernable and deliberate points of formation and growth. This is no mean feat. This project confronts a "history divided between facts and propaganda," adumbrating polarities that include design's canonical heroes (William Morris, Peter Behrens, Walter Gropius), those who remain anonymous, and the gendered nature of writing history (an electrifying intervention poses Catharine Beecher's domestic economy as a precursor to all the men who followed her and tried, and often failed, to rationalize the family home). The book's subtitle, "For a New History of Design," marks out its original contribution, articulating with a unwavering richness of historical and conceptual references a palimpsest of histories, practitioners, and moments that form a landscape distinct from (although always in conversation with) that of architecture or the fine arts.

One of the first projects I have been involved with at my new institution, the Philadelphia Museum of Art, is an exhibition on design and different futures; this book is a timely reminder that one cannot look forward without a holistic and critical understanding of one's past, and that history is not knowledge accumulated but knowledge constructed. Whether the historical path we internalize, teach, or piece together finds its genesis in Morris or Beecher, in the work of Nikolaus Pevsner or Sigfried Giedion, in the anonymous hand, or somewhere entirely different, it is imbricated with politics. Turning such an historiographical journey into a compelling polemic that celebrates and synthesizes the heterogenity of its findings without essentializing is an unenviable task. Yet here, in lyrically composed vignettes, Midal makes this daunting task look almost easy. Within these pages lies a deliberate, powerful, and ambitious manifesto that charts, from the nineteenth century to the present, the emergence of design as an autonomous discipline. As the author asserts, it is a "history of design in its own terms." It is, finally, one for our own times too.

Michelle Millar Fisher
Louis C. Madeira IV Assistant Curator
of European Decorative Arts
Philadelphia Museum of Art

Foreword

Design is central to life, progress, and survival. It is a complex and complete creative endeavor that encompasses science, engineering, art, history, politics, economy, sociology, and more—as well as a deep understanding of human nature. It is a massively important field of physical and intellectual activity. But it has not yet found its firm and just position in academia and in culture.

It is typical of design curators, critics, and academics to "cry over themselves," as they say in Italy, and lament having been intellectually soft and unable to confirm the independence of our field in front of the bench of theory and culture. We have bemoaned the lack of a proper design history as long as we can remember. We have looked up to more established disciplines like architecture and art, envied their gravitas and their ability to create records, histories, and mythologies. We have complained about our intellectual and academic dependency on architecture and art, blamed them for holding on to our umbilical cord, sought emancipation.

However, our real sin seems to have been laziness. Histories and theories, manifestos and aphorisms, unalternative facts can be found in scores to sustain strong design autonomy. Assertions, explanations, and incursions abound, but no one ever bothered to link them, compare them, and gather them in a critical study. Thankfully, Alexandra Midal has never been the lazy—or the passive-aggressive, or the closed-minded—type.

She begins this book by calling upon Joe Colombo's declaration, "Design is a totality which encompasses architecture, urbanism, production, and the means of communication [...]. Design is therefore reality, life, the essential." That is a strong declaration of intent. Indeed, throughout the book she builds up a crescendo of revealing connections and juxtapositions, and ends by affirming in her own voice the current centrality of design and its capacity to accommodate, and even absorb other disciplines. It is at the same time a personal path, and the path of a whole field of academia and practice.

Indeed, this book is an act of design onto itself, where the author uses all the means at her disposal without ever losing sight of the goal, making sure that the final synthesis is elegant and whole, much more than the sum of its parts, and necessary.

It is an important time to present a clarification, to declare the emancipation of design. The field has exploded into a world-building universe of concentrations —visualization design, information architecture, collective design, interaction design, interface design, critical design, and social design are only a few of the possible areas of practice that have been added to the good, old-fashioned products, furnishings, textiles, interiors, and graphics of yesteryear. And, lest we forget, design has embraced also architecture, landscape, urban planning, and beyond.

Spoon to city, lipstick to locomotive, atom to complex system, Alexandra Midal's theory encompasses all scales. Bold and assertive, it claims a territory (both academic and disciplinary) that design has invaded over decades, at times timidly, at times forcefully enough as to be attacked by the antibodies of the architecture and art establishments, often using design's honest and unambiguous relationship to commerce as a way to put it back in its place (the "commercial arts"). But even when it comes to invasions, design proves to be the most vital, useful, and contemporary cultural attitude. Respectful, curious, generous, and hungry for other fields' bodies of knowledge and expertise, designers invade without colonizing. Who can we trust more? They should run the world.

Paola Antonelli
Senior Curator, Department of Art and Design
Museum of Modern Art, New York

Introduction

For the Emancipation of Design

The History of Design: A Tale of Two Architectural Historians

Taken together, Nikolaus Pevsner's *Pioneers of the Modern Movement* and Sigfried Giedion's *Mechanization Takes Command* could be considered the founding texts of the history of design.[1] In his 1936 work, Pevsner retraces the history of the Modern Movement, whose origins he locates in the invention of the machine, from William Morris and British utilitarianism to Walter Gropius and German functionalism. Pevsner points out that "Gropius regards himself as a follower of Ruskin and Morris, of Van de Velde and of the Werkbund," and allows this notion of a direct line of descent to go unchallenged.[2] In fact, he sees in the work of his friend Gropius the culmination of a "cycle" or period of "transition," as he discusses in his first chapter, "Theories of Art from Morris to Gropius." Pevsner seeks to establish a singular, unitary starting point for modernity, which for him necessarily lies between 1890 and the dawn of the First World War. His argument is that "Morris laid the foundation of the modern style [and] with Gropius its character was ultimately determined,"[3] something that is made explicit by the subtitle of his work, "From William Morris to Walter Gropius," which presents a succession of heroic figures who follow one another in a homogeneous lineage. Citing the exemplary nature of the factory plan presented by Gropius and Adolf Meyer at the exhibition organized by the Deutscher Werkbund in Cologne in 1914,

1 Nikolaus Pevsner, *Pioneers of the Modern Movement: From William Morris to Walter Gropius* (London: Faber & Faber, 1936). Sigfried Giedion, *Mechanization Takes Command: A Contribution to Anonymous History* [1948] (New York: Norton, 1969).
2 Pevsner, *Pioneers of the Modern Movement*, 42.
3 Ibid.

Pevsner's historical project considers that the Modern Movement drew upon a nascent industrialization as it was showing its first signs of maturity, and by 1914 had established itself, culminating in 1914 in a way that ensured functionalist ideas alone would determine the future of modern architecture.

Giedion's *Mechanization Takes Command* was published twelve years later and, in terms of both its form and discursive content, it bears little resemblance to *Pioneers of the Modern Movement*. Giedion's book, whose first edition was printed by Oxford University Press in 1948, encompasses a vast range of subjects: locks and bolts, the baking of bread, the butchering of pig carcasses in Chicago's slaughterhouses, furniture, washing, and personal hygiene as well as modes of transport and the rational organization of space. The work thus investigates the exchanges between technological progress and social evolution. Giedion's approach is markedly different from Pevsner's, drawing on everything from the practices of ancient Egypt to those of the French Enlightenment in order to put together a history of innovation—its processes, transformations, and consequences—without turning its back on the history of art. In Giedion's narrative, the evolution of the techniques that unite the aesthetic and the mechanical becomes a triumphant story of progress.

What, then, can be achieved by looking at these two texts together? What do they have in common, aside from offering two versions of the history of design and its origins written almost contemporaneously? Both aspire toward an objective approach and offer a scheme of reference points from which it is possible to analyze design from its very beginnings. Yet rather than offering a history of design tout court, these two works, when read together, offer one possible history of modern design.

If it is unusual to be able to refer with certainty to the founding texts of a discipline, an examination of the intentions behind these two works raises serious questions around the very existence of design. Both texts were produced by authors considered to be major critics associated with the Modern Movement in architecture, for whom design was far from a primary or even secondary concern. Pevsner's project sought to explain the true functionalist origins of the Modern Movement, in order to promote and assert its validity within a hostile context. Pevsner's predecessor as the first secretary of the Congrés internationaux d'architecture moderne (CIAM), Giedion aimed to establish an archaeology of technique. His was a rationalist project that drew on scientific and artistic references in order to demonstrate the coherent internal evolution brought about by the central concept of mechanization. Neither Pevsner nor Giedion set out to establish a history of design as such. For them, design was a functionalist anchor to a wider line of thought. This peculiarity at the very origin of design—its accidental nature—has, until now, gone unexamined.

My title, *Design by Accident: For a New History of Design*, references this ambiguity at the origin of the unintentional project that is design. The notion of the accident frames the history of design as an incursion into a narrative preoccupied by architecture and industrialization. But the emergence of design cannot be approached without taking into account its impact in the fields of art and architecture. As such, *Design by Accident* is also a nod to the 1961 article "Design by Choice" by Reyner Banham,[4] the first historian to break rank with the orthodoxy of modern architecture and set out the conditions for design's singularity.

4 Reyner Banham, "Design by Choice: 1951–1961," *Architectural Review*, July 1961, 43–48; reprinted as "Design by Choice," in Reyner Banham, *Design by Choice*, ed. Penny Sparke (London: Academy Editions, 1981), 97–107.

Banham's essay opposes architecture and design in order to free the latter from the frame imposed upon it by architecture's notion of "total design."

Reading the works of Pevsner and Giedion together with a view to reconsidering the origins of design is an unprecedented project. Historians of design have, for the most part, focused on industrial culture and technology, or have deftly analyzed it in social, economic, and cultural terms. The question of design's origin—and the possibility of constructing a history of design in its own terms—has until now been absent from these debates, with a few rare exceptions. Clive Dilnot's two-part essay "The State of Design History" is one such example.[5] It charts the early forms of design history while noting the absence in the history of design between Pevsner's 1936 work, which relied upon the history of art and of architecture, and Banham's 1960 publication *Theory and Design in the First Machine Age*, which cast a critical eye on Pevsner's theses and broke with them to establish an altogether new historical perspective. Although Giedion's work is cited in the footnotes, Dilnot does not integrate such a historical point of view into his argument, judging it to be too far removed from Pevsner's outlook. Dilnot's interpretation does not shy away from drawing attention to design's improbable origins, nor does it ignore the peculiar way in which its history relies simultaneously upon self-reference and upon the promotion of a distinctly socioeconomic model for its organization. Another perspective comes from Victor Margolin, who was co-director of the journal *Design Issues*,

5 Clive Dilnot, "The State of Design History, Part I: Mapping the Field," *Design Issues* 1, no. 1 (Spring 1984): 3–20; and "The State of Design History, Part II: Problems and Possibilities," Design Issues 1, no. 2 (Autumn 1984): 3–24. Both were reprinted in Victor Margolin, ed., *Design Discourse: History, Theory, Criticism* (Chicago: University of Chicago Press, 1989), on pages 213–32 and 233–50, respectively. Citations here refer to the reprints.

in which Dilnot published his texts on the history and theory of design. Together with design theorist Tony Fry, Margolin subscribes to a tradition that approaches the history of design in terms of its practice, judging any attempt to define design exclusively in its own terms to be necessarily limiting, and maintaining that the discipline's vast scope calls for a "pluralistic vision."[6]

This is precisely why it is necessary to consider the conditions necessary for design's autonomy, an idea previously toyed with by John Blake, then director of the British Design Council, in a 1978 speech:

> What seems to me to be of profound importance is that the history of design should encompass all these aspects so that sooner or later you begin to get a kind of coagulation of ideas into a recognisable body of knowledge which can be unequivocably labelled "design history"—not as an appendage of the history of art, not as an appendage of the history of architecture, not as an appendage of the history of technology, or of anything else for that matter—though with obvious connections to all these things.[7]

The present project seems all the more justified given the fact that Pevsner's and Giedion's texts not only have escaped comparative study but also have yet to be evoked together to investigate the possibility of a singular and objective history of design.[8] To this end, I will return to these two texts to explore their potential role in such a

6 Victor Margolin, "Design History and Design Studies," in *The Politics of the Artificial: Essays on Design and Design Studies* (Chicago: University of Chicago Press, 2002), 218–33.
7 John Blake, "The Context for Design History," in *Design History: Fad or Function?*, ed. Terry Bishop (London: Design Council, 1978).
8 With the exception of the comparison made by Judy Attfield in her text "FORM/female FOLLOWS FUNCTION/male: Feminist Critiques of Design," in John A. Walker, *Design History and the History of Design* (London: Pluto Press, 1989), 199–225.

history, and the complex questions they raise around the foundation, emergence, and evolution of the history of design. Though these two authors have a number of commonalities—their emigration backgrounds, their defense of a Modern Movement still in search of recognition and success—their respective works have clearly distinct objectives. However, both narratives offer visions that, taken together, can be read as a single historiographic project providing a continuum that is an apt space for reflecting upon the construction of a *new history of design*. This work interrogates the validity and permanence of the history that coalesced through and around these texts. I analyze the evolution of this history with reference to its original reception, and explore the key traits that characterized its retrospective construction, with a view to articulating the history of design as a discipline.

The scope of this project is made even vaster by the fact that since 1936 few historiographical works with design as their subject have been published.[9] A recent renewal of interest in this history can be explained by the continued dominance of modernist ideology since Pevsner's time. According to Dilnot, who addresses this question in a number of essays—notably "The State of Design History, Part I: Mapping the Field" and "The State of Design History, Part II: Problems and Possibilities"—this absence can be explained through a combination of factors, but in particular "a rampant anti-intellectualism, combined with the dominance of the fine arts, the history of art, and the idea of 'culture' in art and design schools that served to make all discussions of design in any historical sense more or less impossible."[10] Dilnot posits that the history of design only became possible once Pevsner's model had been challenged, a process set in motion with the 1960 publication of Banham's *Theory and Design in the First Machine Age.*[11] Banham saw the emergence of this history as resulting from the passing of the theoretical torch from architects—in particular by Charles Eames, who Banham called "the last figure from the architectural side to make a significant contribution with his *Ahmedabad Report* to design thinking"[12]—to

9 Clive Dilnot leaves to one side *Mechanization Takes Command*, which he describes as a "problematic" and "curious work," on the grounds that it has never fully been assimilated into design history. He puts the fundamental question in the following terms: "What is implied by the current simultaneous rise of a need for history on all design fronts? And will the answer explain the otherwise puzzling absence of design history between 1936 and the late 1960s?" Dilnot, "The State of Design History, Part I," in Margolin, *Design Discourse*, 218.

10 Ibid.

11 Ibid., 219.

12 Banham continues: "Otherwise, architects have relinquished control of the mind of design to theorists and critics from practically any field under the sun." Banham, "Design by Choice," in *Design by Choice*, 97.

theorists and historians. The first significant milestone in the historiography of design dates to 1972, the year in which the Open University began to offer its first course on the history of modern architecture and design. Overseen by architectural historian Tim Benton and his numerous guests, History of Architecture and Design 1890–1939 gave rise to a number of publications and high quality television and radio programs. These were soon followed in 1978 by *Design History: Fad or Function?*, an anthology of texts that sought to establish the history of design as a discipline.

In the 1980s, the history of design began to appear as a subject in its own right, for example in the 1986 work by Penny Sparke, *An Introduction to Design and Culture in the Twentieth Century*,[13] where she analyzes the tenets of consumerism and sketches a portrait of "the designer" as a free and independent figure in opposition to consumption in its various guises. Two years later, Adrian Forty would prolong this line of thought in his work *Objects of Desire: Design and Society since 1750*, where he drew a distinction between fine art and design according to their sociological and economic dimensions. Despite the clear domination of Anglo-American voices,[14] *La casa calda* by architect Andrea Branzi was published in 1984.[15] An enthusiastic reader of Banham,[16]

13 Penny Sparke, *An Introduction to Design and Culture in the Twentieth Century* [1986] (London: Routledge, 2004).

14 See, for example, Walker, *Design History and the History of Design*, which offers a successive and cursory analysis of the various fields and analytical methods of design. When the text was published in 1989, Walker was the first to call for the history of design to be established as a discipline, making a distinction between the field of study ("history of design") and the academic discipline ("design history"). Walker considers the term "discipline" to mean "the ensemble of assumptions, concepts, theories, methods and tools employed by a particular group of scientists or scholars" (39). Walker goes on to analyze mechanisms of production and consumption in Marxist terms. See also the interdisciplinary journal *Block*, edited by Jon Bird, Lisa Tickner, Barry Curtis, and John A. Walker, and published by the New Art History department at Middlesex Polytechnic from 1979 to 1989. *Block* imagined new methodologies for the history of art by doing away with hierarchical distinctions between fine art, design, and graphic design.

15 Andrea Branzi, *La casa calda: Esperienze del nuovo design italiano* (Milan: Idea Books, 1984); published in English as *The Hot House: Italian New Wave Design*, trans. C. H. Evans (Cambridge, MA: MIT Press, 1984).

16 It is somewhat surprising that Branzi fails to cite Banham in his history.

who had reintroduced the Italian Futurists into the history of architecture, Branzi in turn integrated the group into his history of Italian design. Translated the year of its publication into English (*The Hot House*) and French, the book was highly successful. A founding member of Archizoom Associati, and later Global Tools, Branzi gave his work a gloss of neutrality beneath which he set out key concepts of radical architecture and further developed the group's critical and ironic arguments. As the reference to temperature in Branzi's title implies, the book was the latest salvo in a debate dating back to 1967 around the vulgarization of industrial design and the functionalism that Branzi associated with his proclaimed enemy, designer and Ulm School professor Tomás Maldonado.[17] In addition to the accusations it leveled against modern architecture, Branzi's thesis also dealt with the powerlessness of architecture in and of itself and, due to its position at the very heart of the market, conferred upon design the status of an instrument, one that shapes and reshapes architecture and society at once.

In the United States, in the same period, major works on design were issuing from the hub that formed around the University of Chicago Press and Victor Margolin. With *Design Discourse*, *Discovering Design*,[18] and perhaps most importantly the scientific quarterly *Design Issues: A Journal of History, Theory and Criticism*, founded in 1982 by Margolin and Richard Buchanan and modeled on the

17 Branzi aligned rationalism with lower temperatures and emotionality with higher ones. This thermal take on the history of twentieth-century design was also taken up by Alessandro Mendini in 1990. For Tomás Maldonado, this opposition was not viable for the Modern Movement and its critics. He refuted the notion that postmodern designers held a monopoly over the qualities and meanings associated with "hot design," arguing that these were in fact constant features of design as a whole, across different periods and movements. See Tomás Maldonado, "Design caldo vs. design freddo," in *Disegno industriale: Un riesame* [1976] (Milan: Feltrinelli, 1999), 77–79.

18 Richard Buchanan and Victor Margolin, eds., *Discovering Design: Explorations in Design Studies* (Chicago: University of Chicago Press, 1985).

journal *October*, a space was created for design and its history that more closely resembled the field of cultural studies than art or of architecture. However, the victory of design as an independent discipline was far from set in stone. Whether it was Nigel Whiteley in *Design for Society*,[19] Buchanan and Margolin in *Discovering Design*, or Guy Julier in *Culture of Design*,[20] historians were unanimous in their agreement that the history of design had yet to be fully established.

It was not until the 1980s that the first analyses of design fully distinct from Pevsner's hitherto unquestioned approach began to appear: in the United States, Arthur J. Pulos's *American Design Ethic*,[21] and in the United Kingdom, Sparke's *Introduction to Design and Culture*. However, this current remained minor in the field of design criticism and history, and if it has remained the preserve of Anglo-American design historians, this is doubtless because of the fact that Pevsner was little read by their French counterparts.

In contrast to these methodological texts and manifestos on design, German thinker Siegfried Maser's *A Few Comments on the Problem of a Design Theory* (1972) set out

19 Nigel Whiteley, *Design for Society* (London: Reaktion Books, 1993). Whiteley examines design from an anti-consumerist perspective, rejecting its association with consumer goods that respond to consumerist desires in order to look at the ways in which design enriches society.

20 Guy Julier, *Culture of Design* (London: Sage Publications, 2000). Julier revisits the notion of "design culture" already advanced by Sparke in *An Introduction to Design and Culture* to consider design both as an object of study and an academic discipline.

21 Arthur J. Pulos, *American Design Ethic: A History of Industrial Design* (Cambridge, MA: MIT Press, 1983). Pulos begins his history of American design—the first of its kind—with the New York World's Fair in 1939, which established the profession of the industrial designer as advocating a progressive and future-facing ideology, at the same time as staking a claim to the territories of urbanism, architecture, and the habitat. Pulos locates the origins of design in the projects of the Shakers, founded by James and Jane Wardley in England in 1747, before they were forced into exile in America in 1774. However, he dedicates most of his attention to the creators of American Streamline: Norman Bel Geddes, Raymond Loewy, Egmont Arens, Henry Dreyfuss, et al.

22 Siegfried Maser, *Einige Bemerkungen zu einer Theorie des Design* (Braunschweig: self-pub., 1972); published in English as *A Few Comments on the Problem of a Design Theory*, Design Papers 2 (Halifax: Nova Scotia College of Art and Design, 1979).

a sociological history of design.[22] This work was followed by that of Bernd Löbach and Helmut Schmidt, who approached design through a theory of applied systems,[23] and more recently by *The Shape of Things: A Philosophy of Design*, a collection of texts by the Czech philosopher Vilém Flusser, originally published in German.[24] In Switzerland, by contrast, interest seems to have centered on the history of graphic design, and of typography in particular.[25] Italy, meanwhile, has seen a lively debate driven by figures such as Branzi and the art historian and politician Giulio Carlo Argan,[26] as well as Enzo Frateili, Filiberto Menna,[27] Anty Pansera, and Gillo Dorfles.[28] While Italy boasts a wealth of historians of design, their work tends to focus on the construction of a national history, with proponents of rationalism such as Maldonado[29] facing off against neo-avant-gardists as typified by the radical architect Branzi.[30]

23 Bernd Löbach and Helmut Schmidt, *Design Theorien 1* (Berlin: Internationales Design Zentrum, 1978).

24 Vilém Flusser, *Vom Stand der Dinge: Eine kleine Philosophie des Design*, ed. Fabian Wurm (Göttingen: Seidl, 1993); published in English as *The Shape of Things: A Philosophy of Design*, trans. Anthony Mathews (London: Reaktion Books, 1999).

25 With the exception of economist and sociologist Lucius Burckhardt, who lived and taught in Germany.

26 Giulio Carlo Argan divides the history of industrialization into three phrases, and suggests that rationalism presents an ideological response to the intrusion of technology and the dangers linked to a class production determined by the economy. See Giulio Carlo Argan, "Il disegno industriale" (1955), in *Progetto e destino* (Milan: Il Saggiatore, 1965).

27 Filiberto Menna, *Profezia di una società estetica: Saggio dull'avanguardia e sul movimento dell'architettura moderna* [1983] (Milan: Editoriale Modo, 2001).

28 See especially Dorfles's *Le oscillazioni del gusto e l'arte moderna* (Milan: Lerici, 1958); *Il disegno industriale e la sua estetica* (Bologna: Cappelli, 1963); *L'estetica del mito: Da Vico a Wittgenstein* (Milan: Mursia, 1967); *Simbolo, communicazione, consumo* (Turin: Einaudi, 1967); and *Introduzione al disegno industriale: Linguaggio e storia della produzione di serie* (Turin: Einaudi, 1972).

29 See especially Maldonado's *La speranza progettuale: Ambiente e società* (Turin: Einaudi, 1970); *Avanguardia e razionalità: Articoli, saggi, pamphlets 1946–1974* (Turin: Einaudi, 1974); and *Il futuro della modernità* (Milan: Feltrinelli, 1987).

30 Branzi's publications include *Moderno, postmoderno, millenario: Scritti teoretici, 1972–1980* (Milan: Studio Forma, 1980); *The Hot House* (1984); *Domestic Animals: The Neoprimitive Style* (London: Thames & Hudson, 1987); *Luoghi: The Complete Works* (New York: Thames & Hudson, 1992); *Introduzione al design italiano: Una modernità incompleta* (Milan: Baldini Castoldi Dalai, 1999); *Contemporary Domestic Landscape 1945–2000* (Milan: Skira, 2002); and *Il design italiano 1964–2000: Un museo del design italiano* (Milan: Electa, 2008).

Overall, then, alongside numerous manifestos,[31] and more rare autobiographical texts,[32] the literature on design history consists essentially of object or technical histories,[33] penned by the proponents of different movements, as well as a great number of process-heavy descriptions of projects.[34] The first essays on design itself only began to appear in the 1980s and 1990s. With the exception of Banham's newspaper articles, which playfully critiqued the transformation of pop culture and its objects of consumption, interest in the historiography of design is relatively recent.[35] In his 1961 article "Design by Choice," once more in his capacity as a historian of architecture, Banham revisits the opposition between architecture and design, and takes stock of the previous ten years. He argues in favor of design as an autonomous discipline, distinct from the conception, teaching, and methodologies of architecture. In 1971, Banham drew together a selection of texts

31 See, among others, Le Corbusier, *L'art décoratif d'aujourd'hui* (Paris: Fréal, 1925), published in English as *The Decorative Art of Today*, trans. James Dunnett (Cambridge, MA: MIT Press, 1987); André Hermant, *Formes utiles* (Paris: Salon des arts ménagers, 1959); the writings of Florence's radical architects, including Lapo Binazzi of UFO, Superstudio, Archizoom Associati, and Zziggurat, collected in *Architecture radicale,* ed. Frédéric Migayrou (Villeurbanne: Éditions de l'IAC, 2001); the journal *In* directed by Ugo La Pietra; and Victor Papanek, *Design for the Real World* (London: Thames & Hudson, 1972). The most extensive bibliography to date can be found in Victor Margolin, "Postwar Design Literature: A Preliminary Mapping," in Margolin, *Design Discourse*, 256–88.

32 Such as Raymond Loewy, *Never Leave Well Enough Alone* (New York: Simon & Schuster, 1951); Norman Bel Geddes, *Miracle in the Evening* (New York: Doubleday, 1960); and Charlotte Perriand, *Une vie de création* (Paris: Odile Jacob, 1998).

33 Such as Pierre Francastel, *Art et technique aux XIXe et XXe siècles* (Paris: Gallimard, 1956); Abraham Moles, *Théorie des objets* (Paris: Éditions Universitaires, 1972); Jean Baudrillard, *Le système des objets* (Paris: Gallimard, 1968), published in English as *The System of Objects*, trans. James Benedict (London: Verso, 1996); Lewis Mumford, *Technics and Civilization* (New York: Harcourt, Brace, 1934); Denis Huisman and Georges Patrix, *L'esthétique industrielle* (Paris: PUF, 1961); along with a host of exhibition catalogues and volumes relating to the history of materials.

34 See Victor Margolin, "The Multiple Tasks of Design Studios," in *Essays*, 244–58. Margolin advances the idea of design as a space of integration for visual and material culture. On this subject, Alain Findeli develops the empirical concept of "théorie en design," which seeks to reinsert the project within theoretical research, since "design is not a scientific discipline in the classic sense of the term, but rather a profession or professional practice." Alain Findeli, "Qu'appelle-t-on 'théorie' du design? Réflexions sur l'enseignement et la recherche en design," in *Le design: Essais sur des théories et des pratiques* (Paris: IFM, 2006), 78.

35 For a comprehensive bibliography, see Margolin, "Postwar Design Literature," in Margolin, *Design Discourse*; and Kjetil Fallan, *Design History: Understanding Theory and Method* (Oxford: Berg, 2010).

presented by architects and designers at the International Design Conference in Aspen (IDCA), in order to reevaluate the body of critical work being produced in America at the time.[36] With his growing interest in design, shown through this and other publications, Banham became the first historian to advance, albeit tentatively, the idea that design could attain the status of a discipline. It is worth underlining that Banham's positive disposition toward design is somewhat exceptional for a historian of architecture. Yet even in his work, design is far from being considered an independent current of thought.[37] Over the course of the 1960s and 1970s, design became a significant point of interest for structuralism, for sociology through the work of Jean Baudrillard,[38] for anthropology through the writing of Marcel Mauss,[39] for behaviorism, and for Roland Barthes's semiotics, in *Mythologies* (1957). But design seemed destined to remain a prism through which social change could be explored, rather than an independent field of study in itself. The opening up of design to other areas of theoretical

36 The IDCA was founded in 1951 and hosted its first conference on design that same year in Aspen, Colorado. In addition to the anthology Reyner Banham, ed., *The Aspen Papers: Twenty Years of Design Theory from the International Design Conference in Aspen* (London: Pall Mall Press, 1974); the lectures from the 1966 conference are collected in *Sources and Resources of Twentieth-Century Design: IDCA-66* (Aspen, CO: IDCA, 1967); and those from 1972 in "The Invisible City," special issue, *Design Quarterly*, nos. 86/87 (1973). *Design Quarterly*, originally *Everyday Design Quarterly*, was the first scientific journal of design to be published in the US. These were the only publications produced by the IDCA, despite the renown of the Aspen conferences. The IDCA archives of manuscripts and cassettes are held in the special collections of the University of Illinois at Chicago library.

37 As Nigel Whiteley has pointed out, Banham's books focused on architecture while he discussed design in magazine articles. Penny Sparke was the first to collect these articles in the landmark 1981 anthology *Design by Choice*.

38 See Laurent Wolf, *Idéologie et production: Le design* (Paris: Anthropos, 1972); Adélie Hoffenberg and André Lapidus, *La société du design* (Paris: PUF, 1977); Jean Baudrillard, *La société de consommation* (Paris: Gallimard, 1970), published in English as *The Consumer Society: Myths and Structures*, trans. Chris Turner (London: Sage Publications, 1998); Jean Baudrillard, *Pour une critique de l'économie politique du signe* (Paris: Gallimard, 1972), published in English as *For a Critique of the Political Economy of the Sign*, trans. Charles Levin (Candor, NY: Telos Press, 1981); John Gloag, *Victorian Comfort: A Social History of Design from 1830–1900* (London: A & C Black, 1961); Adrian Forty, *Objects of Desire: Design and Society since 1750* (New York: Pantheon, 1986); John Burnett, *A Social History of Housing, 1815–1985* (London: Methuen, 1986).

39 See also Mary Douglas and Baron Isherwood, *The World of Goods: Towards an Anthropology of Consumption* (London: Allen Lane, 1979).

investigation, rather than cementing its importance, in fact hampered the articulation of its history and ensured it remained yoked to the human sciences.

In the 1980s, postmodern designers refused to explicitly define the object of their work, and flirted with the human sciences, which, in the words of the designer Ettore Sottsass, "opened a broader horizon, as if we had emerged from design's town center to head for new, uncertain peripheries."[40] The social sciences, in turn, would continue to treat design as an object of study.[41] The history of design is characterized by this propensity to figure as an object of study for other disciplines, a phenomenon that would consistently prevent it from affirming its independence. And if, up until now, the history of design has been penned by historians of architecture, to which discipline do today's historians of design belong?

Margolin makes a virtue of the difficulty design poses in terms of disciplinary classification: "The point I want to make here is that *design* does not signify a class of objects that can be pinned down like butterflies. Design is an activity that is constantly changing. How, then, can we establish a body of knowledge about something that has no fixed identity?"[42] He sees design as necessarily involving a principle of transfer, one that raises issues for the recognition, autonomy, and articulation of design as its own discipline.

It is in the following terms that Danish designer Verner Panton railed against the misconceptions surrounding design in the catalogue for the Centre de création industrielle's inaugural exhibition in 1969, "Qu'est-ce que le design?":

40 Ettore Sottsass, "Tel père, Memphis," interview by Anne-Marie Fèvre, *Libération*, January 3, 2008.

41 Notably the field of semiotics, see the work of Yuri Lotman and Baudrillard; and that of sociology, see Wolf, *Idéologie et production*, and Hoffenberg and Lapidus, *La société du design*.

42 Margolin, "Design History and Design Studies," in *Essays*, 224.

> Through some kind of "artistic" mystery, the term "designer" has become a fashionable word robbed of its original meaning. Too many people consider the designer as a figure who adds a decorative touch to everyday objects, or else someone who manipulates habitual forms to produce new and elegant ones. The designer's work is so much more than this, and so much more important for society.[43]

The basic question of the exhibition's title has been a perennial one since the 1950s. Edgar Kaufmann Jr., the founder of the Good Design movement and the curator of numerous design exhibitions at the Museum of Modern Art in New York, made this the central problem of his modernist manifesto *What Is Modern Design?*, and George H. Marcus continues this line of inquiry with his text *What Is Design Today?*[44] The question persists to this day.

In the "Qu'est-ce que le design?" catalogue, a set of twenty-six identical questions are posed to Panton, Joe Colombo, Fritz Eichler, Roger Tallon, and Charles Eames. Colombo responds to a question on the definition of design in the following terms: "Design is a totality which encompasses architecture, urbanism, production, and the means of communication [...]. Design is therefore reality, life, the essential." Eichler's response is more pragmatic, offering a definition of design as "a complex ensemble which is by no means limited to the conception of exterior aesthetic forms that are simply the visible expression of a collective work. Design is an integral part of our evolution. It is neither inherently good nor inherently evil." Tallon, a

43 Verner Panton, quoted in *Qu'est-ce que le design?* (Paris: Centre de création industrielle, 1969), n.p.

44 Edgar Kaufmann Jr., *What Is Modern Design*? (New York: Museum of Modern Art, 1950); George H. Marcus, *What Is Design Today?* (New York: Abrams, 2002).

defender of anonymous design, envisages it as "a stance which rejects the unthinking, the fluke and the random solution."[45] These varied responses demonstrate the different modes of thought and the contradictions raised by so deceptively simple a question. Clearly design is far from being a fixed entity, and contrary to Pevsner's or Giedion's conclusions, it cannot be subjected to a single definition, instead manifesting across concepts that differ from designer to designer. Here it is worth recalling Branzi's conception of the designer as "an inventor of scenarios and strategies [who] must play in the territories of the imagination to create new stories, new fictions, which will add to the thickness of the real"[46] alongside that given by Bruce Sterling—steampunk author, fantasy designer, and "Visionary in Residence" at the Art Center College of Design in Pasadena—for whom design begins with narrative.[47] These conceptions of design rooted in personal strategies and different temporalities show how design cannot reasonably be expressed in a single definition.

It is particularly necessary to underline this due to the proliferation of the term "design" in recent years, which has seen it applied to everything from furniture to haircuts, from objects to services, from style and graphics to user interfaces and industrial production, from spoons to cars, from culinary research to the "intelligent design" of creationism, and even, in a sign of the times, to existence itself.[48] This lexical cannibalization results from a long series of approximate and sweeping definitions. As early as forty years ago, an issue of the journal *L'Architecture d'Aujourd'hui* dedicated to design was already bemoaning this phenomenon:

45 Joe Colombo, Fritz Eichler, and Roger Tallon, quoted in *Qu'est-ce que le design?*, n.p.
46 Andrea Branzi, "Propos recueillis," *Azimuts*, no. 33 (2009): 50–52.
47 Bruce Sterling, *Shaping Things* (Cambridge, MA: MIT Press, 2005).
48 Bernard Stiegler, ed., *Le design de nos existences: À l'époque de l'innovation ascendante* (Paris: Fayard, 2008).

> Design, *le mot à la mode*. [...] In design, some see the total negation of architecture, others its renewal. The architect fancies himself to be a designer, but the designer rejects "architecture." Both strive, using similar means, for a comprehensive command of space. Both suffer from the same misconceptions as to the ends of their work and their role in a changing society. Each object to which they turn their attention has, by definition, its "architecture" or its "design"; yet architecture and design have yet to find their own objects.[49]

Today, the widespread use of the term "design" has done little to aid its comprehension. The fact that art, economics, and lifestyle magazines continue to dedicate covers and entire issues to design as if it were a passing trend is the result of an interdisciplinary openness, or a "crime," to reference the title of Hal Foster's essay collection *Design and Crime*.[50]

49 Marc Emery, introduction to "Le design," special issue, *L'Architecture d'Aujourd'hui*, no. 155 (April–May 1971): 2.
50 Hal Foster, *Design and Crime (and Other Diatribes)* (London: Verso, 2003).

The Art of Design

In his chapter on the Deutscher Werkbund in *Theory and Design in the First Machine Age*, Banham describes architecture as an "art of design."[51] This formula not only applies to the Deutscher Werkbund, but describes as well a wider change in the relationship between art and design, one that Banham himself would experience over the course of his collaboration with Eduardo Paolozzi and the Independent Group between 1952 and 1955.[52] For Banham, the Modern Movement emerged from the academic tradition of beaux arts instruction in Paris. Applied to the field of design, this idea (which is elsewhere reiterated by Roger Newport)[53] forms the central argument of Clive Dilnot's text, in which he asserts that until 1939 historiographical activity surrounding design belonged to the tradition of the decorative arts, which itself belonged to the history of art and architecture. Dilnot sees the collapse of the Modern Movement at the end of the 1960s as evidencing the necessity for design to finally attain an autonomous history.[54] Yet even in 1987, the anthropologist Daniel Miller criticized the lack of originality in the history of design, which he says aspires to be a kind of pseudo-art history.[55]

The situation is no better from an architectural point of view. Since the publication of Pevsner's landmark text,

51 Reyner Banham, *Theory and Design in the First Machine Age* [1960] (Cambridge, MA: MIT Press, 1980), 68.

52 As Sparke points out, Banham's desire to challenge the boundaries between the arts was brought about by his collaboration with the Independent Group around the 1956 Whitechapel Gallery exhibition "This Is Tomorrow." See Sparke, introduction to Banham, *Design by Choice*, 8.

53 Roger Newport, "Design History: Process or Product," in Bishop, *Design History: Fad or Function?*, 89–97; Dilnot, "The State of Design History, Part I," in Margolin, *Design Discourse*, 217.

54 Dilnot, 220.

55 See Daniel Miller, *Material Culture and Mass Consumption* (Oxford: Basil Blackwell, 1987).

it has been widely accepted that design's origins could be located in the Great Exhibition of 1851, the nineteenth century's first great display of technical and industrial prowess. The Great Exhibition of the Works of Industry of All Nations, to give it its full title, took place in the center of London—itself the cradle of the Industrial Revolution in Europe—and brought together the wealth of innovations and inventions of the modern world in the most significant union of arts, sciences, and industry to that date. Against a backdrop of widespread belief in the benefits of technological progress, the machines and products presented at the exhibition were considered to represent a great opportunity for all mankind. For Prince Albert, Queen Victoria's husband and the exhibition's leading proponent, machines promised nothing less than peace and fraternity between nations as well as a reduction in the physical demands of labor, an increase in and redistribution of wealth, and an improvement in the quality of life across social classes. The Great Exhibition, and hence design itself, signified the era's hope for a better and fairer world. It was in this context that William Morris conceived his innovative project: to reconcile the "lesser arts" and "major arts" while drawing upon the decorative arts for the urgent societal reforms necessitated by industrialization. Morris's reconciliation of art and life, however, aimed less to found a new discipline than it did to restore the power of the fine arts, which were at the time in a state of crisis. Pevsner demonstrates clearly how Morris's project shows that design can be considered a response to the emergence of new modes of industrial production and organization, and as the expression of a reconfiguration of fine arts and architecture. In light of this, the invention of design seems to take place in a context of artistic transformation, and so it becomes clearer how and why it was assimilated by the history of art into the continuity of the Modern Movement. The same can be said for the incorporation of the history of design into that of architecture; design, because of the groundwork laid by Pevsner and Giedion, is presented as simply an episode in the history of "the mother of all arts."

Although design doubtless owes a great deal to fine art and—by way of architecture—to engineering, it has nonetheless begun to aspire toward a relative but growing independence. But this is a task made all the more difficult by the refusal of these other disciplines to confer any legitimacy upon design. In such a context, it is difficult for design to stake a claim to disciplinary and historical autonomy, let alone to establish a relationship of equals with art and architecture. While the emergence of any new discipline necessarily involves the borrowing of elements from existing ones, design's location at the crossroads of art and architecture places it in an ambivalent position between recognized discipline and interdisciplinary notion. Margolin draws our attention to these contradictions:

> To think of design history as a discipline based on firm assumptions of what design is and how we might study its past is to ignore the dynamic crossings of intellectual boundaries that are occurring elsewhere. For example, researchers outside design history have discovered design to be a rich topic of historical investigation.[56]

This conception is revisited by Raymond Guidot, who invokes the notion of the "crossroads of the arts,"[57] and by Penny Sparke, who plays it safe with the idea of "unity

56 Margolin, "Design History and Design Studies," in *Essays*, 220.
57 Raymond Guidot, *Design: Carrefour des arts* (Paris: Flammarion, 2003).

in diversity."[58] The idea of the history of design has rarely been proposed, in contrast to the history of architecture.[59] As a result, analyses of its origins are few and far between. Pevsner, in an act of historical irony, places design—and specifically William Morris—at the origin of modern architecture, though never explicitly.[60] Nevertheless, he does little to attenuate the misconceptions and approximations that have tended to confuse the Modern Movement, architecture, and design with each other.

58 See Penny Sparke, *Design in Context* (London: New Burlington Books, 1987).

59 In contrast to design, the modern period has been explored through a succession of books and debates that take contradicting points of view. Henry-Russell Hitchcock locates the origins of the Modern Movement in the Gothic style in *Modern Architecture: Romanticism and Reintegration* (New York: Payson and Clarke, 1929), and builds upon this approach in *The International Style: Architecture since 1922*, co-authored by Philip Johnson (New York: Norton, 1932). Kaufmann would later trace the modern period's origins back to the eighteenth century, while Sigfried Giedion promotes a spatiotemporal fusion of architecture in *Space, Time and Architecture: The Growth of a New Tradition* (Cambridge, MA: Harvard University Press, 1941), before aligning it with progress and technology. The influence of this latter step can be seen in the work of the following generation: on the one hand, Banham, who expanded the modernist genealogy to include the Futurists, De Stijl, and Expressionism and, on the other, Colin Rowe, who used the work of Palladio as his starting point.

60 This point is raised by Mark Wigley in "Whatever Happened to Total Design?," *Harvard Design Magazine*, no. 5 (Summer 1998): 1–8.

Rethinking History

With this in mind, it is worth returning Pevsner and Giedion to the territory in which they located their own work: the history of modern architecture. A survey of texts on the topic points to the conclusion that the history of design can only really be said to emerge from the 1980s onward. While it is possible to speculate as to Pevsner's reasons for not having set out the terms of design's disciplinary autonomy, the time has come to consider what those terms might be. Such an exercise takes aim at received wisdom and its reductive and conventional views that treat design as little more than the production of useful and marketable goods, and the designer as a simple if ingenious hired hand.

While this is a debate for which, sadly, design on the whole demonstrates little enthusiasm,[61] according to Margolin the disinclination can be traced to Pevsner's history of the Modern Movement. Pevsner tended to exclude the everyday object in favor of the masterpiece, and, as Dilnot observes, displayed a clear fascination with William Morris and the Arts & Crafts movement, which resulted in countless historians unquestioningly situating the origin of design in the artistic output of Great Britain in the 1850s and 1860s.[62] I will attempt here to conceive an alternative history of design that might, in turn, change that of modernism.

61 Jeffrey L. Miele, "Design History for What? Reflections on an Elusive Goal," *Design Issues* 11, no. 1 (Spring 1995): 71.

62 See Adrian Forty, "Design History: A Politique and a Pedagogy," *Architectural Association Quarterly* 5, no. 4 (Autumn 1973): 48–49; Tim Benton, "The Past Should Be Looked at through Well-Designed Spectacles," *Times Higher Education Supplement*, October 10, 1975, 7; Clive Ashwin, "Art and Design History: The Parting of the Ways?," in Bishop, *Design History: Fad or Function?*, 98–102; Dilnot, "The State of Design History, Part I," in Margolin, *Design Discourse*, 213–32.

Placing Giedion's *Mechanization Takes Command* in a continuum with Pevsner's *Pioneers of the Modern Movement* allows for a different understanding of the value of the latter work. Pevsner's retrospective designation of Morris as the founder of design and modern architecture has assured that Morris has cast a long shadow over all subsequent writing on design. The first step toward reevaluating design's historical origins can be taken by considering the rational organization of the home—outside the gendered contexts in which this is normally discussed—as an earlier paradigm for the discipline as whole.

In *Mechanization Takes Command*, Giedion succinctly evokes the work of American educator Catharine Beecher and explains how her 1841 bestseller *A Treatise on Domestic Economy* quite literally transformed the American domestic landscape.[63] Revisiting this work today, it becomes clear that its altogether historically valid contribution has rarely been evoked outside of explicitly feminist analyses. When the question of design has been explored from a feminist perspective, it has been approached in terms of the dilemma between the industrial and the artisanal, and by extension according to a male/female opposition, given women's exclusion from industrial production. However, from Beecher's rational organization to Paulette Bernège's "domestic Taylorism"[64] or Christine Frederick's "creative waste,"[65] the ideas and inventions of women have stood

63 Giedion, "Part VI: Mechanization Encounters the Household," in *Mechanization Takes Command*, 512–625. At the height of this chapter Giedion places Beecher—the inventor of "domestic economy"—at the forefront, not only by virtue of her ability to orchestrate the rationalization of the housewife's movements and activities in the home, but because he grants her the distinction of having known how to overcome the question of domesticity and its functional resolutions. Beecher's treatise on domestic economy rapidly became a bestseller. In the book, she describes the home as the departure point for social and political reform extending to society. The concept of a house without domestic servants (the reason for which modern plumbing and technological equipment play a major role in her works) is intended to accompany—and indeed to help bring about—the abolition of slavery.

64 Paulette Bernège, *Si les femmes faisaient les maisons* (Paris: Mon Chez Moi, 1928).

65 Christine Frederick, *Selling Mrs. Consumer* (New York: The Business Bourse, 1929).

the test of time, and their influence has even extended to the domain of architecture, for example in the form of the modernist concept of Existenzminimum.[66] Since the 1980s, the construction of design's history has been examined from a feminine perspective and numerous writers have concluded that any alternative to Pevsner's vision must necessarily challenge and dismantle the heroic lineage it is built upon.[67]

This kind of reevaluation seeks to take advantage of new perspectives to locate an origin of design that would predate Morris. Another such example is that of Sir Henry Cole and Richard Redgrave, who coined the term "design" in 1849 with their *Journal of Design and Manufactures*. Their definition of design not only referred to the spatial organization of the home and the movement of individuals within it, but also aimed to effect social change by way of education, and in particular the creation of specialized schools. These institutions would provide quality education to a generation of young people who would devote themselves not to art or the decorative arts but to design itself. Through the journal they founded, Redgrave and Cole invited all inventors to patent their designs in order to ensure that they retained copyright, encouraging designers to stake a claim to their work and thus marking a break with the anonymity that had until then been

66 Ernst May, Sigfied Giedion, Walter Gropius, Le Corbusier, Pierre Jeanneret, Victor Bourgeois, and Hans Schmidt, *Die Wohnung für das Existenzminimum* [The dwelling for minimal existence] (Frankfurt am Main: Englert & Schlosser, 1930), 20–29.

67 See Dolores Hayden, *The Grand Domestic Revolution: A History of Feminist Designs for American Homes, Neighborhoods and Cities* (Cambridge, MA: MIT Press, 1982); Joan Rothschild, *Design and Feminism: Re-visioning Spaces, Places, and Everyday Things* (New Brunswick, NJ: Rutgers University, 1999); Attfield, "FORM/female FOLLOWS FUNCTION/male," in Walker, *Design History and the History of Design*, 199–225; Ellen Lupton, *Mechanical Brides: Women and Machines from Home to Office* (New York: Princeton Architectural Press, 1993); Penny Sparke, *As Long as It's Pink: The Sexual Politics of Taste* (London: Pandora, 1995); Penny Sparke and Brenda Martin, *Women's Places: Architecture and Design 1860–1960* (London: Routledge, 2003); and Dilnot, "The State of Design History," parts 1 and 2, in Margolin, *Design Discourse*, 213–50.

the norm, which Giedion makes his focus. Cole's support of multiple, individual, and more modest contributions to design was matched by his enthusiastic promotion of the Great Exhibition, which may explain why Pevsner, with his heroic lineage, largely glosses over this landmark 1851 event, whereas Giedion chooses to refer to it from the very start. Reconsidering these alternative contributions allows for an interrogation of the validity of a history constructed around a succession of white, male Europeans.

Design in Its Own Terms

To begin the history of design with *Pioneers of the Modern Movement* is to begin with a paradox. To suggest that this work, which declines to confer upon design the status of a discipline, and whose subject is not design but the prehistory of modern architecture, is clearly problematic. Nor does *Mechanization Takes Command* simplify the issue. Giedion was barely more interested in design itself than Pevsner. But the weaving together of these two histories sets out the basis for a critical awareness necessary for the construction of an autonomous history of design. Morris is no longer design's heroic figure, but is preceded by a heroine—or rather, non-heroine—in the form of Beecher. Women come to occupy a more important role, Morris is no longer presented as the sworn enemy of the machine, and so on. It is not a question, however, of dethroning Pevsner's great figures, but rather of reintroducing into the history of design and its origins major events that may redefine the discipline's central questions.

A close reading of the logic and evolution of a discipline's historiography is necessary to understand its foundations. In the field of architecture, these questions were posed by a generation of historians whose certainties had been thrown into question by the violence and totalitarianism of the Second World War. The generation that followed, no longer faced with these same historical imperatives, challenged the modernist project and questioned its coherence and legitimacy. They contested the ostensible timelessness of its concepts of pure form, functionalism, standardized products, and mechanization. They railed against the lack of credence paid to the consequences of applying standardization to life itself, as Giedion describes.

This new cohort of historians, with Banham at its fore, attacked the rational analyses of modernity and what they saw as the biased positions of its proponents. Their approach, which relied upon a careful and critical rereading of history that would lead to its reevaluation, can easily be applied to our present subject. Since the first history of modern architecture has long served as a history of design, a reevaluation of the latter surely calls for an examination of the Modern Movement.

Banham first raised the incompatibility of the history of design with that of the architecture of the Modern Movement in a 1966 speech at the IDCA:

> Too many of the great unquestioned assumptions on which modern design is based have begun to peel and flake of late; neither they nor their advocates appear to be quite such stainless representations of the shining new world as once we thought. It is high time we checked to see which ones have rusted through and must be junked, which need to go back in the plating tank, and which only need a wipe over with the silvercloth.[68]

To stay with Banham's silver cloth metaphor, could we affirm in much the same way that the history of design might benefit from a similar "polishing"? Or perhaps the choice to discuss the history of design through a comparative critique of Pevsner and Giedion runs the risk of perpetuating and further diffusing a certain myth. These clarifications make possible the critical distance necessary for a veritable history of design, and although this often raises contradictory hypotheses, the history of ideas is

68 Reyner Banham, "All That Glitters Is Not Stainless," in Banham, *Aspen Papers*, 160.

undeniably the material par excellence from which to construct this debate. Without dwelling on the contradictions inherent to Pevsner's formulation of design's origins and the consequences this had for its subsequent scope, it is fair to say that he articulates the founding principles of design. He links his hero, Morris, to the reform of relationships between the fine arts and decorative arts in the context of the British Industrial Revolution, and of the forces that governed the interaction between disciplines, as well as to the importance conferred upon functionality in the wake of the Great Exhibition.

Giedion also describes design with reference to the advent of the Industrial Revolution, although he selects a different initial focus—the city of Chicago: "[From] 1880 to the time of the Columbian Exposition of 1893 the 'Loop' area in Chicago (its business quarter, that is) was the center of architectural development not merely for the United States but for the whole world."[69] Giedion thus locates the origin of design in a social and cultural transformation that took shape over the course of the nineteenth century through the work of American engineers and inventors who applied functionalist principles inherited from Philadelphia native Frederick Winslow Taylor, and from innovations and patents pioneered on the factory floor. I will return later to the contribution of Beecher, whom Giedion cites and whose work involved adapting these industrial optimizations to the rational organization of the home, a significant political project in the history of design.

The invention of design has often been attributed to the German Peter Behrens, considered to be the first industrial designer. From 1907 to 1914, he worked for Allgemeine Elektricitäts-Gesellschaft (AEG), designing

69 Giedion, *Space, Time and Architecture*, 10 (see note 59).

everything from the company's advertising campaigns to its buildings, graphic identity, and the electrical goods it manufactured. This collaboration unfolded after his decisive encounter with the German industrialist Emil Rathenau, who afforded him an exceptional degree of independence, and with whom he shared a perspective on the cultural role of industrial projects. Behrens created a design identity and distinctive signage system for AEG that could be rolled out across the board: from products to distribution points, factories, catalogues, shops, posters, and promotional materials. But if design is to be considered in terms of the driving force of industrialization, then late nineteenth-century Viennese furniture manufacturer Gebrüder Thonet, or Ford's American factories in the 1920s, could also be considered possible points of origin. Elsewhere, the inaugural declaration of the Bauhaus by its founder Walter Gropius in 1919 has been posited as design's formative moment, a point of view that closely associates design with functionalist principles. Banham and Franco Raggi, among others, have meanwhile pointed to the creation of the Deutscher Werkbund in 1907, which firmly established the notion of standardization.

While these different origins may seem to cancel each other out, they are not in fact incompatible with Pevsner's genealogy. Banham and Sparke in Britain, and Margolin and David Watkin in the United States, have underlined that with *Pioneers of the Modern Movement* Pevsner lauded the absolute value of functionalism—a stance that these same authors have also on occasion challenged. Reconsidering these events together reveals the extent to which design's history is an accidental one, since, as Margolin writes, "Design history has not developed on the basis of a well-understood subject matter or a set of methods and principles to guide research. Instead, it has grown as a response to the initial literature in the field, first celebrating it and then criticizing it."[70] As a result, it remains to be seen whether or not design as a discipline can benefit from an autonomous history.

It is Sparke who first raises this possibility in 1978, at a conference on the history of design in Brighton, where she emphasizes its uniqueness as a discipline:

> As an academic discipline it is undoubtedly the child of the art schools, where the increasing number of design students need a historical perspective more relevant to their immediate needs than the one provided by traditional fine art history, and it is largely within their confines that it has blossomed and yielded fruits.[71]

Giedion's approach to the question is somewhat too closely linked to the history of art and its methods to offer an altogether satisfying alternative. In this light, it is worth considering the events that could allow for a conception of a theory of design truly independent from all other disciplines.

As it has become clear, the questions surrounding the history of design's origins call for a reformulated history that pays careful attention to a number of oft-neglected movements and events, from Bauhaus Expressionism to the Streamline movement, a genealogy I briefly outline in *Design: Introduction à l'histoire d'une discipline*.[72] While it would have been possible to construct this timeline around the rectifications necessary from the point of view of contemporary design, I chose as my starting point 1969, the

70 Margolin, "Design History and Design Studies," in *Essays*, 221.
71 Penny Sparke, introduction to Bishop, *Design History: Fad or Function?*, 5.
72 Alexandra Midal, *Design: Introduction à l'histoire d'une discipline* (Paris: Press Pocket, 2009).

year in which Joe Colombo published his antidesign manifesto.[73] This work represents a turning point for the historiography of design, radically challenging the established narrative and demanding that design be considered in an entirely new light. A moment of rupture, 1969 unlocked potential historiographies hitherto unconsidered by design historians, who were still weighed down by the original discourse of Pevsner and his successors. Colombo's idea of antidesign challenges the notion of design as something singular and unified. As such, antidesign offers an illuminating entry point for a reconsideration of the origin, history, and significance of design. It is a question not of placing antidesign at the origin of design's political dimension—whether rational organization and its proponents in the United States or Morris and his successors in Britain—but rather of using the notion as the basis for the interrogation, deconstruction, and reconstruction of design's existing historiography.

Antidesign aims for nothing less than the total independence of design, which it seeks to attain by overturning the hierarchy between objects, furniture, architecture, and urbanism. Colombo draws upon philosopher Herbert Marcuse's notion of one-dimensionality and transposes it to the field of design, laying the foundation for a dynamic and critical vision of the discipline. Colombo rails against the traditional notion of design and its references to timeless modernist standards. Colombo goes beyond this conventional approach to explore social, familial, and psychological behaviors in all their complexity. Though he reaffirms the importance of rationalism while also criticizing its formal, modernist interpretation as being disconnected from reality, he creates a kind of ambiguity through his use of classic modernist terminology. What is

73 Joe Colombo, "Antidesign," *Casabella*, no. 342 (November 1969): 28.

clear is that Colombo has no overly fixed position: he challenges the heritage of modernism yet kneels at the altar of functionality, and he attacks consumerism while designing countless gadgets. In this way, he offers an entirely new and unparalleled conception of design.

Antidesign must nonetheless be considered within a wider and more complex context. It may be contrasted with the furniture-as-architecture of the radical architects' controdesign, which formed in Florence around two key groups, Archizoom Associati and Superstudio. Whereas Colombo's antidesign affirmed design's authority over architecture, the proponents of radical architecture treated the concept as a means of reforming architecture. The radical architects used the term "controdesign" to describe their output of furniture and objects, which they positioned according to a cynical analysis: imagining their creations as both commercially viable merchandise and a way of criticizing industrial production from within—something that they felt *designers* were incapable of doing. In 1971 the radicals also adopted the term "antidesign," but with a different connotation. While for its original coiner Colombo, antidesign was the tool that would bring about design's revolution, the radical architects saw antidesign as a means of renewing their own discipline.

Colombo's vision of antidesign, as elaborated by the insights afforded by my study of his private archives, further supports a rereading of design and of its historical interpretations.[74] The debates across different disciplinary territories were so numerous and intense in the 1960s that I have chosen to exclude fine arts from my analysis here in order to allow for a deeper exploration of the significance of antidesign, which signaled a definitive rupture with the

74 The archives of Joe Colombo are held in the designer's former office in Milan.

traditional axiology that has valued architecture over design. Again drawing on archival material—here, that of Superstudio—I will demonstrate how the radical architects sought to find solutions for the crisis that had beset their discipline since the collapse of modernist ideology. The 1962 manifesto "Absolute Architektur" by Hans Hollein and Walter Pichler and Hollein's 1968 text "Alles ist Architektur," are two such antidotes.[75] What Colombo and the radical architects shared was a desire to overturn the hierarchy in which, as Branzi writes, "the progressive abandonment of the traditional limits of design, now seen as a form of territorial planning, fostered an understanding of the new reality of the metropolis, which could now be defined as a market for consumer goods, and of architecture caught up in the new dimensions of design but still unable to come up with a renewed image of itself, i.e. a credible role of its own."[76]

Overthrowing existing hierarchies, Colombo proposed a territorial and historical restructuring of his discipline. He explored this restructuring in the last three years of his life through experiments into the model of the capsule, which he gave a wholly original meaning and ideological charge. With his *Total Furnishing Unit*, designed for the 1972 MoMA exhibition "Italy: The New Domestic Landscape," Colombo combined the various functions of a typical home into a small, independent, and totally self-contained unit. He thus expressed his desire for design's emancipation, its independence as a discipline, and ultimately its authority; with the metaphor of the capsule, Colombo aimed to completely redefine the place of design and its exchanges with architecture.

75 Hans Hollein and Walter Pichler, *Architektur: Work in Progress* (Vienna: Galerie St. Stephan, 1963), n.p.; Hans Hollein, "Alles ist Architektur," *Bau*, nos. 1–2 (1968): 138–39.

76 Branzi, *Hot House*, 66.

The architects of the Modern Movement considered design to be within the remit of their practice: simultaneously an architectural synecdoche and architecture in a concentrated form. Yet the opposition between antidesign and controdesign demonstrates the authority and expansionist nature of two disciplines—architecture and design—competing over the same territory. This tension creates a crucial turning point from which to formulate a new history of design liberated from the perspective of "design by accident" raised by modernist architectural theory through the founding writings by Pevsner and, subsequently, reformulates the historical foundations of any interdisciplinary approach between art, design, and architecture.

This rewriting of the history of design draws upon Colombo's conception of the discipline in terms of antidesign, expanding its territory and asserting its dominance over the built environment. Antidesign allows us, for the first time, to see the history of design, from its origins through to the present day, in terms of expansionism. With the principle of Existenzmaximum, a neologism coined from the famous Existenzminimum of the modern architects,[77] the history of design begins to emerge as an all-encompassing paradigm. Existenzmaximum becomes the metonym for a design situated at the center of the field and extending outward as far as possible, for a design that proclaims its independence while absorbing other disciplines, and for a design that decisively articulates its own history, from Morris through to the present day. This time, it is a history without accidents. The rupture effected by antidesign liberates design, at last, from the yoke of modern architecture, and creates the conditions that make possible a new history of design.

77 "Existenz Maximum" was an exhibition held at Ospedale degli Innocenti, Florence, in 1990. Alessandro Mendini discusses the exhibition in "Existenz Maximum," in *Scritti*, ed. Loredana Parmesani (Milan: Skira, 2004), 95.

Part I

The History of Design's Origins

Before rethinking the history of design and exploring the new and unpublished sources that make this task possible, it is nonetheless worth returning to its two founding texts.

The Origin Story of Design: Pevsner and Giedion's Parallel Histories

Pevsner's history of the Modern Movement developed from the classes that he gave on the history of architecture between 1930 and 1932 at the University of Göttingen, and in work published in 1931 in the *Göttingische gelehrte Anzeigen*. (The Hegelian notion of Zeitgeist that he employs is borrowed from his former professor, Heinrich Wölfflin.) *Pioneers of the Modern Movement* opens with a portrait of Morris written in a biographical style, retracing the steps of his life that led to the founding of his decorative arts company Morris, Marshall, Faulkner & Co., Fine Art Workmen in Painting, Carving, Furniture and the Metals, in 1861. Pevsner then ends his work with a similar portrait of Walter Gropius, lauding the achievements of German rational functionalism, which for him reaches its pinnacle in the form of designs for a model factory drawn up by Gropius and Adolf Meyer and presented at the 1914 Deutscher Werkbund exhibition in Cologne.

In his opening chapter, "Theories of Art from Morris to Gropius," Pevsner sets out the core of his argument, and presents Morris in a somewhat ambiguous light.[78] Whether Pevsner sees him as a premodern or a backward-looking figure—albeit one with strong intuitions—remains uncertain. The first step of his narrative charts Morris's revolt against his era's woeful architecture and shoddy industrial goods. Pevsner praises Morris's project for two major reasons: the first being what he sees as Morris's decisive break with his period as the first figure to reconsider

78 Pevsner, "Theories of Art from Morris to Gropius," in *Pioneers of the Modern Movement*, 17–43 (see note 1).

the condition of the artist in the modern age, and the first to attempt to restore the dimension of craft that had been part of the artist's identity until the Renaissance, even going so far as to return to the idea of the artist and craftsman as unified entity. By recounting the story of Morris's pioneering campaign, Pevsner seeks to legitimize his construction of a coherent and unified history of modern architecture.

The second reason for Pevsner's keen interest in Morris, and the most important, relates to the democratic dimension of his revolutionary project, particularly evident in Morris's writing and numerous speeches. The most well known of these, an 1877 speech entitled "The Lesser Arts," is but the first of thirty-five that he would go on to deliver. Morris took a theatrical approach to these lectures, with his passionate opening words, "I do not want art for a few any more than education for a few, or freedom for a few,"[79] becoming a famous expression later borrowed by Pevsner. With this declaration, Morris—whom Pevsner elsewhere refers to as a "genius" and a "prophet"—outlines the moral virtues inherent in the alliance of art and society within his political project, insisting that "it is not possible to dissociate art from morality, politics, or religion";[80] the true richness of art can only come into being through the shared happiness of the conception and making of an object and its use by all.

Pevsner's enthusiasm for Morris does, however, have its limits, and he is critical of what he sees as Morris's backward-looking, perhaps even reactionary, tendencies. Pevsner suggests that, faced with rioting workers and an uncompromising British government, he sought refuge

79 William Morris, "The Lesser Arts," in *The Political Writings of William Morris*, ed. Arthur Leslie Morton (London: Lawrence & Wishart, 1984), 42.
80 Pevsner, *Pioneers of the Modern Movement*, 23.

from reality in the values of the past, in Nordic epics and the ballads of the Middle Ages: "This is the decisive antagonism of Morris's life and teaching. His work, the revival of handicraft, is constructive; the essence of his teaching is destructive."[81] Thus Pevsner's praise for his hero is not unconditional, despite his admiration of Morris's stirring call for a truly democratic art. Elsewhere, for example, he accuses Morris of having unfairly vilified industrialization, blaming it for the poor quality of manufactured goods, and, graver still, for having alienated the worker by reducing him to a machine. Pevsner's account of Morris renders him as a rather lackluster pioneer, one who failed to understand that the machine would define the century to come. Pevsner attempts to justify the marked coherence of his narrative, which covers a period of roughly seventy years, writing that "the assertion on which the present work is based [is] that the phase between Morris and Gropius is an historical unit. Morris laid the foundation of the modern style; with Gropius its character was ultimately determined."[82] His principal concern is to clearly identify the origins of the Modern Movement and to definitively assert its validity. Although he does not explicitly state as much, it is in fact *design* that Pevsner places at the origin of modern architecture. Pevsner acknowledges that it was on Gropius's advice that he chose the figure of Morris—who had abandoned his initial studies of art and architecture to devote himself to the decorative arts—to initiate his chronology.[83] Gropius had expressed to Pevsner the sense of indebtedness that he

81 Ibid., 24.
82 Ibid., 39.
83 Pevsner states as much on a number of occasions, for example, on "From William Morris to Walter Gropius," a BBC radio program aired on March 6, 1949: "They are, precisely as Gropius quotes, Ruskin and Morris, then Van de Velde—or rather Voysey and Art Nouveau including Van de Velde—and then Behrens and the Werkbund. The last stage then was the Bauhaus." Nikolaus Pevsner, *Pevsner on Art and Architecture*, ed. Stephen Games (London: Methuen, 2002), 36–37.

felt toward Morris, and thus naturally encouraged the historian to consider it the key to understanding the origin of the Modern Movement. But to which discipline can Morris, who was more an artist and designer than an architect, be reasonably assigned?

Pioneers of the Modern Movement is therefore indicative of the long-standing uncertainty as to the boundaries between design, architecture, and functionalism, and the first reference work for the history of design. To better understand the nature of Pevsner's project, it is worth paying attention to his subtitle, "From William Morris to Walter Gropius." Though this clearly establishes the beginning and end of his genealogy of pioneers, it inadvertently and fatally compromises his initial intention: given Pevsner's fervent advocacy of architecture and his lack of interest in design, it is altogether remarkable that he should place Morris, a designer and not an architect, at the source of modern architecture. Contradicting himself, Pevsner confers an unexpected importance upon design: without having set out to do so, he crowns Morris as history's first designer, and credits design with the inception of modern architecture. Pevsner's position thus gives rise to a trio of incongruities that undermine his architectural history project, while not giving design its full due.

Had he wished to do so, Pevsner could have resolved this ambiguity on a number of occasions. Several editions of his text were republished in his lifetime, and *Pioneers of the Modern Movement* became a project that developed over the course of almost thirty years. Invited by MoMA to republish his work in 1948, Pevsner made a series of amendments. Not only did he add a new preface and alter the title of the book, but he opted for a larger format with more images, and revised his text in places. For example, he selected a new epigraph, replacing a quote from Morris's first employer, Sir George Gilbert Scott, "Architecture is the decoration of construction,"[84] with a similar one from John Ruskin, "Ornamentation is the principal part of architecture."[85] By referencing Ruskin (whose work Morris closely followed) Pevsner underlines the lineage his work sought to establish while also alluding to his belief that decor, previously on an equal footing with architecture, was now its subordinate.

But this is the extent of Pevsner's revisions. He retains his critique of the aesthetic theories that had developed since 1800 following the first Industrial Revolution. He accuses them of having had so devastating an effect on art that Morris had no choice but to devise a reform of the arts and architecture as a whole, and to anchor this in a project of social and artistic reform that would be effected through the production of quality objects created for all. Pevsner carefully develops his retrospective analysis around this succession of events in order to establish and legitimize a Modern Movement that in 1936 was still fragile. Pevsner maintains that Morris's stance made inevitable the universal and industrial style of the Modern Movement as initiated by its "pioneers," and that, in 1914, the question had already been settled.

Yet if the reasons for Pevsner's presentation of the Modern Movement are relatively clear, they fail to explain the significant change made to his title, which he declines to comment on. For the second edition, Pevsner's pioneers go from being those of the "Modern Movement" to those of "Modern Design," a change that remains for the third edition published in 1960. The change was apparently made at the request of his friend Allen Lane, the

84 Pevsner, *Pioneers of the Modern Movement*, 19.
85 Nikolaus Pevsner, *Pioneers of Modern Design: From William Morris to Walter Gropius* (New York: Museum of Modern Art, 1949), 7.

owner of Penguin Books. While the term "design" would have brought to mind, for speakers of French, German, or Italian, at least in 1960, the industrial production of everyday objects, in English it had no such specific connotation. As such, it is quite possible that the use of this term represents a deliberate editorial decision to prevent the work from seeming like a defense of the Modern Movement, which by 1960 had become outdated to the point of crisis.

A partial answer can perhaps be found in a similar revision that Pevsner made to his 1964 publication *The Sources of Modern Art*, the second edition of which was retitled *The Sources of Modern Architecture and Design*.[86] What can be learned from this substitution of "the Modern Movement" with "Design"?

In *Pioneers*, Pevsner employs the term "designer" on a number of occasions, notably to describe Morris's contemporary Lewis Day: "Day, a well-known industrial designer of his time, wrote as one who prefers a life in the real world to dreams of a medieval and idyllic existence."[87] Yet when describing the various figures working in the shop belonging to cabinetmaker Karl Schmidt in Dresden in 1898, which "employed from the beginning modern architects and artists as designers,"[88] Pevsner does not specify the difference between them nor the role that each played. He returns to the figure of the designer to emphasize that, in the Europe of the early twentieth century, "there were hardly any instances outside Germany of outstanding artists or architects working not for decorative art but for industrial design."[89] Pevsner links design

86 Nikolaus Pevsner, *The Sources of Modern Architecture and Design* (London: Thames & Hudson, 1968).
87 Pevsner, *Pioneers of the Modern Movement*, 28.
88 Ibid., 37.
89 Ibid., 38.

with industrialization, the manufacture of furniture, and the fruits of the labor of architects or artists rather than of designers.[90] These contradictions render obscure the meaning that the term "design" holds for Pevsner: Does it refer to a question of craftsmanship, of the creation of furniture by architects, of standardized production, or of a modern style? Whose work ought to be considered in terms of design? The case of Charles Voysey demonstrates the ambiguity of Pevsner's terms: he is referred to variously as an "artist," "a designer of furniture, [and] not a craftsman," and the author of "decorative designs" who would eventually develop "an architectural style." Pevsner's lack of precision on the subject, given his devotion to the cause of modern architecture, might in fact betray a lack of interest in any subordinate disciplines.

None of these questions would be addressed in the third edition of Pevsner's work, which instead sought only to rectify certain omissions, affording a greater importance to wrought-iron architecture, the work of Charles Rennie Mackintosh, and the Futurists. The long-overdue inclusion of the Futurists can be attributed to advice from Banham, whose 1958 doctoral thesis was supervised by Pevsner, and published in 1960 as *Theory and Design in the First Machine Age*.[91] Banham's work reevaluated the Modern Movement through an original theoretical framework, seizing upon its contradictory narratives in order to bring to light an altogether more complex counter-history. He asserted in particular the significance of the influence of De Stijl upon the Bauhaus, after Gropius and Herbert Bayer had minimized the contribution of this movement in

90 Pevsner makes an exception for Germany, which he describes as the only country to boast industrial designers at the turn of the century.

91 Reyner Banham, *Theory and Design in the First Machine Age* (London: Architectural Press, 1960). I refer to the 1980 MIT Press edition in this book; see note 51.

their 1938 exhibition at the MoMA in New York.[92] Banham thus detected historical inconsistencies in order to challenge established consensus and define a methodological starting point for critical revision. I aim to take a similar approach here, drawing attention to the equally glaring contradictions within the history of design—a history divided between facts and propaganda. I will question the reasons for such blind spots, and, as I have already begun to, consider the relationship between the history of design and the history of the Modern Movement. While I draw inspiration from Banham's work, this text will also cast a critical eye upon his contribution; as I will later attempt to show, even as he proposes a more nuanced role for modern architects, he fails to escape from their disproportionate influence.[93]

In 1948, twelve years after the appearance of *Pioneers of the Modern Movement*, and the year of its first reissue, Giedion published *Mechanization Takes Command*. Having set out to write a historical treatise provisionally titled *The Origins of Modern Man*, Giedion's first effort in the 1930s took the form of a manuscript entitled *Konstruktion und Chaos*, before it evolved into the text that I will discuss here.[94] Giedion brought together what he called "fragments" and set out "the origins of everyday life,"[95] building on research and lectures from his time at Yale, where he had taught since 1941. Yet Giedion's perspective on modernity did not lead to an analysis of design that resembles Pevsner's even vaguely, and instead he proposes a new set of

92 The exhibition "Bauhaus 1919–1928" was organized by Walter Gropius and Herbert Bayer at the invitation of Alfred H. Barr Jr., and held at the MoMA in New York, December 7, 1937–January 30, 1938.
93 Banham, "Design by Choice," in *Design by Choice*, 97–107 (see note 4).
94 Between 1929 and 1938, Giedion worked in Paris, London, and Switzerland on the manuscript of *Konstruktion und Chaos*. Sokratis Georgiadis discusses this unpublished work in "Giedion and the Third Factor," *Daidalos*, no. 27 (March 1988): 63–64.
95 Giedion, *Mechanization Takes Command*, 21, 22 (see note 1).

origins, referencing figures other than Morris and Gropius. He sets out an alternative historical model, based on the ingeniousness of anonymous inventors, and describes the processes of modernization set in motion by new technologies such as lighting, gas heating, and electricity. In a work heavily illustrated with diagrams and photographs, he charts the historical evolution of technology and progress across seven chapters, beginning with "Anonymous History" and concluding with the human body in a chapter entitled "The Mechanization of the Bath."

Constructing his theory from case studies, the anonymous history of Giedion's subtitle alludes to his intention of retracing, across all domains where automation had taken place, the stages of the revolution that saw what he terms "handicraft" give way to mechanical production.[96] Giedion views the world as a unified system in which each manufactured object can be related to a wider whole, and the general is to be found in the particular.

Giedion draws on European thought, from Hellenistic philosophy through to the Middle Ages and the scientific progress of the nineteenth century. A central part of his study of mechanization and movement involves a presentation of the sphygmograph, a device developed by Étienne-Jules Marey around 1860 to capture movement, creating a linear trace of variations in pulse and blood flow. A later chapter on the home features a critique of recent prefabricated units, including Buckminster Fuller's 1927 Dymaxion House, which Giedion labels "grotesque," likening it to a "merry-go-round" and a "half-pumpkin."[97] While recognizing the utility of the mechanized central

96 Giedion's *Mechanization Takes Command* is part of a lineage initiated by Abbott Payson Usher, who compiled a study of the origins of industrialization in *A History of Mechanical Inventions* (New York: McGraw-Hill, 1929), and Lewis Mumford, in *Technics and Civilization* (see note 33).

97 Giedion, *Mechanization Takes Command*, 576.

core in Fuller's proposition, Giedion rejects outright the industrial production of homes more broadly, which he views as an imposition of tyrannical mechanization upon the individual: "As a standard form, multiplied by millions these self-enclosed huts becomes a city planner's nightmare."[98] But it is possible to go beyond this apparent dialectic between the deployment of technology and the outright condemnation of its application for the home by returning to the argument set out by a reflective Giedion in his introduction. He explains how his project was born of the desire to return to the origins of the "split that exists in our period between thought and feeling" and to carry out his work exclusively through the examination of

> humble things, things not usually granted earnest consideration, or at least not valued for their historical import. But no more in history than in painting is it the impressiveness of the subject that matters. The sun is mirrored even in a coffee spoon.[99]

For Giedion, every fragment and every object, no matter how seemingly insignificant, is worthy of historical study—the key point of differentiation between his work and Pevsner's mythology. This is why Giedion's text, encyclopedic and rich in detailed descriptions of different innovations, lauds mechanization in terms of both the "miraculous" automaton and the "utilitarian" rational organization of labor. He applies his approach to all areas of life, from the organic to the inorganic, from bathing

98 Ibid.
99 Ibid., 21.

to cooking, and even to artificial insemination. Whereas Pevsner had carefully assembled a convincing genealogy around a coherent set of events and personalities, Giedion rejects this methodology and in doing so challenges the Modern Movement's hagiography. By referencing documents and patents drawn up by inventors, both famous and unknown, Giedion offers an alternative narrative: a methodology that had already been formed for his 1941 work *Space, Time and Architecture*. Rejecting the idea of neutrality, he proposes a typological approach reminiscent of an encyclopedia of furniture. Giedion treats history as dynamic, acknowledging the usefulness of the dates of the historian's "yardstick," but warning that "in themselves or when pinned to isolated facts, they are as meaningless as the numbers on a ticket."[100]

The geographical scope of Giedion's work also differs from that of Pevsner, encompassing the United States as well as Europe. He suggests that the "constituent furniture of the twentieth century" is the work of "pioneers,"[101] a term he borrows from Gustav Stickley, who uses it with reference to the conquest of the American West (though it is difficult to avoid recalling Pevsner's use of the term at this stage),[102] and of "geniuses," his preferred accolade for European designers and architects.[103] Having established a founding myth different to that of his predecessor Pevsner, he touches briefly upon Morris's work

100 Giedion, *Space, Time and Architecture*, 29.
101 Ibid., 401.
102 See Gustav Stickley, *Craftsman Homes* (New York: Craftsman Publishing, 1909), 202.
103 "Finally, it might even be said as a postscript that William Morris was destined to become the best designer of the 19th century in all Europe at least where flat surfaces are concerned (that is in chintzes, wallpapers, and the like) because he was English and had grown up with a sensitive and intelligent appreciation of English traditions in design. Morris's designs are paraphrases of natural growth. His observation of tree and flower was as close and intense as that of any English landscape painter. But his genius lies in the conversion of these observed data into perfectly fitting surface patterns." Nikolaus Pevsner, *The Englishness of English Art* [1956] (Harmondsworth: Penguin Books, 1988), 107.

and skims over Ruskin, while Muthesius receives only the briefest of mentions. Giedion does, however, dwell upon the formal invention of designers such as Marcel Breuer, Gerrit Rietveld, and Alvar Aalto. There is something of a contradiction in this tying together of heroic individuals (whose trajectories he had initially resisted telling) with the anonymous figures usually excluded by history, whose contribution he celebrates from the outset, as evidenced in his subtitle.

The designer per se does not exist for Giedion in the nineteenth century, though he does discuss the decorator-upholsterer.[104] Like Pevsner before him, Giedion goes on to chart the changing role of the craftsman in the twentieth century, describing the transition to "decorative artist," to "reformer designer," and then to architect trained by the Deutscher Werkbund, suited to the design of furniture.[105] It is not until he describes the Modern Movement that Giedion evokes, with reference to a unified conception of architecture, the emergence of the "designer-architect" or the "architect-designer." The two roles are, in his view, one and the same:

> It was not a matter of designing single pieces or even complete suites of furniture. Now, for the first time since the eighteenth century, the room and its contents were felt as a single entity. By the new standards, the decorative artist, superficially changing forms, had failed. The initiative passed into the hands of architects. Architect and designer merged into one person.[106]

104 Decorator-upholsterers came to be in the nineteenth century—with the taste of elites for upholstery, "the upholsterer becomes identical with the decorator." Giedion, *Mechanization Takes Command*, 364.
105 Ibid., 400–402.
106 Ibid., 484.

However, behind the apparent dissolution of these two once separate roles persists a traditional conception of the architects of the Modern Movement, with the attendant inseparability of the interior and exterior. There is still a refusal to recognize the role of the designer as the figure in charge of the interior, and the architect as responsible for the exterior. Giedion leaves his reader in no doubt: "Many who began as designers later revealed themselves as architects."[107] In the closing pages of his argument, Giedion further clarifies his position as he evokes the "American industrial designer" of the 1920s, if only to condemn them. Evaluating this profession in terms of the Streamline movement alone, Giedion offers a moral judgment, accusing its designers of having subjected the entire nation to the movements of commerce. Yet he contradicts himself soon after, tempering his criticism before reconsidering the designer in the context of mechanization more broadly:

> The industrial designer as such is not a new phenomenon. We have seen how around 1850 Henry Cole exercised direct influence on English industry by the encouragement of artists and by criticism. The activity of the German Werkbund around 1910 also moved in this direction.[108]

With this evocation of the Deutscher Werkbund, and the reforms that it promised for the relationship between design and industry, Giedion echoes Pevsner's project and the conclusion of Pevsner's text. The relationship between man and industry-driven technological progress represents

107 Ibid.
108 Ibid., 497.

a crucial question, and despite having previously raised the issue in *Space, Time and Architecture*, it remains unresolved for Giedion. With *Mechanization Takes Command*, he sets out to sketch the history of this dynamic, and calls for a restoration of the delicate balance between man and machine. In doing so, he reasserts the critical role of the historian, and problematizes the origins and the nature of man's relationship with mechanization, progress, and science.

The Heroic Designer and the Anonymous Designer: Two Opposing Narratives

Discussing the respective narratives proposed by Pevsner and Giedion together raises essential questions as to the complexity and constitution of design's history and origins. Taken together, they can be read as a single historiographical project: Pevsner articulates his history around a series of so-called geniuses and heroes, exceptional figures who proposed some resistance to the decadent societies of their time, while Giedion offers a panorama of the evolution of inventions and machines. In this sense, although each of these historians constructs his own version of history, their visions can be brought together to form a single history of ideas and ontological, moral, and social forms. Pevsner was born in Leipzig in 1902, yet *Pioneers of the Modern Movement* draws for the most part upon the history of Britain, the country that became his home after he emigrated in 1933. British figures are so comprehensively represented in his work that it is worth questioning to what extent his exile, before he obtained UK citizenship in 1946, might have influenced his choice of references, given that he credits his adoptive nation with nothing less than the invention of design and the origin of modern architecture.[109]

109 Pevsner refers to Gilbert Scott, Lord Palmerston, Keats, Coleridge, Shelley, Ruskin, Morris, Ashbee, Crane, Day, and Sedding. He believes that Morris's ideas vanished from England, however, in the ten years following his death: "The initiative now passed to the Continent and the United States, and, after a short intermediate period, Germany became the centre of progress. English writers have not failed to acknowledge this fact; but hardly anybody has tried to explain it. One reason may be this: so long as the new style had been a matter which in practice concerned only the wealthier class, England could foot the bill. As soon as the problem began to embrace the people as a whole, other nations took the lead, nations that lived no longer, or had never lived, in the atmosphere of the *ancien régime*, nations that did not accept or did not know England's educational and social contrasts between the privileged classes and those in the suburbs and the slums." Pevsner, *Pioneers of the Modern Movement*, 29.

Giedion, meanwhile, was born in Switzerland and emigrated to the United States in 1938, shortly before the outbreak of war; the inventors, patents, and references of his "contribution to an anonymous history" are largely American, though some of them appear in works that predate this transatlantic move.[110]

The two historians differ not only in terms of the nations that they privilege for discussion but also in terms of their ideological imperatives. Pevsner's absolute belief in the moral value of modernism contrasts with the taxonomic and functionalist ideology developed by Giedion through the analysis of selected forms, materials, and industrialized objects. Giedion does not, however, limit his study to the stated positions of their creators, but rather avoids the potential naivety of such an approach by investigating the diverse ramifications of mechanization, a phenomenon he had already detailed in *Space, Time and Architecture*. Giedion explores the evolution of modernity while expressing concern about its consequences, and in this respect *Mechanization Takes Command* can be considered the echo of his previous work. Far from offering an unambiguous history, the contradiction within *Mechanization Takes Command* manifests in a kind of double language. While the overall tone of the text is progressive, invoking a multitude of descriptions and examples to express the benefits and achievements of mechanization, in the preface and conclusion another tentative voice is discernible, warning the reader against the dangers of mechanization. Pevsner and Giedion reference different sources and periods, but their sagas share a narrative mode underpinned by a similar progressive perspective, wherein each character and invention advances history ever closer to its

110 F. & L. Gilbreth, Wholesale Grange Supply House, Chicago, 1878; Joseph Bramah (patent 1974); Linus Yale Jr.; Walter A. Wood; Thomas Jefferson, etc.

conclusion, which for both historians lies in the glorious achievements of the Modern Movement.

Particularly striking in Giedion's reading is the role that he attributes to women at the start of the sixth chapter, "Mechanization Encounters the Household." Giedion outlines a lineage of American women in stark contrast to Pevsner's exclusively male, British genealogy, describing a domestic revolution that occurred through an adaption of the Taylorist experiments in rational organization that were being carried out at the same time in factories across America. He links these women's struggle for improved status, and in particular for the right to vote, with a broader promotion of democratic values, including a condemnation of slavery, which was still in force in the United States at the time. Using hitherto unexplored sources, Giedion constructs a pantheon of female innovators presided over by Catharine Esther Beecher, who created the notion of "domestic economy."[111] Beecher elevated the organization of the home to the political sphere, as "housekeeping for her was not an isolated problem, but one that grew out of the feminine question as a whole."[112] Giedion's American perspective, to which Beecher is key, provides a useful counterweight to Pevsner's squarer focus on Britain. Through her adaption of the rationalization of movements and actions to the domestic sphere, Beecher demonstrated that slaves were no longer necessary for the upkeep of the home. Beyond her promotion of rationality, and behind her functionalist discourse, Beecher expounded an ideology that aimed not only to ease the labor of women but more importantly to lend weight to her abolitionist convictions. Giedion's evocation of Beecher reveals his belief that design is necessarily tied to a form of political functionalism.

111 Giedion, *Mechanization Takes Command*, 426–27.
112 Ibid., 425–26.

On the other side of the Atlantic, the Industrial Revolution prompted a reflection on the consequences of standardization, led by Morris, who chose decorative arts as his conduit while maintaining the reform of the political sphere as his end goal. By restoring Beecher to the history of innovation, Giedion is able to simultaneously challenge and complete Pevsner's conception of design in which Morris reigns supreme. In Giedion's work Beecher supplants Morris as he retraces her impact over the course of the following century and the debt owed to her by innovators such as Christine Frederick. This original historical perspective confers an unprecedented importance upon the contributions of women, and confronts *Pioneers of the Modern Movement*—not least Pevsner's presentation of his male pioneers as virtue incarnate, in particular Morris, whose combination of moral, political, social, and environmental values represented those of the Victorian era. Secondly, he presents functionalism as a picture of the humanist values necessary for the successful functioning of democracy, finding its antithesis in redundant and superfluous ornament. And lastly, Pevsner draws on both exceptional works by individuals of note and the production of unremarkable, everyday objects. Giedion's work is, in part, a response to this last omission. Both women and the anonymous inventor are given pride of place in his text, as Giedion sets out to pay tribute to those forgotten by the narrativized movements of history, believing their contribution to be fundamental to the history of industrialization. So why evoke simultaneously female and anonymous inventors?

It is possible that Giedion was in fact consciously attempting to destabilize Pevsner's heroic model, in order to better rewrite the history of the Modern Movement. In the nineteenth century, women were particularly active in the private sphere, and although the boundaries of public and private life had begun to blur, their roles and prerogatives remained unchanged. Giedion's decision to discuss the inventiveness of women is all the more necessary given the fact that, far from being a neutral space, the private sphere was highly gendered and considered to be the only site for female creativity. Despite women's increasing transgression of the bounds of the traditional domestic sphere and the changes they were making in society, historians of modernity consistently fail to recognize their contribution: the ideas, inventions, and strategies developed by women in the home, even given the subsequent impact of these upon the public sphere. It was not until the 1980s that their contribution finally received the recognition that it deserved, in the work of Cheryl Buckley, for example.[113] However, a careful reading of Giedion makes it possible to contest the consensus among historians of design that the exclusion of women can be attributed to their relative distance from industrialization and their confinement to the domestic sphere, and, by extension, the historical model that followed.

Pevsner portrays the history of design as being influenced by the conception of men as engineers, architects, and artists. Women are glaringly absent. In defining mechanization in terms of "cheaper substitutes for handicraft work,"[114] on the one hand, and the more radical solutions of "practically unknown and uncounted" inventors that "belong to the anonymous history of the century,"[115] on the other, Giedion necessarily alludes to the role of oft uncredited women. Yet after discussing Beecher and Frederick he moves on, leaving only this pair of exceptional women

113 Cheryl Buckley, "Made in Patriarchy: Toward a Feminist Analysis of Women and Design," *Design Issues* 3, no. 2 (Autumn 1986): 3–14.
114 Giedion, *Mechanization Takes Command*, 335.
115 Ibid.

as examples. The integration of Pevsner and Giedion's histories makes it possible to reconcile a heroic lineage with the current of anonymous invention. Pevsner proclaims the progressive reign of democratic values as the exclusive domain of modernity; Giedion responds with his project glorifying history's forgotten figures. The result of their combination is a newly organized historical account—one richer for the critical eye cast upon its constitution—which represents the foundation of a new history of design.

Part II

Design Histories—Beyond the Modernist Perspective of Pevsner and Giedion

In writing his history of modern architecture, Pevsner established a model for design, in spite of the fact that he considered it to be little more than an episode within the history of architecture. At the same time, Pevsner also inadvertently elevated design to a position of paramount importance by demonstrating the debt owed by modern architects such as Henry van de Velde, Hermann Muthesius, Adolf Loos, and Walter Gropius to William Morris, and hence to design. From the point of view of design, this parallel history is all the more intriguing for the analogy it implies between architecture and design, and between the Modern Movement and design; the latter relationship would become the generally accepted reference for the history of design as a discipline. This double analysis makes it possible to dispute the notion that design's origins can be definitively located in modernity, and justifies the necessity of looking beyond the histories of Pevsner and Giedion, regardless of whether they are to be considered biased or truly critical. Faced with the twin cults of the heroic individual and technological progress, it is essential to reconsider the paradigms that underlie the history of design, following the example set by Banham in the field of the history of architecture.[116] In his introduction to *Theory and Design in the First Machine Age*, Banham returns to the conclusion of Pevsner's *Pioneers of the Modern Movement* to propose an alternative genealogy for modern architecture. Banham's work is punctuated with critiques of academism,

116 Banham sets out his historical approach in clear terms in the preface to *Theory and Design*: "To understand what went wrong and what went right with the Modern Movement we must still understand, even try to re-experience, the revolution in sensibility which was wrought by, and upon, the Futurists and their contemporaries like Le Corbusier and Mies van der Rohe, we must understand the irrational mechanistic urges that underlay the rationalist platitudes with which the Bauhaus has been justified to later generations; what romantic dreams of prismatic crystalline splendours, cathedrals of light and colour, are imprisoned in the snug and inexpressive towers of glass that form our current downtown scenes." Banham, *Theory and Design*, 12 (see note 51).

and in John Ruskin he finds his bête noire,[117] yet he does not challenge the underlying principle of filiation, which places Morris at the origin of modern architecture.

In light of the tendency of historians of architecture to treat architecture and design together, the present study aims to identify and investigate the sources that can be said to belong exclusively to design, in order to obtain a new perspective on the discipline. For the historians of the 1950s, historical revision represented a kind of generational catharsis, with Banham recalling in his introduction, "In the Fifties we were all revisionists, and spoke sneeringly of our elders and betters who still clung to the 'tired certainties of the Thirties.'"[118] Following their example, I aim to present a revision of the history of design, with the acknowledgement that the term "revision" is itself not without conflict.[119]

117 See Nigel Whiteley, *Reyner Banham: Historian of the Immediate Future* (Cambridge, MA: MIT Press, 2002), 20.

118 Banham, *Theory and Design,* 10.

119 See Reyner Banham, "History under Revision: History and Psychiatry," *Architectural Review*, May 1960; in *Design by Choice*, 20–22 (see note 4). In the very first line, Frédéric Migayrou discusses in his introduction to the French edition of Banham's *Theory and Design*: "Banham himself uses the word 'revision,' a term that is ambiguous to say the least—particularly given the fact that this clearly important text does not reappear in the anthology *A Critic Writes* [...]. Revision is conceived as an instrument for re-reading the modern period, one that will bring to light its 'zones of silence.' Banham likens this process to a kind of 'psychiatry' or even psychoanalysis, which ratifies this interpretation of modern architecture by celebrating its leading figures (the quest for respectable grandfathers)." Frédéric Migayrou, introduction to Reyner Banham, *Théorie et design à l'ère industrielle*, trans. Christelle Bécant (Orléans: Éditions HYX, 2009), 32.

Proto-design: The Advent of Industrialization, or Design before Pevsner

In order to avoid the potential for manipulation inherent to historically marked terms such as "decorative arts," "minor arts," and "applied arts," I will discuss design at the advent of industrialization in terms of what I call *proto-design*. As I have already attempted to show, the hypotheses of Pevsner and Giedion are at once unavoidable in any discussion of design, and wholly exterior to the discipline. It is important to bear in mind that Giedion and Pevsner set out respectively to identify the constellation of forerunners of the history of modern architecture and to celebrate the laws of reason, logic, and even functionalism—neither of these authors was concerned with writing the history of design. However, as I have previously discussed, these authors and their hypotheses established an "accidental history." It is an undeniably ambiguous history, preoccupied with issues that are indifferent to design though they do not openly dismiss it, yet in reading between the lines of these texts, it becomes clear that the elements and sources assembled by Pevsner and Giedion are nonetheless compatible with a potential history of design.

Women and Proto-design: Politics, Feminism, and Domestic Organization

Toward the middle of the nineteenth century, American women adopted functionalist principles from the factory production line to shape the organization of the domestic realm that preceded Taylorism by some decades. These proto-designers, led by Catharine Beecher, would become a reference for Giedion in the United States, and for Paul Breton, the organizer of the Salon des arts ménagers from 1929 to 1976, in France.[120] The eldest of twelve children of a well-to-do Boston family, Beecher pioneered the notions of domestic economy and hygiene. Though best known for her various instructive works offering practical advice to young women, Beecher was also a shrewd businesswoman: the educational bodies that she founded included the Hartford Female Seminary, a private school for young women; the Western Female Institute; and the Ladies' Society for Promoting Education in the West. Beecher's contribution ranges from practical inventions, such as devices for ventilation and air circulation, or the continuous work surface (1869), to broader principles such as the rational layout of different rooms, the regulation of temperature, practical storage, and even good posture and

120 Beecher's works include: *Suggestions Respecting Improvements in Education, Presented to the Trustees of the Hartford Female Seminary, and Published at Their Request* (Hartford, CT: Packard & Butler, 1829); *An Essay on the Education of Female Teachers, Written at the Request of the American Lyceum and Communicated at Their Annual Meeting, New York, May 8, 1835* (New York: Van Nostrand & Dwight, 1835); *The Elements of Mental and Moral Philosophy, Founded upon Experience, Reason, and the Bible* (Hartford, CT: Peter B. Gleason, 1831); *An Essay on Slavery and Abolitionism, with Reference to the Duty of American Females* (Boston: Perkins & Marvin, 1837); and *Educational Reminiscences and Suggestions* (New York: J. B. Ford, 1874). For evidence of Beecher's influence beyond America, see Paul Breton, ed., *L'art ménager français* (Paris: Flammarion, 1952), and Catherine Clarisse, "En Europe, la grande ancêtre prestigieuse officiellement revendiquée est la cuisine américaine de Catharine Beecher," in *Cuisine, recettes d'architecture* (Paris: Les Éditions de l'Imprimeur, 2004), 61.

body care. Her advice aimed to save the homemaker time and spare her unnecessary fatigue.[121] Her bestselling 1841 text *A Treatise on Domestic Economy* lauds the virtues of rational organization, treating the domestic economy as a science, and domesticity as a profession.[122] Beecher promotes a rationalist aesthetic that relies upon practical analyses. She visited the Lowell Mills to confirm her intuitions and observe up close the production line, coupling this with the political conception of the domestic economy with which Giedion would later credit her.[123] For Giedion, Beecher's writing establishes a kind of enclave in the history of design in which women establish the domestic sphere as a space of social and political reform intertwined with national ramifications. This aspect of Beecher's work was consolidated in 1869 when, together with her younger sister Harriet Beecher Stowe, the author of *Uncle Tom's Cabin*, she penned a notable text entitled *The American Woman's Home*, in which the emancipation of women is equated with the rational organization of their homes.[124]

Richly illustrated with diagrams showing optimum storage strategies for everything from shoes to spices to fabric, as well as anatomical charts and plumbing models, this work marks a clear change in the status of the housewife, recognizing homemaker as a profession. The Beecher sisters explain in their introduction that, just as men begin their careers only after many years of study, it is only through some form of instruction that women can fully assume their professional responsibilities as mothers, wives, and homemakers. Implicit in this reappraisal of the

121 See Anson Rabinbach, *The Human Motor: Energy, Fatigue, and the Origins of Modernity* (Berkeley: University of California Press, 1992).
122 Catharine Beecher, *A Treatise on Domestic Economy for the Use of Young Ladies at Home and at School*, rev. ed. (New York: Harper & Brothers, 1846), 5.
123 Giedion, *Mechanization Takes Command*, 424–31 (see note 1).
124 Catharine Beecher and Harriet Beecher Stowe, *The American Woman's Home; or, Principles of Domestic Science* (New York: J. B. Ford, 1869).

domestic space was a demand for the same rights men enjoyed, as well as a reinforcement of the Victorian separation between private and public spheres. The workplace had long been open to the world and its movements, and the domestic space a refuge; with the Beechers, it too would become a place of work. The adaptation of the industrial model to the home brought with it a revolutionary corollary: the Beechers called for women who had trained and been educated in the upkeep of the home to be granted financial independence. Giedion emphasizes the fact that, for Beecher, the upkeep of the home "was not an isolated problem, but one that grew out of the feminine question as a whole."[125] This stance is reflected in the analogy used by the sisters in a pamphlet wherein they called for housewives to be considered "house physicians [who would] be as liberally educated and paid as men for curing diseases."[126] In among the recipes and advice on maintaining good health, one finds a redefinition of women's place in nineteenth-century industrial society. This remains the case, in the context of the time, even though Beecher—at once a fervent reader of Tocqueville's *Democracy in America* and an advocate for domesticity as an ideological expression of virtue—saw a woman's role first and foremost as that of devoted wife and mother, and her place definitively in the home.

Beecher's notion of the rational home problematizes the conception of functionalism as the efficient, impersonal servant of capitalism, to form the basis of an ambitious educational mission with genuinely political implications. Beecher used the rationalization of movements and actions in the home to demonstrate the feasibility of a

125 Ibid., 514.
126 Katheryn K. Sklar, *Catharine Beecher: A Study in American Domesticity* [1973] (New York: Norton, 1981), 268.

reduced staff, and thus the possibility of maintaining a home without slaves. Her functionalism ultimately anticipated the outcomes of a future ideology that aimed not only to lessen the burden of women but also to lend weight to abolitionist arguments.

Proto-design promoted a vision of the modern world purely in terms of objects and things through the application of the methods and materials of industrialization. Beecher's example shows that functionalism has been used from design's outset as a means of imposing a social responsibility upon the designer, and of legitimizing the more dissenting, political, and revolutionary aspects of design. An examination of Beecher's work makes it possible to articulate this angle, as well as to counter misconceptions that all discussion of design by women should reductively replay the tensions between industrial and craft production, and in turn between men and women. Returning to Beecher, the legacy of her educational mission, and the many theories it subsequently informed, which would in turn be reinterpreted by the generations that followed, dispels the notion of design as an exclusively masculine phenomenon. Since the 1980s, a feminist perspective has challenged the reductive critical discourse surrounding design and its origins, and has gradually dismantled the orthodoxy initiated by Pevsner.

Beecher's conclusions were just the starting point for an ongoing reflection on the mechanization of domestic tasks, which began with the next generation and would continue throughout the twentieth century across the globe. One such example was the concept developed by Christine Frederick of "creative waste." Frederick was a professor of domestic science and a regular contributor to titles such as *The Designer* (1920–29) and *Ladies' Home Journal*. She began her research by looking at the organization of the kitchen, but soon expanded her scope to encompass social and economic concepts. Her progressive notion of creative waste, according to Ellen Lupton and Jack Abbott Miller, mirrors the digestion of nutrients in the body:

> Her phrase "creative waste" elevated the garbage of consumer culture into a form of positive production, valuing the destruction and replacement of objects as a pleasurable and socially instrumental act. Frederick and other promoters of consumerism conceived of "waste" not merely as an incidental by-product, a final residue, of the consumption cycle, but as a generative, necessary force. In the consumer economy, "production" finds a place inside the process of consumption, a cycle that reiterates the body's own form of "creative waste," excrement.[127]

Similar organizational principles can be found in the "domestic Taylorism" of Paulette Bernège; the two women held each other in high regard, with Bernège inviting Frederick to speak on a number of occasions and publishing several of her texts, and Frederick applauding Bernège for her efforts to spread the gospel of optimized housekeeping in Europe.[128]

Beecher's domestic economy was inspired at least partially by her belief in abolitionism, and in the 1920s the application of rational principles by the likes of Bernège

127 Ellen Lupton and J. Abbott Miller, *The Bathroom, the Kitchen, and the Aesthetics of Waste: A Process of Elimination* (New York: Kiosk, 1992), 7.

128 "In France a small but brave attempt is being made by my brilliant, self-sacrificing friend, Mlle. Paulette Bernège, who has sponsored and directs that unique home-management periodical, *Mon-Chez-Moi* which more than perhaps any other in Europe is attempting to educate the woman in modern scientific housekeeping." Christine Frederick, *Selling Mrs. Consumer* (New York: The Business Bourse, 1929), 284–85.

and Frederick once again underpinned a project of reform that was far from apolitical. Beecher wrote in a religious, political, demographic, and economic context shaped by the unprecedented technological revolution set in motion by industrial capitalism, which attempted to institute a belief in a democratic, theological, and moral individualism. It is significant that the ramifications of these changes extended to the organization of the family and the home. These areas remained relatively faithful to family traditional models, if only to offset the transformations of production, which moved from within the family unit to the factory floor, and eventually to the home again, enhanced by systems developed on the assembly line. Despite the social and political ramifications of their work, however, none of these women set out to reform the relationship between the sexes. In extolling the value of domesticity and seeking to influence the education of an elite class of young women, Beecher aimed not so much to raise the status of American women as to make them aware of their grave responsibilities in the context of a nation in peril. The ambiguous nature of her revolution reflected the contradictions in her own life philosophy: while she was uninterested in altering the balance of power within the home, as historian Janice Williams Rutherford observes, "Beecher espoused the doctrine of separate spheres, yet she sought the power and influence available only to men under the terms of that doctrine."[129]

The same can be said for Frederick, who never missed an opportunity to reassert the importance of traditional family values. She repeatedly extolled the virtues of modesty and the submission of wives to their husbands, rejecting

129 Janice W. Rutherford, *Selling Mrs. Consumer: Christine Frederick and the Rise of Household Efficiency* (Athens: University of Georgia Press, 2003), xix.

feminist values in her speeches and even pleading the cause of men, whom she saw as victims of the new balance in roles between the sexes. More than simply declining to conceive of her work in terms of the emancipation of women, she readily disparaged the political dimensions of Beecher's work. However, it would be incorrect to suggest that Frederick's contribution was confined to the transformation of the home. Frederick traveled the world to promote the benefits of consumerism and efficiency, while simultaneously adhering to the notion that a woman's place is in the home. In this she reflects fundamental transformations brought about by the Industrial Revolution, namely, the collapse of morality in the face of commerce and the reconfiguration of the relationship between the sexes with women's newfound independence through paid factory work. Frederick has been considered variously a feminist by Samuel Haber,[130] a "double agent" by Gwendolyn Wright,[131] and an "antifeminist" by Dolores Hayden,[132] who levels this charge on the grounds that she drove women into the arms of consumerism. Ultimately, any portrait of Frederick must take into account the political and social context of her class.

The genealogy of these American women who carried out research into the organization of the home raises something of a paradox. Their projects reinforce a marked separation between the public and private spheres, yet at the same time promote a reform of domestic organization and the education of women with a view to their emancipation. They strive for domestic chores to be recognized,

130 Samuel Haber, *Efficiency and Uplift: Scientific Management in the Progressive Era, 1890–1920* (Chicago: University of Chicago Press, 1964), 62–63.

131 Gwendolyn Wright, *Building the Dream: A Social History of Housing in America* (Cambridge, MA: MIT Press, 1983).

132 Dolores Hayden, *The Grand Domestic Revolution* (Cambridge, MA: MIT Press, 1982); and *Redesigning the American Dream: The Future of Housing, Work, and Family Life* (New York: Norton, 1984).

not as the socially inexistent activity of the subaltern, but as a profession in their own right. However, while they succeeded in maintaining society's stability by reconciling the division of roles along gender lines with the modernization of the private sphere that threatened to destabilize them, they also allowed men to retain their power and the spaces associated with it. This is why the advent of a female conception of design actually preserved divisions along gender lines rather than challenging them.

Frederick's work had a pragmatic dimension at a time when domestic employees were becoming scarcer and more expensive. Taking up Beecher's mantle, she promoted the professionalization of housework, and took cues from the scientific field, insisting that white uniforms ought to be worn, using a technical vocabulary, and approaching the kitchen as if it were a laboratory. She readily used the tools of self-promotion to disseminate her views: in a photograph taken for the inside cover of her book *The New Housekeeping: Efficiency Studies in Home Management*, she is pictured in a white apron and bonnet, the uniform of a professional homemaker.[133] The domestic space, once the preserve of private and emotional life, is transformed according to a rational framework. While these innovations undeniably saw a masculine rationality enter the feminine, supposedly irrational, private sphere, the opposite movement was also taking place. Though the metamorphosis of the domestic sphere was ostensibly along rational lines, the entry of the laws of consumption into the home brought with them the danger of irrational choices and purchases. Frederick anticipated this assault and built her barricades in the kitchen. The reform of the domestic

133 Christine Frederick, *The New Housekeeping: Efficiency Studies in Home Management* (New York: Doubleday, 1913).

environment was to be achieved through material culture and the acquisition of innovative, efficient, and rational tools. In *Selling Mrs. Consumer*, Frederick decrypts what she deemed to be female consumer psychology in chapters such as "Feminine Instincts and Buying Psychology" and "Women and Eye Appeal." She explains to business owners and admen that it is essential that they pay close attention to women's "tastes," given that the consumer is essentially a female figure: "Women react very sharply to the appearance and exterior of articles or merchandise, are often indeed hypersensitive on the subject. Every seller should realize this clearly and plan his merchandise and advertising accordingly."[134] She explains that it is the manufacturer's responsibility to find convincing sales pitches to seduce female consumers, alluding to the field of advertising that was beginning to interest American industrial designers at the time.

Frederick's innovations were inspired by those of Taylor, the inventor of the scientific management of labor in factories across the country, the governing principles of which he lays out in his work *Principles of Scientific Management*.[135] Frederick began to publish her series of articles on the adaptation of these rules with a view to increasing domestic productivity in 1912, before collecting them in 1913 in *The New Housekeeping*. By this point, the domestic model of slavery had been replaced by a contractual model in which the mistress of the house and her employees formed a standardized team, where each member had individual obligations to fulfill.

Like Beecher before her, Frederick adapted methods that had been pioneered in American factories, which she

134 Frederick, *Selling Mrs. Consumer*, 152.
135 Frederick W. Taylor, *The Principles of Scientific Management* (New York: Harper, 1911).

had learned about at business dinners she organized for her husband and his colleagues. She recalls, "I became acquainted, through my husband's interests, with several men in close touch with the new movement of industrial efficiency. From them I learned what the new science of work was accomplishing for the office, the shop, the factory." She decided to experiment with these innovations, even though, she writes, "At first it did not occur to me that methods which were applicable to organized industries, like shoe factories, and iron foundries, could also be applied to my group of very unorganized industries the home."[136] Her text is at once manifesto and manual for the organization of housekeeping, and promotes the minimization of movements and a reduction of fatigue. Associated with the effort of labor, fatigue became a subject of fascination in the nineteenth century. It was seen as embodying the malaise of the Industrial Revolution, and as a sickness that could be cured through the reorganization of the home and the workplace.

Frederick proposes to achieve this with a number of key ideas, the first of which she demonstrates through a diagram of her own invention which has since become universal: the "before and after."[137] Describing the correct method for preparing an omelet, Frederick eschews ingredients and recipes in favor of two side-by-side illustrations. The first panel shows the traditional and poorly organized kitchen; it is contrasted with a second, which presents a space organized according to Frederick's principles. She further lends weight to her argument by employing arrows and dashes to track the movements of the housewife in each one. While the left-hand panel is crisscrossed by the

136 Frederick, *Selling Mrs. Consumer*, viii.
137 Christine Frederick, *Household Engineering: Scientific Management in the Home* (Chicago: American School of Home Economics, 1923), 22–23.

diagonal lines of the cook's to-ing and fro-ing in the traditional kitchen, the right-hand panel features just two continuous lines. Frederick thus invented a simple visual method of illustrating the increased efficiency which her innovations made possible in any given context, and the "before and after" has since been widely reused, particularly in the advertising industry. The homemaker working in the logically organized kitchen could avoid unnecessary fatigue by applying these principles. These straightforward demonstrations were republished widely outside of the United States, by Bruno Taut and Erna Meyer in Germany and by Bernège in France. Frederick deconstructed her initial Taylorist frame of reference by contrasting the relative ease with which the worker's clearly defined and endlessly reproduced task was simplified with the multiple and varying movements of the housewife in her kitchen.

With her second central idea, set out in the chapter "The Efficient Tool," Frederick shifts her focus from the organization of space to the appliances and utensils available to the housewife. Critical of the money wasted on appealing but expensive gadgets of limited use or that consume disproportionate amounts of energy, she demonstrates her argument with photographic plates presenting her four categories of admissible appliances: fuel savers, step savers, labor savers, and time savers. She presents more complex inventions, such as an icebox that can be stowed with a system of counterweights, alongside more simple ones, such as the *Lazy Susan*, a rotating circular plaque mounted on a base and placed in the center of the table to facilitate the serving of food. This inventory of ingenious devices reveals the link between the recent domestic revolution and the consumerism that Frederick sought to instill in her readers, America's homemakers. She concludes her work with a description of the *Applecroft*

Home Experiment Station, a laboratory installed in her home where she tested the potential domestic applications of scientific management, as well as products and inventions for cooking and preparing meals. Each of the 1,800 experiments she conducted contributed to her new, more efficient principles for housewives. By establishing a parallel between the home and the laboratory, Frederick sought to apply her personal vision of scientific principles as a coherent system of immediately applicable and effective techniques. However, her Taylorist principles were conceived in the spirit of a new and different form of consumption. By proposing to ease the burden placed upon housewives through the purchase of innovative appliances, she justified the necessity of a productive consumption that played an important role in society.

Frederick's work echoes that of the economist Thorstein Veblen, who had previously explored the relationship between consumption and the ostentatious in *The Theory of the Leisure Class*. However, her own analysis ran contrary to the one set out by Veblen in his chapter "The Pecuniary Canons of Taste." Referencing William Morris and Augustus Pugin, Veblen demonstrates the decisive influence of monetary value on the aesthetics of objects, often at the expense of their function. From this, he extrapolates the principle that the less functional an object is, the more desirable it becomes. He warns against a tendency among consumers to associate costliness and beauty with preciousness and rarity, a phenomenon he fears could lead to the perception that a lack of embellishment is a mark of poor quality.[138] The cycle of taste, with its dual driving forces of imitation and distinction, demonstrates the

138 Thorstein Veblen, *The Theory of the Leisure Class: An Economic Study in the Evolution of Institutions* (New York: Macmillan, 1899).

futility and redundancy of waste. But this perception was challenged by Frederick's concept of creative waste,[139] developed in 1929 following her experiments and explained in her chapter "Luxury Buying and Mrs. Consumer," which lauds waste as essential to the national economy:

> It is now time to assert and proclaim for the American family, on all levels above the Minimum Comfort Level, a bold new Policy, already in existence, without fear of being called extravagant or wasteful. This is the policy of creative waste in spending.[140]

Promoting the idea of an economy subject to a permanent cycle of consumption and the resupplying of goods, Frederick makes a distinction between real waste, "to buy goods which do not fit or will not be used at all, or which are willfully wasted," and creative waste, which is equated to a form of "progressive obsolescence," a term coined by her husband J. George Frederick the previous year.[141] This notion blurred consumption and pleasure, and made the former a civic duty. The economy of consumption that Frederick advocated went beyond the traditional obsolescence of wear and tear, as she espoused the moral obligation of the homemaker to regularly replace the products in her home.[142] To justify her concept, Frederick turned to the ideology of the American advertising industry.[143] This was

139 This contradiction is mentioned by Rutherford in *Christine Frederick and the Rise of Household Efficiency*, 150–52.
140 Frederick, *Selling Mrs. Consumer*, 79.
141 Ibid., 81.
142 Ibid.
143 On consumption see Daniel J. Boorstin, "Welcome to the Consumption Community," *Fortune*, September 1967, 118–38. For an analysis of consumption in America, see T. J. Jackson Lears and Richard Wrightman Fox, eds., *The Culture of Consumption: Critical Essays in American History, 1880–1980* (New York: Pantheon, 1983). For an analysis on the origins and interpretations of consumption, see Grant McCracken, *Culture and Consumption: New Approaches to the Symbolic Character of Goods and Activities* (Bloomington: Indiana University Press, 1988).

summed up in 1932 by the executive Earnest Elmo Calkins, for whom the role of marketing was to ensure that products were used up or no longer usable, in order to guarantee the endless replacement and renewal of products. Items such as radios were to be treated as perishable goods that could be worn out and came with an expiration date.[144]

Defying the perception of housework as a series of inconsequential chores and decorative touches, Frederick anticipated the modernist aesthetic of the machine:

> The machine and power era makes it not only possible but vital to apply in the home the doctrine of creative waste. By this term I mean the relaxation, by those who can afford it, of the old desperate grip most of us had upon values and utility in goods; a desperate grip which became a necessary instinct of self-preservation during our long and bitter hand struggle with our environment before the machine and power emancipated us.[145]

She saw in America's overabundant production of ever more sophisticated appliances and gadgets the expression of a new space of modern creativity distinct from individual craft production. It must be noted, however, that critics have denounced this belief with relative ease as a naive surrender to limitless consumption. But above all, her project can be criticized for having treated consumption and the scientific management of the home as part of the same symbolic system. Insofar as it expresses a broader national cause while drawing on the inventiveness of individuals, Frederick's omission of all questions of style and form is also noticeable.

144 Roy Sheldon and Egmont Arens, *Consumer Engineering: A New Technique for Prosperity* (New York: Harper & Brothers, 1932), 32.
145 Frederick, *Selling Mrs. Consumer*, 81.

Beecher has been criticized for having betrayed women by encouraging their subjugation to their families and husbands, even while she extolled the virtues of freedom. Frederick was in turn condemned for developing ostensibly emancipatory theories that in fact confined women to the narrow roles of housewife and consumer, acting as gendered agents of consumerism. Yet these criticisms should not detract from the truly original solutions and renewed conception of the home these two women proposed. Frederick differs from Beecher in the importance she accords to technology and the rules of form, which had been central to the golden age of engineering-influenced thought since the nineteenth century. This absolute deference to logic is one of the weaknesses in Frederick's argument, which upholds that aesthetic considerations play a secondary role to technical solutions, and implies that any approach which takes aesthetics into account is conceptually lacking and devoid of all complexity.

With its breadth and consequences yet to be determined, the relationship between design and both science in general and the sciences of consumption and engineering continued to gain ground through the rational organization of the home. It reached Europe through the work of Paulette Bernège, editor of the magazine and publishing house Mon Chez Moi and founder of the Ligue de l'organisation ménagère (League for Household Efficiency). Bernège sought to remedy the fatigue of the housekeeper, citing a number of examples of waste that could in no way be considered productive, not even through Frederick's definition. These included the "escalier saboteur" (sabotaging staircase), "matériaux qui épuisent" (exhausting materials), and "distances vampires" (vampiric distances). This last term was coined by Bernège to describe the wasted energy of the housewife's incessant to-ing and fro-ing, and opens the third chapter of her 1928 book, *Si les femmes faisaient les maisons* (If women made houses): "I call them vampires, these poorly studied distances which suck human strength. You must not believe that I am exaggerating. Mathematics is the most rigorous of sciences and the figures I present here are exact."[146] She combines her figures with illustrations: the equation "climbing the stairs 5 times a day for 40 years is the equivalent of raising the 9 million kilograms of the Eiffel Tower to a height of 2.3 meters" is accompanied by a drawing of a slender, elegant woman holding out the Eiffel Tower at arm's length.[147] Bernège's findings echo those of Frederick, whose work she had discovered in 1915 in the magazine *Revue de Métallurgie*, and whom she had met in 1927 at a conference on rationalist principles held in Paris. At Bernège's invitation, on April 22, 1927, Frederick presented her principles in a rudimentary French to the League for Household Efficiency, the Association for Household Electric Appliances, and Bernège's Mon Chez Moi, at a conference chaired by the French minister of housing. A communiqué of the event was published under the title "American Home Economist in Paris after Lecturing English Housewives."[148] The meeting proved to be significant and inspiring for both women, with Bernège publishing Frederick's texts in her magazine and Frederick giving an admiring account of Bernège's work in the United States: "In France a small but brave attempt is being made by my brilliant self-sacrificing friend, Mademoiselle Paulette Bernège, who has sponsored and directs that unique home-management periodical, *Mon-Chez-Moi* which more than perhaps any other in Europe is attempting

146 Bernège, *Si les femmes faisaient les maisons*, 13 (see note 63).
147 Ibid., 6.
148 Paulette Bernège, "Mrs. Christine Frederick," *Mon Chez Moi*, May 1927, 350.

to educate the woman in modern scientific housekeeping."[149] In the years that followed, these two colleagues would continue their epistolary exchange on the science of domesticity.[150]

This domestic and scientific approach grew in renown, reflecting a tentative recognition of the importance of women in American society. The contribution of female innovators was celebrated at a 1935 ceremony at the Astor Hotel given in honor of thirty-five of New York's most important women. Frederick was among the invitees, and on the occasion met her contemporary, the engineer Lillian Gilbreth, whose research into movement represented a further extension of the scientific current initiated by Frederick.

Giedion sets out the foundations for a genealogy of female proto-designers in *Mechanization Takes Command*, but after a brief description of Frederick's work, he leaves them to one side and returns to the Modern Movement and Gropius's Bauhaus. Giedion retraces the evolution of the methods for recording the movement in the chapter "Means of Mechanization," a process which begins in the book's opening pages with a discussion of the work of Marey. Giedion references the work of Frank Bunker Gilbreth, a disciple of Taylor who was hired in 1914 as a consultant by the lighting company Glasglühlicht Auer-Gesellschaft. At this stage, Lillian Moller Gilbreth is mentioned only in conjunction with her husband, yet it was she who, following his premature death, not only took the reins but largely expanded and improved upon the research they had conducted together. Long before Frank's death in 1924,

149 Frederick, *Selling Mrs. Consumer*, 284–85.
150 Very little of this correspondence is still accessible. See Series I. Correspondence, Papers of Christine Frederick, Schlesinger Library on the History of Women in America, Radcliffe Institute for Advanced Study, Harvard University, Cambridge, MA.

the pair of engineers had begun to combine their research into movement with the theories of Taylor, Beecher, and Frederick in order to propose systems, furniture, and tools to ease the burden of fatigue for housewives, workers, and sportsmen alike. They engineered systems to refine their study of the body, and were able capture its movements as it performed an astonishing variety of actions, from the construction of a brick wall to the assembly of soap boxes to the application of stickers to packaging.

One of the innovative instruments that they devised for observing the body and its movements was the microchronometer. As its name suggests, this device measured very short time spans, allowing the Gilbreths to record sequences of gestures with an increased precision. They soon turned to film in order to further refine their results, partnering with the New England Butt Company. Capturing the movements of workers going about their tasks, the Gilbreths recorded some 635,000 meters of film. In order to visually represent and isolate the correct and incorrect gestures, they also used another device from their arsenal, the cyclogram. This lightweight system of bulbs and wires was placed at different strategic points around the body according to the task in question. Their test subjects would then perform their tasks over and over again in front of a camera, in a room fitted with a system of grids to render the readings more legible. Using the resulting plates, the Gilbreths were able to produce, with the aid of nothing more than a system of simple wires, a luminous schema representing the movements involved in each action. With motions thus fixed in space as if they were physical forms, the difference between useful and superfluous actions was immediately visible: the necessary gestures were represented by fluid lines while wasted effort was betrayed by the halting, discontinuous ones it produced. The plates also revealed the length of time required by each movement, along with hesitations, pauses, and errors, and thus clearly showed the postures necessary for more efficient, less tiring labor. In this way, the Gilbreths' studies sought to correct poor physical habits and to find appropriate solutions to relieve the body and mind of the worker as they carried out repetitive tasks.

"No waste is so startling, so enormous, so criminal as the waste of human efforts."[151] Such is the lament that opens the second edition of *Fatigue Study: The Elimination of Humanity's Greatest Unnecessary Waste; A First Step in Motion Study*, published at the end of the First World War. The Gilbreths sought to address fatigue in all its forms and envisaged an extraordinarily ambitious project that would ultimately remain unrealized; their Museum of Fatigue would have consisted of "a collection of devices for and information concerning the elimination of fatigue, or for affording rest for overcoming fatigue. Its purpose is to serve as an object lesson as to how the fatigue problem may be approached practically."[152] Their discussion of fatigue was not new in itself: it had been a much debated notion in the nineteenth century, with the writings of Étienne-Jules Marey and the engineer Charles Frémont particularly important for the popularization of the issue. Yet as Giedion shows, the Gilbreths' work on fatigue was exceptional due to their collaboration with inventors and the ingenious devices that resulted, which prefigured the design landscape in the industrial era.

And it is indeed in Giedion's work that the first comparison between Nicolas Oresme's theory of motion,

151 Frank B. Gilbreth and Lilian M. Gilbreth, *Fatigue Study: The Elimination of Humanity's Greatest Unnecessary Waste; A First Step in Motion Study*, rev. ed. (New York: Macmillan, 1919), ix.
152 Ibid., 99–108.

the work of physiologist Étienne-Jules Marey, and of the Gilbreths can be found: "The American production engineer, Frank B. Gilbreth, is but one link in the great process of mechanization [...]. Gilbreth [...] detached human movement from its bearer or subject, and achieved its precise visualization in space and time. Gilbreth is an innovator in the field of scientific management. His thinking and his methods grow out of the great body of nineteenth-century science."[153] He draws a parallel between the methods developed by the Gilbreths for recording and analyzing the movement of the body and Marey's invention of chronophotography in 1890, praising Marey's ability "to visualize movement as it evolves in space" in the following terms: "This scientist sees his objects with the sensibility of a Mallarmé. Marey called his procedure 'time photography'; its object is to render visible 'movements that the human eye cannot perceive.'"[154] While today it may be tempting to see their work as an exercise in technological control that aimed to simply improve workers' productivity, the Gilbreths were motivated by a sincere belief in progress as a means of improving the conditions of labor and reducing the hardships of work through the elimination of wasted effort. The Gilbreths were immortalized in the young adult novels *Cheaper by the Dozen* and *Belles on Their Toes*, jointly written by Frank Jr. and Ernestine, two of their twelve children, who describe how their parents' research was inspired by their to-ing and fro-ing between the workplace and the kitchen, the factory and the home.[155] This back-and-forth and transfer of techniques is characteristic of the work of proto-designers as a whole, and with the Gilbreths

153 Giedion, *Mechanization Takes Command*, 25.
154 Ibid., 24.
155 Frank B. Gilbreth Jr. and Ernestine Gilbreth Carey, *Cheaper by the Dozen* (New York: Thomas Y. Cromwell, 1948); and *Belles on Their Toes* (New York: Thomas Y. Cromwell, 1950).

it became the starting point of an applied ergonomics that sought to ease work in the factory and the home alike. Lillian continued to promote these nascent scientific principles alone following the death of Frank. In addition to raising their children and continuing their research, she went on to establish a school for the "study of movement" in order to better win the confidence of industrialists who were suspicious of a lone female engineer. Much more than a wife, an assistant, or a collaborator, Lillian Gilbreth was—to cite an accolade she received during her lifetime—very much the "First Lady of Engineering." She held a doctorate from Brown University, was the first woman to join the prestigious American Society of Mechanical Engineers, and the first woman to teach on her subject at Purdue University. She also brought her research into contact with the field of psychology by linking it with scientific management. In her 1919 book, *The Psychology of Management: The Function of the Mind in Determining, Teaching and Installing Methods of Least Waste*, she recognizes motivation, satisfaction, and stress as elements just as important as rational organization, standardization, and ergonomics.

From Beecher to Gilbreth, pioneering women would take the first steps in the history of design and demonstrate the extent to which its origins lie in the feminine and political issues with which it has rarely been associated. Alone in their field, these women operated outside of the model proposed by Pevsner.

Everyday Form versus the Law of the Market: Design, Democracy, and the Nation

While the benefits of technical progress were welcomed with enthusiasm by America and its housewives, in England industrialization was a source of some anxiety for those who worried about its impact upon the lives of their countrymen. This fear of the machine, and, by extension, of industrial production itself, marked design and in particular its relationship with the capitalist economic model. Even proponents of manufacturing who praised its relationship with the industrial arts were ambivalent or even critical of its impact upon the environment, people, and the products it was capable of producing. Among the most influential defenders of industry was Sir Henry Cole, who also worked as a designer under the pseudonym Felix Summerly. Felix Summerly's Art Manufactures, the company he operated, produced tableware, ceramics, metal, glasses, and furniture which referenced antique styles while employing the recent industrial techniques.

With the *Journal of Design and Manufactures*, which he published together with Richard Redgrave between 1849 and 1852, Cole was the first to use the term "design" in print as it is understood today. The journal signaled modernity's expansion, along with nascent industrialization, standardization, functionalism, and the Industrial Revolution's entry into the home, the factory, and, of course, the media. Cole and Redgrave used their journal to promote the principles of industrial production, which they hoped would blend function, decoration, and intelligence. Together with their European contemporaries, such as Owen Jones, author of the 1856 text *The Grammar of Ornament*, or the

German architect Gottfried Semper, and with the help of the Great Exhibition, they were able to construct a discourse whose impact upon modern architects is undeniable. They believed that industrial production could be improved only through a systematic investigation of all its elements. They emphasized the importance of patents, with the reproduction of photographic plates playing a central role in the social and educational project that underpinned their journal. They aimed to reassure their readership and position their publication as an advocate for the copyrights of the designer-inventor.

These same motivations led Cole to call for an alliance between the fine arts and industry, and he would have a significant influence on this process through his tireless promotion and constructive criticism of artists who employed industrial methods. His proposal of a "Great Exhibition" to demonstrate Britain's supremacy in the field of industrial art would become a defining moment in the country's history. Cole and Redgrave's journal aimed to promote the union of art and industrialization, and to create a space for reflection on the subject.

Pevsner's desire to focus on individual inventors explains why he declined to include Cole in his history; Giedion, on the other hand, deems Cole's contribution highly significant, writing in *Mechanization Takes Command* that "Cole exercised direct influence on English industry by the encouragement of artists and by criticism."[156] Cole is of particular interest to my study as he acts as a pivot between Pevsner and Giedion, his work representing a site where their two histories meet. Pevsner's heroes—Morris, Ruskin, and C. R. Ashbee—would all recognize the importance of Cole's work, particularly in terms of the political

156 Giedion, *Mechanization Takes Command*, 610.

and cultural institutions that were his legacy, and which would play an integral role in the future of English design. As such, it is easy to see how Cole could be incorporated into Pevsner's genealogy of pioneers. At the same time, the emphasis the *Journal of Design and Manufactures* placed upon patents and anonymous invention means that Cole's work is in perfect harmony with Giedion's anonymous history.

Art and Industry: Ambitions and Reality

Cole was the first to voice concern over the irrational nature of industrial production. He advocated not a return to artisanal techniques but a harmonization of art and machine, which he believed necessarily called for changes in the era's tastes. To this end he organized a string of exhibitions, Felix Summerly's Collection of Art-Manufactures, as well as setting up competitions and publishing articles expounding his views on the subject in the *Journal of Design and Manufactures*. He readily took aim at the views of Ruskin and the group that had formed around Morris. A contrast with Cole raises questions as to Pevsner's progressive portrayal of Morris: in the articles published in his journal, Cole set out a conception of the relationship between man and machine that was infinitely more bold than the one Pevsner attributes to Morris, and in this Cole seems apt to precede or even replace Morris as design's "pioneer." However, Cole's work was, in a sense, lacking an important element, as Giedion would later argue: "The great disadvantage of Henry Cole and his circle in comparison with the movement of 1920 was their inability to proffer a new artistic vision. This denied them lasting influence."[157] Giedion contrasts Cole's earnest archiving and social and political reforms with the generation of Pre-Raphaelites, led by a passionate Morris, striving for a new aesthetic in the decorative arts. However, this political characterization seems somewhat unjust given Cole's crucial influence upon British design. He founded the body that would give rise to the Victoria & Albert Museum, created the

157 Ibid., 349.

Journal of Design and Manufactures as well as Britain's first design schools, and encouraged designers to apply for patents to protect their copyrights, but his influence was not only institutional: he also contributed to the development of the aesthetics of industrial art. His dedication to the improvement of design's quality and aesthetics was exemplified by a tea set created by his company between 1844 and 1846. The all-white set contrasts sharply with the elaborate aesthetic of the period, which fills the pages of the catalogue of the 1851 Great Exhibition. Its sober forms eschewed habitual ornamentation and drew inspiration from Hellenistic decoration. Rather than meeting disapproval from a public more used to the opulence of decorative luxury, it earned Cole a silver medal from the Royal Society of Arts in 1846.

Despite the relatively narrow role Giedion assigns to him, Cole can be credited with the establishment of an industrial aesthetic in England as well as the subsequent vitriolic critique when it failed. Cole instigated the Great Exhibition, with Sir Matthew Digby Wyatt as secretary of the exhibition's executive committee, Owen Jones as superintendent of works, and J. W. Wild as its decorative architect. Cole implored Prince Albert on a number of occasions to support his proposal for an exhibition modeled on the Exposition des produits de l'industrie française, which had brought together 3,960 exhibitors in the Grand Carré des Jeux des Champs-Elysées in Paris between May 1 and June 30, 1844. Cole's project, which finally came to fruition in 1851, began the tradition of universal exhibitions as the showcase for a triumphant Industrial Revolution, and was the first event to reflect the extent and complexity of the political and aesthetic considerations underlying the history of design. The exhibition took place in Hyde Park in the center of London between May 1 and October 11, 1851, and brought together industrial, scientific, technological, architectural, and artistic innovations in one location, making it possible for the first time to envisage an alliance of art, industry, and science. It featured the works of some 14,000 exhibitors, industrialists, and craftsmen from over forty countries; though most participating nations were industrialized, the superiority of the British exhibitors was immediately obvious. The main exhibition was housed in the Crystal Palace, a monumental glass structure thirty-six meters tall with 70,000 square meters of exhibition space, erected in just seventeen weeks and overseen by architect Joseph Paxton. Its vast scale was made possible, as Pevsner observes, thanks to the first-ever use of standardized methods of construction and recently developed materials in the form of a steel structure and a factory-produced system of prefabricated modular elements. The building symbolized as much as any of the exhibits the technological might of British industry. The exhibition had both political and commercial ends, aiming to present a survey of the state of art and industry in order to usher in a new era founded upon international trade and the expansion of human knowledge. Widespread faith in progress saw great enthusiasm for the exhibition, with machines and the objects they produced widely considered to be critical for the future of humanity. An impassioned Prince Albert viewed them as the culmination of man's work, looking to machines to lessen the burden of labor, increase wealth, and improve the quality of life for all, with the trade of goods guaranteeing peace and fraternity between nations.

While the organizers expected that faith in progress and the abundance of machines and objects presented would provoke an unprecedented wave of enthusiasm and a universal consensus that the machine was a vital expression of humanity, this was not to be. Even Prince Albert, who at the outset of the project had proclaimed, "The distances which separated the different nations and parts of the globe are rapidly vanishing before the achievements of modern invention," and "Nobody [...] who has paid any attention to the peculiar features of our present era, will doubt for a moment that we are living at a period of most wonderful transition, which tends rapidly to accomplish that great end, to which, indeed, all history points—the realisation of the unity of mankind," despaired at the results.[158] The exhibition's proponents and organizers were equally disenchanted, including Cole, who recognized that the craft and industrial products displayed in the Crystal Palace did little to glorify the present state of production. Beyond replacing craft style and ornament with their industrial equivalents, the results were inconclusive and unsatisfying: the standardized products of European countries were inconsistent and largely deferred to the tastes of past eras, and bourgeois taste was still characterized by ostentation and imitation. This bitter and unexpected outcome resulted in a reappraisal of the hierarchy governing industrial, craft, and artistic products, with conclusions that were largely hostile to mechanization. So while Cole and his friends had organized an exhibition that was wildly successful in terms of attendance, drawing some six million visitors and winning over the general public, they were left feeling frustrated, in particular by the absence of governing principles that would be necessary for industry to serve the nation in its drive toward modernity. They found the current output of decorative arts or "industrial arts" mediocre, despite the enthusiasm of the public. Manufacturers meanwhile considered taste and

158 Prince Albert, speech at the Mansion House, March 21, 1850; in John Tallis, *History and Description of the Crystal Palace and the Exhibition of the World's Industry in 1851* [1851] (Cambridge: Cambridge University Press, 2011), 11.

commerce to be two separate and irreconcilable entities, insisting the best was what sold the best. Despite its original intentions, the Great Exhibition made it painfully obvious that industrial prowess guaranteed neither refinement nor virtuosity.

Worse still, the contrast between the modern architecture of the Crystal Palace and the products on display, which sought to flatter bourgeois tastes with a busy and dated style, as well as the contrast between objects produced by machines and those created by craftsmen, caused alarm and prompted a wave of opposition. Proponents of industrial production published numerous pamphlets and critiques despairing at its current state and calling for reform, such as Redgrave's *Supplementary Report on Design* or Semper's *Wissenschaft, Industrie und Kunst*.[159] The latter called for a new form of industrial art and proposed a taxonomy of objects, each with a number of predetermined functions, referencing one previously established by the naturalist Georges Cuvier. This uncertain period gave rise to a wave of dissent led by English intellectuals. Its forerunners were the theater decorator, designer, architect, and theorist Augustus Pugin, who called for a return to the Gothic style; the controversial Scottish author Thomas Carlyle, who advocated for social reform; and the pamphleteer, author, artist, and collector John Ruskin, who had a major influence on his contemporaries and his students alike. Each of them launched scathing attacks on the industrialization of Britain and the materialism that accompanied it, preferring the former grandeur of the Gothic style, which they believed had, by contrast, expressed the moral and spiritual values indispensable to the survival of society.

159 Gottfried Semper, *Wissenschaft, Industrie und Kunst: Vorschläge zur Anregung nationalen Kunstgefühles bei dem Schlusse der Londoner Industrie-Austellung* (Braunschweig: Vieweg, 1852).

Given his role in its promotion, it was surprising that Cole found himself the instigator of the first protests against industrial production, which he now feared was disastrous and irrational. Though far from proposing a return to craft methods, Cole aspired to a new relationship between art and the machine, which he believed necessarily called for the modification of tastes. Along with publishing articles in his journal, Cole ran the aforementioned series of exhibitions, Felix Summerly's Collection of Art-Manufactures, and organized competitions to combat the poor standard of industrial production, which had turned its initial celebration into a bitter disappointment, only accentuated by the flagrant contrast between the architecture of the Crystal Palace and the exhibitions it housed. The cutting-edge building was a popular and critical success, whereas the products, which tried to appeal to contemporary tastes in order to be as commercially successful as possible, had a largely outdated aesthetic. Paxton's building, whose aesthetic was partly determined by the industrial processes of its production, proved to be the only real masterpiece of the exhibition, the only element that truly expressed the progress promised by the Industrial Revolution. This point of view was not shared by all, however, with Ruskin dismissing the building as "a cucumber frame between two chimneys,"[160] whose iron structures detracted from the dignity and integrity of the building, one of the key aesthetic values that he had set out in his 1849 book *The Seven Lamps of Architecture*.[161] He was no kinder to the merchandise it housed. A young Morris, meanwhile, refused to visit the exhibition. Despite the vast space it dedicated to machines of all kinds, from

160 John Ruskin, *Praeterita*, vol. 1 (London: George Allen, 1907), 57.
161 John Ruskin, *The Seven Lamps of Architecture* (London: Smith, Elder, 1849).

wheat threshers to cigarette rollers, and countless pumps, wagons, and locomotives, the exhibition's failure was clear to its organizers. They had believed that the advent of the machine, with the decent working conditions and the plentiful, quality manufactured goods it promised, would naturally promote democratic principles and social progress; but with the Great Exhibition it became apparent that, if not completely incompatible with industrial advancement, the values they cherished were far from the results they were expecting.

The Origin of Design in England: "The Classic Tradition of Design Worry"[162]

For all its initial promise, industrialization had proven to have a bitterly disappointing side and an array of adverse consequences. However, this tragic realization encouraged its proponents to envisage a new way of collaborating that was to be highly rewarding, namely the alliance between the engineer and the designer based on functionalist principles. Design was charged with a noble mission: the renewal and improvement of life itself. But the peasant-turned-worker would fall victim to the same industrial civilization that had made promises of happiness.

For Pevsner, this history begins with Ruskin, a tireless and passionate advocate for the reconciliation of life and art. By seeking to bring together fine arts and applied arts, he prepared the contextual and theoretical terrain upon which Morris would later build. A "prophet" for Gillian Naylor,[163] and a "first thinker" for Pevsner, Ruskin's work allowed his contemporaries "to realize how precarious and decayed the social functions of art had become during the centuries since the Renaissance, and especially during the years since the Industrial Revolution."[164] Pevsner's work reflects Ruskin's belief in a close relationship between society and the arts; it is no coincidence that the first edition of *Pioneers of the Modern Movement* opens with an account

162 For this subtitle, I have again borrowed a phrase from Banham: "Two of the most important resources of modern design are about a hundred and twenty years old now; one is the plastics industry, the other is the tradition of worry about the state of the art [...] I don't have to remind you that design worry was founded by old John Ruskin and young William Morris [...] the classic tradition of design worry." Banham, "All That Glitters Is Not Stainless," in Banham, *Aspen Papers*, 55–60 (see note 36).

163 Gillian Naylor, *The Arts and Crafts Movement: A Study of Its Sources, Ideals and Influence on Design Theory* (Cambridge, MA: MIT Press, 1971), 25.

164 Pevsner, *Pioneers of the Modern Movement*, 22 (see note 1).

of the famous "battle of styles" and a quote from Sir George Gilbert Scott: "Architecture is decoration of construction." In the second edition, this quote is replaced by a near-identical one from Ruskin: "Ornamentation is the principal part of architecture." It is ornamentation that confers upon a building "certain characters venerable or beautiful, but otherwise unnecessary." Pevsner adds further emphasis to this surprising assertion by citing Gilbert Scott's recommendation that architects favor the Gothic style because its "great principle is to decorate construction."[165]

What Pevsner does not discuss, however, is Ruskin's revisiting of the moralistic position developed around Gothic architecture by Pugin in his 1836 book *Contrasts*, and further explored in the 1841 book *The True Principles of Pointed or Christian Architecture*.[166] For Ruskin, the Gothic style was the only valid expression of Christian values, and his examination of it led him to question the moral values associated with each different style, the relation of each to its particular context, and whether or not they reflect the society around them. For Ruskin, the Gothic style represented the absolute and unquestionable model for the life and behavior of man in the Victorian age. He also continued Pugin's combat against the decadent tastes of the era, which Pugin had discussed with both humor and genuine concern. Britons like Pugin and Ruskin aspired to the virtuous Gothic style, and enviously watched its successful

165 The first quote, from Gilbert Scott, is drawn from M. S. Briggs, *The Architect in History* (Oxford: Clarendon Press, 1927), though Pevsner acknowledges that Briggs was unable find the original source (Pevsner, *Pioneers of the Modern Movement*, 19). In the 2nd edition, Pevsner quotes from a lecture given by John Ruskin in Edinburgh, November 1853, published in John Ruskin, *The Works of John Ruskin*, vol. 12: *Lectures on Architecture and Painting* (London: George Allen, 1904), 82–83; Ruskin, *Seven Lamps of Architecture*, 7; and Sir George Gilbert Scott, *Remarks on Secular and Domestic Architecture* (London, 1858), 221 (Pevsner, *Pioneers of Modern Design,* 19).

166 Augustus Pugin, *Contrasts* (London, 1836); *The True Principles of Pointed or Christian Architecture: Set Forth in Two Lectures Delivered at St. Marie's, Oscott* (London: J. Weale, 1841).

revival in Belgium, France, and Prussia from the 1830s onward. This led them to set up committees whose aim was to improve the state of industrial production. Pugin, like Cole before him, did not question the machine itself, and in this he differed from Ruskin, who distanced himself from Pugin to side with Carlyle against industrialization, progress, and the machine, which he believed to be the symptoms of a spiritual and intellectual mediocrity. Carlyle set out his principal ideas in *On Heroes, Hero-Worship, and the Heroic in History* and *Past and Present*, published in 1841 and 1843, respectively. In the first book, he brings together six lectures to create a single history, which begins with Odin and ends with the modern revolution, considered to be the "last form of heroism."[167] According to the theory he develops throughout the work, and which can be easily identified in Pevsner's writing, the forward march of civilization is the result of individual feats of heroism:

> As I take it, Universal History, the history of what man has accomplished in this world, is at bottom the History of the Great Men who have worked here. They were the leaders of men, these great ones; the modellers, patterns, and in a wide sense creators, of whatsoever the general mass of men contrived to do or to attain; all things that we see standing accomplished in the world are properly the outer material result, the practical realization and embodiment, of Thoughts that dwelt in the Great Men sent into the world: the soul of the whole world's history, it may justly be considered, were the history of these.[168]

167 Thomas Carlyle, *On Heroes, Hero-Worship, and the Heroic in History* (London: Chapman & Hall, 1841), 233.
168 Ibid., 3.

Carlyle discusses in succession "gods," "prophets," "poets," "priests," "men of letters," and "kings," each in their own way leaders of humanity. These exceptional beings are endowed with superior moral force, intelligence, bravery, a sense of justice, and sincerity. He believes that these values give meaning to history and propel the masses toward spiritual fulfillment. It is worth considering whether Carlyle's notion of the hero, to which Ruskin proved sensitive, might have also informed Pevsner's heroic history of the origins of modernity.

Ruskin openly drew inspiration from Carlyle's work, extending his critique of civilization's ostensible progress, which saw people go hungry while shops were full of merchandise and workers toil endlessly for pitiful salaries while wealth and riches grew around them. Carlyle lays the blame squarely on thriving mechanization—"On every hand, the living artisan is driven from his workshop, to make room for a speedier, inanimate one"[169]—and despairs that in the political and social sphere "men are grown mechanical in head and in heart, as well as in hand. [...] Their whole efforts, attachments, opinions, turn on mechanism, and are of a mechanical character."[170] He continues his argument denouncing industrialization, which, rather than bringing together and satisfying the greatest number of individuals as it had promised, had instead brought about an exodus, the misery of the slums, and entirely new forms of poverty. Ruskin, though inspired by Carlyle, was by no means his disciple. An unorthodox thinker, he went beyond the ideas of his contemporary to develop an original understanding based on a rejection of the difference between the artist and the worker, and between art and

169 Thomas Carlyle, "Signs of the Times," *Edinburgh Review*, June 1829, 441.
170 Ibid.

the everyday. He considered art as the product of a society and of the needs of its members. Ruskin's most significant contribution to the field of design came in the form of his outright condemnation of the machine, and in particular the dehumanization it brought about:

> It is not, truly speaking, the labour that it divided; but the men—divided into mere segments of men—broken into small fragments and crumbs of life; so that all the little piece of intelligence that is left in a man is not enough to make a pin, or a nail, but exhausts itself in making the point of a pin or the head of a nail.[171]

Forced to carry out thoughtless tasks and deprived of a chance to exercise their capacity for creativity, workers would inevitably come to despise themselves, as "the kind of labour to which they are condemned is verily a degrading one, and makes them less than men."[172] Ruskin favored artisanal production, even with its flaws, which he saw as signs of humanity ("Men were not intended to work with the accuracy of tools, to be precise and perfect in all their actions") and the imperfect product of the craftsman as a reassuring reflection of the imperfection of human nature itself:

> Understand this clearly: you can teach a man to draw a straight line, and to cut one; and to copy and carve any number of given lines or forms, with admirable speed and perfect precision; and you find his work perfect of its kind: but if you ask

171 John Ruskin, "The Nature of Gothic," in *The Stones of Venice*, vol. 2, *The Sea Stories* (London: Smith, Elder, 1853), 165.
172 Ibid., 163.

> him to think about any of those forms, to consider
> if he cannot find any better in his own head,
> he stops; his execution becomes hesitating; he thinks,
> and ten to one he thinks wrong; ten to one he makes
> a mistake in the first touch he gives to his work
> as a thinking being. But you have made a man of him
> for all that. He was only a machine before, an
> animated tool.[173]

Such a critique of industrial production represents the first step toward the realization of Ruskin's aesthetic project. While some of his texts, such as *The Political Economy of Art*, *The Two Paths*, or the more complete *Unto This Last* are sometimes considered minor relative to his other writing on art and architecture, it is in these works that Ruskin develops the ideas that would be essential for the development of a conception of the decorative arts which was simultaneously political and moral.

With a deliberately moralistic vision, Ruskin proposes a new framework for determining the value of an object. No longer a question of price or profitability, and less still of usage, Ruskin sets out the principles of "Sacrifice," "Truth," "Power," "Beauty," "Life," "Memory," and "Obedience," which together can fully account for intrinsic value. An object has no value beyond its ability to be placed in the service of life, whether that of the body or the mind; wealthy people who do not know how to make good use of their possessions are rich only in appearance.

In *Unto This Last*, Ruskin brings together four of his articles on the economy previously published in the *Cornhill Magazine*, and sets the tone from the very beginning:

173 Ibid., 161.

> Among the delusions which at different periods have possessed themselves of the minds of large masses of the human race, perhaps the most curious—certainly the least creditable—is the modern *soi-disant* science of political economy, based on the idea that an advantageous code of social action may be determined irrespectively of the influence of social affection.[174]

Ruskin developed bold critiques of Britain's market economy, and long before the Deutscher Werkbund and the Bauhaus, he established a link between the economic and the aesthetic, between the production of goods and the conditions of life. A critic and a visionary, his project sought to bring about a revolution of everyday life. Ruskin imagined a version of the welfare state well before it became a reality, envisaging a structure that would meet the physical, spiritual, and cultural needs of all, including the poor and disabled. The project for a utopian society in *Unto This Last* was met with attacks from all sides, with the author accused of "eruptions of windy hysterics."[175] Carlyle was the only exception to his near-unanimous condemnation, and Ruskin was fired from the *Cornhill Magazine* following the publication of his text. The experience made it clear to Ruskin that his long-held desire for artistic reform was far from compatible with the traditional values of Victorian England. The realization that his program would be destined to fail as long as the political landscape of the country remained the same led Ruskin to withdraw from intellectual life and divert his energy into a project that was modest in scale but

174 John Ruskin, *Unto This Last* (London: Smith, Elder, 1862), 1.
175 John Ruskin, *The Collected Works of John Ruskin*, ed. E. T. Cook and Alexander Wedderburn, vol. 17 (London: George Allen, 1905), xxviii.

even more ambitious: he set out to establish an ideal community of craftsmen modeled on the guilds of the Middle Ages, and in 1871, founded the Guild of St George. This brief endeavor lasted just four years, but is notable for the fact that, contrary to Pevsner's characterization of Ruskin, its rejection of the machine was by no means total: its rules stated that "machinery is only forbidden by the Guild where it supersedes healthy bodily exercise, or the art and precision of manual labour in decorative work [...] (electricity perhaps not in future refused)."[176] Ruskin's reservations were mostly directed toward the waste produced by machines, such as steam, which was "absolutely refused, as a cruel and furious waste of fuel to do what every stream and breeze are ready to do costlessly."[177]

To better understand Ruskin's position, it is essential to understand the context in which he was writing, and to recognize that his more direct opposition to capitalism was counterbalanced by his desire to reform it. Ruskin's stance, which would significantly influence Morris, was far from the anti-progressive one described by Pevsner, and later by Filippo Tommaso Marinetti and László Moholy-Nagy, who saw Ruskin as a reactionary. Upon closer study, it becomes clear that Ruskin passed on to Morris a form of resistance to the capitalist economy and the aesthetic forms to which it gave rise. The overly simplistic interpretations which have mischaracterized the thought of Ruskin and his contemporaries as a straightforward attack on the machine can be seen, Adrian Forty suggests, as a useful myth to deftly obscure the objectives of capitalism:

176 John Ruskin, *The Collected Works of John Ruskin*, ed. Cook and Wedderburn, vol. 30 (London: George Allen, 1907), 48.
177 Ibid.

The practice of blaming machinery for bad design conveniently diverted criticism away from capitalism and focused attention on the technical problems of production rather than on the much more difficult and contentious social ones. It was, after all, much easier to see how machines might be redirected to make better design than to conceive how the social relations of capital and labour might be reconstituted to the same end.[178]

178 Forty, *Objects of Desire*, 61 (see note 38).

Design and Society: William Morris's Exemplarity

From 1854, Ruskin taught at the Working Men's College in London alongside Dante Gabriel Rossetti and Edward Burne-Jones, before being named the first Slade Professor of Fine Art at the University of Oxford, where he would teach Morris. For Ruskin, who aimed to bring together fine arts and applied arts to offset the contradictions of industrialization, for Carlyle, who denounced the age as "a Cockney Nightmare,"[179] and for Pugin, who railed against Victorian materialism and accused industrial production of dividing men more than work itself, design represented the best means of opposition in a modern society which "would keep you machines as you have been so long, fed like machines, tended like machines, made to work like machines—and cast away like machines, when you are no longer capable of being kept in working order."[180] From its very origins, as Ruskin's example shows us, design and its history opposed the dominant liberalism and, contrary to the received wisdom, were not merely concerned with the production of useful goods. The founders of design, led by Morris, were political in their work, lending design an interpretative and speculative dimension from the outset and going beyond societal and commercial questions to initiate a genuine debate.

In his youth, Morris was a keen observer of the applied arts in England, which he judged to be rather pitiful in their current state. He attributed this to a lack of interest on

179 Thomas Carlyle, quoted in William Morris, "The Society of the Future" (1887), in *Political Writings*, 202 (see note 79).
180 William Morris, "Makeshift" (November 18, 1894); in *William Morris: Artist, Writer, Socialist*, vol. 2, ed. May Morris and George Bernard Shaw (Cambridge: Cambridge University Press, 1936), 480.

the part of industrialists, for whom productivity was the absolute priority, at the expense of quality and any artistic dimension. The resulting abyss between the decoration and function of objects inspired him to work for the reform of the decorative arts. Once engaged in this almost sacred mission, he distanced himself from religion, where he had for a time believed his destiny lay, and instead dedicated himself to the cause of decorative arts and artists "working helplessly among the crowd of those who are ridiculously called manufacturers, i.e. handicraftsmen, though the more part of them never did a stroke of hand-work in their lives, and are nothing better than capitalists and salesmen."[181] For Morris, salvation depended upon craftsmen, who had "the duty and honour of educating the public,"[182] and upon the creation of pleasing objects that promised the satisfaction of both individual expression and of a quality product. The craftsman thus gleans from his work not only a sense of pride but a real happiness.

181 William Morris, "The Lesser Arts," in *Political Writings*, 42.
182 Ibid., 51.

Morris, Marshall, Faulkner & Co.: A Case Study

With this noble mission in mind, in 1861 Morris founded the firm Morris, Marshall, Faulkner & Co., Fine Art Workmen in Painting, Carving, Furniture and the Metals, together with his friends Peter Paul Marshall, Charles Faulkner, Edward Burne-Jones, Dante Gabriel Rossetti, Ford Madox Brown, and Philip Webb. With this enterprise he hoped to restore craft production to its former glory. The first of its kind, the company proposed artisanal works and quality interior decoration. Its structure was inspired by the medieval guilds, with a series of workshops that specialized in the creation of different products, each overseen by a particular craftsman. Morris was omnipresent in the company, drawing, inventing, weaving, and mastering different techniques, even as he oversaw the various workshops and the sale of goods—having acquired this last skill during a tedious first job with architect George Edmund Street. In 1875, he split from his associates and reorganized the firm as Morris & Co., continuing to produce textiles, upholstery, prints, rugs, and carpets. The business gradually expanded, and in 1877 Morris opened a new shop on Oxford Street. Recognized for his talent, he was appointed as an advisor to the South Kensington Museum, later the Victoria & Albert Museum. Even in the last years of his life, he dedicated himself to new endeavors, founding the Kelmscott Press in 1890, just six years before his death, a publishing house that printed political pamphlets, essays, poems, and novels. Morris was also directly involved in England's political scene during this time, organizing meetings for the Hammersmith League in the basement of his London home and protesting in support of workers.

For Morris, the importance of design lay in the fact that it allowed for a reflection around the conditions necessary for the alliance of the fine arts with the applied arts. He sought to develop his own artistic theories in order to restore the integrity of the object and the dignity of man, both of which had been lost over the preceding decades. With his belief that the artist prizes beauty and aesthetic perfection above all else, Morris denounced the alienation of the worker that had resulted from industrialization and despaired at the new conditions of production and labor:

> How good a foundation it would be towards getting good Decorative Art, that is ornamental workmanship, if we craftsmen were to resolve to turn out nothing but excellent workmanship in all things, instead of having, as we too often have now, a very low average standard of work, which we often fall below.[183]

Once this dream was realized, he added,

> we may adorn life with the pleasure of cheerfully buying goods at their due price; with the pleasure of *selling* goods that we could be proud of both for fair price and fair workmanship; with the pleasure of working soundly and without haste at *making* goods that we could be proud of?—much the greatest pleasure of the three is that last, such a pleasure as, I think, the world has none like it.[184]

For Morris, a working life devoid of the joy of creativity spelled nothing less than the death of civilization. With its

183 Ibid., 50.
184 Ibid., 42.

nascent industrialization, Britain thus ran the risk of the total destruction of beauty, and even of life itself. However, in order to respond to the growing number of orders his firm received, Morris did make use of industrial production techniques, which for numerous historians from Pevsner onward would represent an insurmountable contradiction at the heart of his work, and one he would rather have left unaddressed. Yet Morris's project was never concerned with cultivating an opposition between art and industry, but rather with searching for a viable alternative to capitalism and the dichotomy between craftsmanship and industrial production. Though the machine undeniably crystallized a number of Morris's anxieties, he also argued on numerous occasions in favor of the mechanical production of everyday objects. On the condition that this should be carefully managed and be in no way harmful to man himself, Morris praised "those almost miraculous machines, which if orderly forethought had dealt with them might even now be speedily extinguishing all irksome and unintelligent labour, leaving us free to raise the standard of skill of hand and energy of mind in our workmen."[185] Clearly it would be both unjust and inaccurate to perpetuate here the misconceptions that reduce Morris's work to a reactionary call for a return to the craftsmanship of the Middle Ages and a simplistic, direct attack upon mechanization. In reality, Morris sought to restore the qualities of the craftsman to the worker and to reintroduce human dignity into industrial production. This would liberate workers from their subjugation by capitalism and the market, which reduced them to the playthings of "greedy gamblers on the Stock Exchange."[186]

185 William Morris, "Art and Socialism," in *Political Writings*, 124.
186 See William Morris's manifesto, "To the Working Men of England," written under the pseudonym "A Lover of Justice," partially reproduced in Fiona MacCarthy, *William Morris: A Life for Our Time* (London: Faber & Faber, 1994), 382.

Design, Politics, and Morris's Total Commitment

While a number of valid comparisons can be made between Ruskin and Morris, the major difference between teacher and student lies in the latter's firm desire to address the ill effects of the Industrial Revolution upon natural and domestic environments through concrete action. Like Ruskin before him, Morris envisioned a reorganization of society based on the model of medieval guilds, but he did not imagine such a project in terms of a utopia located outside of time; rather, he revisited the tradition and put its guiding principles into practice within his own firm. Morris added a democratic and anti-capitalist dimension to the notion of happiness through work and of the artist for whom the pleasure of creation is its own reward. Present throughout his work, it was perhaps expressed most clearly in his very first lecture, "The Decorative Arts, Their Relation to Modern Life and Progress," which he gave to an audience of workers belonging to the Trade Guild of Learning on April 12, 1877, at the Cooperative Hall in London. Morris prepared for his speech by rereading Molière and Daniel Defoe, and approached it as an event and oratory spectacle, rehearsing his gestures and intonation. Published the following year and better known under the title "The Lesser Arts," it was on this occasion that Morris set out the foundation for a redefinition of the decorative arts as part of a wider social project:

> I do not want art for a few, any more than education for a few, or freedom for a few. No! Rather than art should live this poor thin life among a few exceptional men, despising those beneath them for an ignorance

> for which they themselves are responsible, for a brutality that they will not struggle with [...]. I hope that we shall have leisure from war,—war commercial, as well as war of the bullet and the bayonet; leisure from the knowledge that darkens counsel; leisure above all from the greed of money, and the craving for that overwhelming distinction that money now brings [...]. Then having leisure from all these things, amidst renewed simplicity of life we shall have leisure to think about our work, that faithful daily companion, which no man any longer will venture to call the Curse of labour [...] men will then assuredly be happy in their work, and that happiness will assuredly bring forth decorative, noble, popular art.[187]

Morris, who considered himself among the "servants of a Cause,"[188] would return time and again to the decorative arts as a vital terrain at the crossroads of the aesthetic and the political, whether in his lectures on the subject or in his uchronic and utopian socialist novel *News from Nowhere*.[189] It is no coincidence that he read Karl Marx's *Das Kapital*, purchased in 1883 in French, since it had yet to be translated into English, and maintained a correspondence with Friedrich Engels, whose texts he would later publish through the Kelmscott Press. Morris looked toward the decorative arts to achieve nothing less than freeing the worker from the degradation of industrialization, and even the end of class war. For Morris, the industrially produced object heralded the advent of a dangerous capitalism that it

187 Morris, "The Lesser Arts," in *Political Writings*, 54–55.
188 William Morris, "The Beauty of Life" (1880), in *The Beauty of Life*, ed. G. D. H. Cole (London: Brentham Press, 1974), 564.
189 *News from Nowhere* was first serialized in *Commonweal* before being reprinted in England as *News from Nowhere; or, An Epoch of Rest, Being Some Chapters from a Utopian Romance* (London: Reeves & Turner, 1891).

was imperative to master, and to that end he grappled with the economic theories of Adam Smith, John Stuart Mill, and David Ricardo. Aware of the battles fought and lost by Ruskin before him, Morris knew that his program for the decorative arts would be impossible to bring to fruition without fundamental changes in society. Preoccupied by this realization, he confessed in a letter to Austrian socialist Andreas Scheu, with whom he maintained a rich correspondence between 1883 and 1895, "Both my historical studies and my practical conflict with the philistinism of modern society have forced on me the conviction that art cannot have real life and growth under the present system of commercialism and profit-mongering."[190] These beliefs led him to join the Social Democratic Federation, Britain's only socialist organization, in January 1883. He was a highly active member, hosting meetings of the Hammersmith League and later the Hammersmith Socialist Society, whose manifesto he published along with two political newspapers, the *Hammersmith Socialist Record* and *Commonweal*. This activity complemented his practice as a designer, through which he sought to return the means of production to the worker rather than the investor and the speculator.

190 William Morris to Andreas Scheu, 1883; in *William Morris: Selected Writings and Designs*, ed. Asa Briggs (London: Penguin Books, 1962).

Politics through Fiction: The Educational Value of Utopia for Design

With the 1890 publication of *News from Nowhere*, the development of Morris's convictions took a turn that was perhaps less expected. In order to give his imagination free rein in remodeling reality, he created a second self in the novel's protagonist, William Guest, who wakes up from an apparently ordinary night's sleep to embark upon a fantastical voyage. Still half-asleep, he leaves his home and begins to notice subtle changes that eventually lead him toward the discovery of a new world. Using the well-known construct of the utopia to criticize the supremacy of industrial values and the modern civilization to which they had given rise, Morris sets out in minute detail the political, social, and environmental virtues of a society restructured and renewed by a harmonious marriage between art and life in all its forms.

With *News from Nowhere*, Morris was able to share his critique of capitalism with his readers under the cover of a utopian vision, and to use the fictional mode to set out his project for a bucolic and egalitarian society. Morris was in fact but one of a number of Victorian authors to publish speculative texts—including H. G. Wells, author of *The Time Machine* (1895) and *The Island of Doctor Moreau* (1896)—featuring imagined alternative worlds as a means of critiquing contemporary society. Morris's novel thus belongs to a wider genre in which a situation outside the historical continuum creates a space for demonstrating that another, parallel world is possible. In the case of *News from Nowhere*, this displacement allows for an indirect critique of contemporary society as well as a detailed counter-proposition: man cannot be happy, Morris suggests, unless he is free to practice a craft of his own choosing, to create useful objects, to set the pace at which he wishes to work, to enjoy long periods of rest and leisure, to vary his activities throughout the day, to decorate his surroundings as he chooses, and so on. In order to attain this state and truly enjoy the pleasing objects they create, people must inhabit a healthy and agreeable environment, free from pollution and the thick smog of industry, which lay heavy on England's industrial cities as Morris wrote his novel. The dreamlike frame of *News from Nowhere* belies its real subject: the redefinition of society and its value system, whose place in his wider project is evident. Even as an author of fiction, Morris is compelled by the same desire to struggle against the destruction engendered by modern life, materialism, and the exploitation of man by his fellow man. He goes as far as to criticize the laws of marriage, imagining in its place a three-year contract that would be renewed only with the consent of both parties—a revolutionary proposition in notoriously prudish Victorian Britain, made possible only by the spatio-temporal displacement of the literary utopia. With *News from Nowhere*, Morris found a new critical tool through which to bring to life his belief in the possibility of a world where art and life could be truly united.

I will now return to the various interpretations of Morris's ideas in order to question whether or not it is accurate to hold him up as the pioneer of design. Pevsner's position in *Pioneers of the Modern Movement* seems valid, but it is worth reexamining, given that Morris's personality and his conception of decorative arts were both rather more complex than Pevsner's depiction would suggest.

Morris's thought is highly nuanced and cannot be reduced to the one that Pevsner presents to his readers: a hybrid between the pioneer of modernism and the anti-modern reactionary—opposing progress at all costs, nostalgic for the past, and incapable of comprehending the changes society was undergoing. It is not impossible to reconcile these two contradictory dimensions, especially through due consideration of the changing course of Morris's life; but Morris cannot and should not be reduced to this simple paradox. The antagonism that Pevsner puts forward only stands for the purposes of his own argument. Though anointed a "pioneer" and elevated to the status of a mythic patriarch of the discipline, to define a more accurate place for Morris within the history of design is not, however, to do him a disservice. He has often been presented as a figure whose desire to create beautiful and useful objects saw him torn between an art against the machine and an art of the machine. In reality, Morris articulated and promoted a certain way of understanding the relationship between the tangible world of objects and more abstract political ideas, considering design to be the catalyst of his own politics and his desire for proletarian revolution. Rejecting the bourgeois liberalism of his milieu to pursue an anti-capitalist aesthetic project, Morris challenged the established notion of design as a servant of the market. This stance contradicts the more straightforward reconciliation of art and the machine that Pevsner made the structuring historical principle of his canonical text, and which allowed him to conclude his timeline with the advent of the Modern Movement. A close reading of Morris's texts shows that he considered the decorative arts to be the best means of resisting not so much the machine as the values of an economic system that was both alienating and oppressive. Morris's English and European successors would draw on his conception of design and its strong moral imperative, and in this respect Pevsner's reading of Morris and his genealogy remain essential, even if they cannot, in isolation, give a sufficient account of design in all its complexity.

After Morris: Morris's Heritage and Design between Sense and Sensibility

We are beginning to uncover some of the ways in which existing narratives of design have overlooked certain areas and nuances in its history. Emphasizing the critical and politically engaged dimensions of Morris's work, which he was careful to articulate but which have often been neglected in the numerous texts and theories he has inspired since Pevsner's time, brings other aspects of his legacy to the fore. Informing not only the famous Arts & Crafts movement but also the Vienna Secession, Jugendstil in Germany, and the Tiffany style in America, Morris's theories would be a reference point for the discipline for generations to come. Echoes of the redemptive dimension that Morris introduced to design can be detected in the theories of hygienist doctors, French Art Nouveau, or the work of Henry van de Velde in Belgium. His influence can also be found in the thinking of the founders of the Deutscher Werkbund, in the Bauhaus, and in Charles L'Eplattenier's Cours supérieur, a revolutionary educational project in Switzerland.[191] Both within and outside the Modern Movement, Morris's footprints quickly spread across Europe, and to the United States and Australia.

191 Inspired by Ruskin's and Morris's writings, the twenty-three-year-old Charles L'Eplattenier became the director of the Cours supérieur at La Chaux-de-Fonds. The revolutionary educational project was too provocative for the school and in March 1914 L'Eplattenier resigned. See "The School, from the Cours supérieur to the Bauhaus" in this book: pages 154–169.

Hygienist Design, or The Doctor as Designer

Morris's ideas would arrive in France by way of the work of the physician Henri Cazalis. A friend of Stéphane Mallarmé and a poet in his own right, Cazalis was an avid reader of Morris, analyzing and promoting his ideas in France. His pen name, Jean Lahor, was an anagrammatic homage to "Le Horla," a short story by Guy de Maupassant, whom Cazalis treated following his suicide attempt. After his day's consultations were over, he would write tracts on the optimum layout of the home to promote the virtues of a clean and hygienic interior decoration. He considered walls covered with chalk to be the reflection of a healthy body and soul, with aseptic, whitewashed interiors making cleanliness visible. Cazalis demonstrated a link between illness and overcrowded, unhygienic living conditions, and drew on his findings to develop principles for the planning and renovation of homes, which he then disseminated through numerous publications. In *Les habitations à bon marché et un art nouveau pour le peuple* (Inexpensive homes and a new art for the people), Cazalis lays out the link between a simple, stripped-down interior decor and improved domestic hygiene, arguing, "The inexpensive home, already a reality, is not enough; we call, too, for inexpensive interior decoration and furniture; a light, pleasant decor and solid furniture, with simple forms of the utmost taste."[192] Cazalis further imagined extending these principles from the home to the entire nation. With his advocacy for simplified of forms and decoration, and

192 Jean Lahor [Henri Cazalis], *Les habitations à bon marché et un art nouveau pour le peuple* (Paris: Librairie Larousse, 1905), 50.

promotion of their hygienic and spiritual potential, Cazalis aimed to better both the moral and decorative state of the world. He charged design with the creation not only of a more salubrious home but also a cleaner civilization, body, and soul, envisaging this program as a means of making good on the promises of a better life that had spurred a rural exodus to the cities, only for them to be dashed by miserable, overcrowded living conditions. A number of reformers, often physicians like Cazalis himself, worked to combat the disastrous pathologies that arose from the Industrial Revolution, seeking concrete treatments for a civilization suffering from its own excesses.

From the very start of the Industrial Revolution, doctors and philanthropists joined forces to combat the deplorable conditions in workers' homes, where access to clean water and sanitation were rare. One contemporary writer summed up their unhappy fate in the following lines:

> Two words sum up your present:
> deprivation and misery.
> Your future?
> More misery and greater deprivation.[193]

Such was the daily reality of workers whose daily labor barely earned them enough to feed and shelter their families, and who endured lives marred by famine, alcoholism, illness, cold, danger, and filth. Charles Baudelaire evocatively described dawn in Paris in his 1852 poem "Le crépuscule du matin":

193 "Deux mots résument votre présent: privations, misères. Votre avenir? Encore la misère et de plus grandes privations." Jules Burgy, *Détresse des ouvriers au XIXe siècle, le travail avili ramène l'esclavage, rompt les liens de paix et prépare un orage* (Paris: Burgy, 1848), 12.

> Pauper women, dragging their thin, cold breasts,
> Blew on their brands and blew on their fingers.
> [...]
> And the agonized in the depths of asylums
> Uttered their last death-rattles in irregular hiccups.
> The debauchees returned, broken by their business.[194]

In the small hours, as the vagrants returned to their lodgings, exhausted workers returned to small, dirty, foul-smelling, and disease-ridden rooms, crowded with family members or other workers from the same region. In Paris in 1880, some 220,000 individuals were sleeping in small dormitories with five or more beds, with some housing as many as twenty people. Furnished rooms offered little improvement: with seven or eight inhabitants in each, horrified visitors would describe their fetid atmosphere and miserable conditions. One such witness, a Doctor Bayard, on a visit to a Parisian hovel, reported, "I found in a fourth-floor bedroom of barely five square meters, twenty-three individuals, men and children, lying hither-and-tither on five beds. The air in this room was so foul that I was overcome by nausea."[195] Close quarters and serious overcrowding defined the living conditions of workers housed in ramshackle accommodation. The foul odors were signs of the dilapidated and unhygienic state of such lodgings, and overcrowding and filth posed a danger more serious than the lack of comfort; they were breeding grounds for deadly diseases that workers were unable to treat, let alone cure.[196]

194 "Les pauvresses, traînant leurs seins maigres et froids, Soufflaient sur leurs tisons et soufflaient sur leurs doigts. [...] Et les agonisants dans le fond des hospices Poussaient leur dernier râle en hoquets inégaux. Les débauchés rentraient, brisés par leurs travaux." Charles Baudelaire, "Le crépuscule du matin," in *Les fleurs du mal* (1857); trans. Geoffrey Wagner, in *Selected Poems of Charles Baudelaire* (New York: Grove Press, 1974), 84.

195 Quoted in Félix Laroulandie, *Les ouvriers de Paris au XIXe siècle* (Paris: Éditions Christian, 1997), 131.

196 Roger-Henri Guerrand, *Les origines du logement social en France* (Paris: Les Éditions ouvrières, 1967), 193–232.

The poor were soon represented as prisoners of the industrial city, and after numerous studies drew attention to the dangers of the miserable conditions they endured, various hygiene commissions were created. The situation was exacerbated as factories opened in urban areas throughout the Industrial Revolution. The residents affected by these factories complained about their new neighbors, but workers seemed to remain largely unaware of the dangers inherent to their labor conditions, and most objections were quickly silenced to safeguard commercial interests. Despite numerous social and environmental problems, the discussion between observers of social and urban transformation was usually in vague terms of workers' quality of life, even after a link was established between the industrial city and the illnesses afflicting its inhabitants, as historian Roger-Henri Guerrand writes:

> It is also the enormous growth in cities that, more and more, is emptying the countryside, that grand reservoir of humanity. The city, whose air and life itself tend to have dire consequences for the health of the young girls and the young women, multiplying their special illnesses, also threatens the health of men. The reasons are multiple and various: the costliness of life and lodgings, the meanness and narrowness of the apartments where a family cannot develop with ease.[197]

The harmful consequences of the Industrial Revolution were not limited to the miserable material conditions philanthropists and hygienist doctors sought to address, but

197 Ibid., 216.

extended to problems associated with overpopulation, malnutrition, and epidemics. The situation was exacerbated by the pollution that resulted from activities such as coal burning. The home was a center for hygienic and scientific study, a key site for reforms that aimed to institute a cleaner domestic environment and the purification of society as a whole. At first, the relationship between poor health and the city was envisaged as one of cause and effect, but the two quickly became synonymous, with illness contaminating urban areas and the city becoming sickness incarnate. This interchangeability explains the growing numbers of exhibits that displayed hygienic homes at universal exhibitions from 1867 onward. The demand for these new domestic models grew ever greater, and, combined with low construction costs and the promise of preventing illness and promoting well-being, it gave rise to a new hygienic aesthetic.

The efforts of doctors were paralleled by those of interior decorators, and together they sought to promote good health by introducing principles gleaned from the latest discoveries in the medical field into the home. Morris had previously afforded a central place to these preoccupations by defining the decorative arts as an association of the healthy and the beautiful, while also insisting upon their democratic dimension. This conception is reiterated by Cazalis on a number of occasions:

> It was therefore necessary to seek a decor, a formula of art that could be applied in equal measure to the most modest homes and the wealthiest [...] this formula, applicable to the entire home, from the poorest to the richest, is already provided in part by hygiene, because above all, we want a healthy home, and as such the artistic formula that

> we seek must reconcile our hygienic needs with our aesthetic ones.[198]

In the field of architecture, it was only at the start of the twentieth century that the promises of a new world founded upon hygienic principles began to take shape. The links between hygiene and the Modern Movement are well known, with its advocates promoting cleanliness and sanitation at every turn. To truly conform to modern tastes, the home had to be uncluttered and free of random, superfluous decoration. It had to offer visible proof of good health and reflect the values of its inhabitants. Cleanliness thus became an emblem of modern civilization.

In a medical context, hygiene promoted prevention over treatment, and this structuring principle would be appropriated by its proponents in architecture and design. A fear of disease informed the architecture of the Modern Movement and their preference for simple, white forms devoid of ornament that would visually represent cleanliness. The expression of hygiene in architecture can be traced back to the principles established with the construction of sanatoriums around the turn of the twentieth century. Modern architects expanded upon these ideas by incorporating spaces dedicated to sport and exercise into their housing plans, in the hope that the muscular and flexible bodies of the inhabitants would reflect the healthy lifestyles made possible by these new homes. Cazalis's promotion of Morris's ideas shows the extent to which designers were in many ways as instrumental as doctors in the development of hygienic values, in that they offered a vital framework for the interaction between the body and the domestic space.

198 Jean Lahor [Henri Cazalis], *William Morris et le mouvement nouveau de l'art décoratif* (Geneva: Eggimann, 1897).

Le Corbusier would in turn encourage the application of hygienist principles in architecture as a solution to unsanitary housing conditions. In 1925, he set out the Law of Ripolin in his manifesto *The Decorative Art of Today*, outlining the relationship between the values of hygiene and of space.[199] The death knell of decoration and ornament heralded the inscription of hygiene as an integral part of space: "Gilding is fading out and the slums will not be with us for long before they are abolished."[200] The abolition of decor was a victory for Le Corbusier, who was waging nothing short of a "crusade for whitewash" where a coat of white would eliminate dark, dirty corners, and ensure that "everything is shown as it is."[201] Le Corbusier considered the "coat of whitewash" equivalent to a "productive morality" capable of rendering healthier spaces and spirits alike: "On white ripolin walls, these accretions of dead things from the past will be intolerable; they would leave a mark. Whereas the marks do not show on the medley of our damasks and patterned wall-papers."[202] Le Corbusier dreamed of legislation for the cleansing of all surfaces: "Suppose there was a decree requiring all rooms in Paris to be given a coat of whitewash. I maintain that that would be a police task force of real stature and a manifestation of high morality, the sign of a great people."[203] By calling for the use without exception of smooth, white, and easy-to-clean surfaces, Le Corbusier suggests an equivalence between cleanliness and visibility. The implication is that the interior and the very atmosphere of the home are the sole preserve of the architect, whose work is to construct not only a healthy space but an equally healthy body.

199 Le Corbusier, *Decorative Art of Today*, 188 (see note 31).
200 Ibid., 42.
201 Ibid., 188.
202 Ibid., 189.
203 Ibid., 192.

Le Corbusier, Mies van der Rohe, Charlotte Perriand, and others would all approach architecture in these hygienic terms, integrating health and physical exercise into their projects. Robert Mallet-Stevens's Villa Noailles, designed between 1923 and 1933, featured, for example, a number of terraces, a swimming pool, a squash court, a gymnastics room, and even a miniature golf course. Every room was defined in accordance with the body's cycles, and each was equipped with a meticulously calibrated and synchronized clock to govern the program of sporting activities throughout the day. The villa's workings were demonstrated by the bodies in movement of Man Ray's *Les Mystères du Château de Dé*, filmed there in 1918.

This conception of design as a site where moral and social elements cohere and combine leads back to Cazalis's work. With the hygienist aesthetic that he articulated and brought into dialogue with design by way of Morris's ideas, Cazalis sought solutions to public health problems through principles for decoration, and thus attempted to prove that a habitat could heal its occupants.

From Hygienic Design to Eugenic Design

The causal relationship that had been firmly established in Paris between the deteriorating health of workers and overcrowding and poor sanitation would in turn inform hygienic principles for the organization and decoration of homes. Cazalis sought to extend these to the nation as a whole and to demonstrate that scientific thought ought to govern the planning of the home in the century to come. Yet despite their importance, these hygienic ideas were rarely applied and were even attacked by critics of industrialization.

Cazalis seemed either unaware or unconcerned by the symbolic differences between design and hygienism. From a strictly disciplinary point of view, the parallel between the work of the doctor and that of the designer belies the different register of values of each profession, a distinction that was of little interest for Cazalis, who authored works on sexually transmitted diseases and hereditary illness such as *La science et la mariage* and *A propos des risiques pathologiques du mariage*,[204] in which he defended hereditary capital and with which he hoped to halt the spread of syphilis in France. With these works written in support of eugenics, he hoped to develop new measures for fighting disease and to that end called for the authorities to adopt draconian public health measures and sanitation laws. He presented them as an extension of the simple principles for decoration borrowed from Morris, who was highly unlikely to have approved of Cazalis's project.

204 Henri Cazalis, *La science et le mariage, étude médicale* [Science and marriage, medical study] (Paris: Octave Doin Éditeur, 1900); and *A propos des risques pathologiques du mariage, des hérédités morbides et d'un examen médical avant le mariage* [On the pathological risks of marriage, morbid heredities, and medical examination before marriage] (Brussels: Imprimerie C. Vande Weghe, 1902).

He justified his eugenicist ideas by pointing to the consequences of urbanization and the Industrial Revolution in world capitals such as Paris at the end of the nineteenth century; by combining eugenics with democratic ideals, Cazalis formulated principles that the history of design would rather forget. Yet it was around similar eugenic ideas that the Streamline movement would develop from 1910 onward, particularly in the 1920s and 1930s. Where the Modern Movement had lauded an aesthetic of hygiene, the Streamline movement promoted smooth, aerodynamic forms where healthy objects were conflated with healthy bodies. Christina Cogdell has brought to light the relationships between the discourse of the Streamline movement and biological efficiency and selection in the United States.[205] Principles encouraging eugenicist social reform embodied not only a certain attitude toward public health, but also the rhetoric of some industrial designers, in particular Norman Bel Geddes's notion of the progress of the human race. Confident of the moral imperative of their work, the Streamline designers made no distinction between objects and human beings: they hoped to save an endangered humanity by transforming the human race in the image of this new sleek, powerful, and supposedly progressive industrial design.

Long before the Streamline movement, however, Cazalis looked for solutions to public health issues in Morris's ideas on decoration. His praise for Morris's life and work was limitless:[206] Morris was "a man of genius," "one of these heroes" who, "in spite of all resistance, are able to articulate the intellectual, moral or material conditions

205 Christina Cogdell, *Eugenic Design: Streamlining America in the 1930s* (Philadelphia: University of Pennsylvania Press, 2004).
206 See Thomas Walton, "A French Disciple of William Morris," *Revue de Littérature Comparée*, no. 15 (September 1935): 524–35.

of the time."[207] At the University of Geneva on January 13, 1897, a year after Morris's death, Cazalis organized a conference in his honor, and would go on to dedicate no less than four works to Morris: *William Morris et le mouvement nouveau de l'art decorative* (William Morris and the new movement for the decorative arts, 1897), *L'art nouveau* (1901), *L'art pour le peuple à défaut de l'art par le peuple* (An art for the people, or else, an art by the people, 1902), and *Les habitations à bon marché et un art nouveau pour le peuple* (Inexpensive homes and a new art for the people, 1905).[208]

Cazalis proposed a number of readings of Morris's work, portraying him as a man of action and the founder of *magasins artistiques*, who opposed "the tyranny of the machine, and the tyranny and the epidemic that is the factory and the city," and as a poet issuing a "cry of revolt."[209] With his dual portrayal of Morris, Cazalis sought to pay tribute to his hero's poetic and theoretical work, writing that he, "as much or more than Ruskin, the group's theorist, seems [...] to have been the leader and standard bearer of this movement, this revolution."[210] Cazalis noted the same contradictions in Morris's work that Pevsner would later observe: the prohibitive costliness of the work that he intended for all, his rejection of the machine despite it being the only means to produce affordable objects, and the archaic aspect of his revolutionary project. Yet Cazalis insisted on the artistic dimension of Morris's life: "Morris shows us that all coheres in life"; "Morris's masterpiece was above all his very life."[211]

207 Lahor, *William Morris*, 51, 8.
208 Jean Lahor [Henri Cazalis]: *L'art nouveau, son histoire, l'art nouveau étranger à l'exposition, l'art nouveau au point de vue social* (Paris: Lemerre, 1901); and *L'art pour le peuple à défaut de l'art par le peuple* (Paris: Librairie Larousse, 1902).
209 Lahor, *William Morris*, 39.
210 Ibid., 34.
211 Ibid., 55, 70.

In *L'art pour le peuple* Cazalis relates Morris and the decorative arts to his own practice as a physician. After explaining that art is as essential to man as air, and that the decoration of the home has a determining influence upon the mental well-being of its inhabitants, he discusses hygiene as a "branch of aesthetics."[212] He draws on his study of the causal links between unsanitary living conditions and illness to define a series of governing principles for interior decoration and organization, ideas he hopes to extend to the scale of the entire nation through industrial processes. In *Les habitations à bon marché* he offers a more mature vision of design, discussing architecture and inexpensive industrial furniture, as well as lighting and decorative motifs. The Exposition internationale d'art populaire et d'hygiene that he hoped to organize and the whitewash that he recommended applying to sanitize interiors demonstrate Cazalis's belief that the mission of design is to disinfect, bleach, and lend to the home a visible cleanliness that would reflect the moral propriety of its inhabitants.[213]

Of all the architects, historians, and designers who drew inspiration from Morris, Cazalis was one of the few to have actually met him. He describes this encounter and the indelible impression it made upon him in *William Morris*:

> In my mind I can see him once more, four years ago, a very simple figure in his simple home in Hammersmith, with the Thames flowing calmly by [...] I can see his powerful face, leonine, his high and broad forehead below his thick mass of graying hair, his bristly beard which was also going white,

212 Lahor, *L'art pour le peuple*, 9.
213 Ibid., 54.

> his large blue eyes, the eyes of an idealist glistening with self confidence, his work, his hope for great victories still to come.[214]

Yet even those who would never encounter Morris in the flesh were deeply inspired by his work. Hermann Muthesius lived in London between 1896 and 1903, having been dispatched there by the Prussian finance minister as an envoy to Great Britain. Charged with observing the country's technological advances and innovations, he was introduced to Morris's work by Willy Finch. Returning to his home country from London, he brought with him his own interpretation of English ideas about the home, which differed greatly from Cazalis's Art Nouveau. Muthesius published his ideas on the state of the development of the English house in three large volumes,[215] in the hope that his work would inspire his own country to put in place the measures necessary to ensure a level of quality in industrial production, and encourage a distinctive national style that would allow his country to equal, if not surpass, the then dominant industry of Britain.

214 Lahor, *William Morris*, 11.
215 Hermann Muthesius, *Das englische Haus* (Berlin: Wasmuth, 1904); published in English as *The English House*, trans. Dennis Sharp (New York: Rizzoli, 1979).

Uniformity and Individuality: Production in Germany in the Industrial Age

It was with these same objectives in mind, and in response to the polemic that followed the Third German Decorative Arts Exhibition in 1906, that twelve industrialists, artists, architects, and businessmen founded the Deutscher Werkbund on October 6, 1907. The exhibition, held in Dresden, had brought to the surface the latent opposition between the proponents of traditional, artisanal decorative arts, and reformers who favored industrial artistic production; the latter group included Hermann Muthesius, Peter Behrens, Karl Schmidt, Friedrich Naumann, and Henry van de Velde. In the years that followed, they sought to bring about a newly productive economy based upon exchange between industrialists and designers. Led by Muthesius, who came to assume an ever more important role in the group, the Deutscher Werkbund could not escape design's political dimension, and expanded its activity to promote a socially minded economy. Muthesius reflected on the role of each of his country's different economic actors in the development of industry: "the form of production with which we will have to contend,"[216] according to the words of the architect and Werkbund member Fritz Schumacher. Muthesius saw in mechanization not only the promise of material benefits—that is, the potential for a new culture and a reformed economy—but also the embodiment of equality and social justice:

216 Quoted in Julius Poesner, "Entre l'art et l'industrie, le Deutscher Werkbund," in *Le Werkbund: Allemagne, Autriche, Suisse*, ed. Lucius Burckhardt et al. (Paris: Éditions du Moniteur, 1981).

> It is not handcraft, but rather machine work which prevails in our life today, which surrounds us at every step, which is economically decisive [...] It has become a primary promoter of Culture, has made available means of creation, has given freedom to those without means; and since all rely on the same objects it has prepared the way for the levelling of classes.[217]

With these ideas, Muthesius went beyond the bounds set out by Morris, who only accepted the machine on the condition that it be mastered by and of service to man, and left behind his predecessors' tentative positions on the subject to openly laud the liberating power of industrial production.

Believing that the fault for the declining quality of goods did not lie with the industrial situation itself, he envisaged a project of reform that would master the chaos and unbridled competition of the market with a view to developing a controlled and civilized economy. At the same time he laid the groundwork for an aesthetic of the machine in service of mass production. While the Deutscher Werkbund fit seamlessly into this pro-capitalist context, it is important to note that a number of its members considered Ruskin and Morris the forerunners of their project. This was *despite* its emphasis on the division of labor and the development of new relations between the consumer and the producer. The Werkbund's vision of industrial production and its relationship to the individual differed significantly from that of its predecessors.

217 Hermann Muthesius, "Handarbeit und Massenerzeugnis" (1917), quoted in Frederic J. Schwartz, *The Werkbund: Design Theory and Mass Culture before the First World War* (New Haven, CT: Yale University Press, 1996), 101.

Since the turn of the century, labor had taken on a new role as an expression of culture. At the same time, industrially produced objects had come to crystallize critiques of capitalist alienation, a process described by Georg Simmel in *The Philosophy of Money* (1900) and Karl Kraus in *Die Fackel* (1899–1936). Frederic J. Schwartz explores this shift in his analysis of the Deutscher Werkbund:

> The negative effects of the commodity in the factory or workshop were transcended as it was brought into the *intérieur*, either the department store or the upper-middle-class salon and its lower social equivalents. In Marx, Ruskin and Morris (who first set the terms for the discussion), the cultural impact of the commodity was seen at the level of production (the closed social circle defined by the production of objects or their use in further production); with the Werkbund, the mass-produced objects of everyday use came to be considered (and both criticized and celebrated) in their cultural effects as a matter of the surface appearance of objects bought at a far remove from the sphere of labor. From figuring culturally in pre-industrial societies as a product of labor, the commodity would, under capitalist conditions, perform its spiritual closure as *a carrier of signs.*[218]

It was not until 1914 that Muthesius officially broke from Morris and put an end to the pretense that the Werkbund could be considered his successors. This was the same year in which he coined the term *Typisierung* to describe an object possessing a style. The term can be translated into English as "type" or "typing." Germs of this idea can

218 Schwartz, *The Werkbund*, 72.

be found earlier in a speech Muthesius gave in 1911, entitled "Wo stehen wir?," in which he reflects upon the state of German production and anticipates a new aesthetic independent of the quality of materials:

> A cup, for example, is in its general form the same in all nations and at all times; it remains in principle unchanged, whether in wood, clay, glass, or executed in any other material. The basic idea of an artwork which emerges from its use and function is independent of fashions of material, and of temporal and local conditions.[219]

With Typisierung, Muthesius hoped to introduce forms suited to new industrial production capacities that would possess what Pevsner names *Sachlichkeit*, usually translated into English as "objectivity." With geometric or cubic forms, and smooth surfaces devoid of ornaments, the standardized forms of Typisierung were supposed to restore the link between consumer and producer that had been lost with the advent of modern capitalism, and give rise to a national style capable of inaugurating a new and truly democratic national culture. Muthesius significantly altered the definition of design by positioning it as the determining cultural element within the market: he placed the concept of Typisierung at the heart of the economic field.

1914 was also the year in which the Deutscher Werkbund, now seven years into its existence, would organize its first exhibition. Muthesius drew up a series of theses for the occasion, ostensibly on the group's behalf but in fact without their knowledge. His theses directly addressed industrialists

219 Hermann Muthesius, "Wo stehen wir?" (1911), in *Durchgeistigung der deutschen Arbeit: Wege und Ziele in Zusammenhang von Industrie/Kunst* (1912); quoted in Schwartz, *The Werkbund*, 123 (Schwartz's translation).

to alert them to the imperative of creating a national style based upon standardization through which it would be possible to defend German industry. However, Van de Velde, Gropius, Bruno Taut, Paul Scheerbart, and other members of the Werkbund, maintained a different conception of industrial production, one not subject to the laws of the market and of industry but which would give the artist free rein in the creation of useful objects through industrial techniques. Among them, Van de Velde was the staunchest defender of the artist's creative freedom, insisting that their only duty was to express an original and individualistic artistic position. As such, he demanded that a second text be published, in which he refuted each of Muthesius's points in turn. This now famous confrontation has been interpreted in a number of ways. For Pevsner, it represents a final moment of friction before the smooth ascent of the Modern Movement, and such is its high drama that he concludes both *Pioneers of the Modern Movement* and *The Sources of Modern Architecture and Design* with the episode. He presents this moment of hesitation in the following terms:

> It must have been a memorable moment—Art Nouveau at its best resisting the needs and declining the responsibilities of the new century.
>
> In fact the victory of Muthesius was assured even before the Cologne meeting. The meeting was held apropos the first Werkbund exhibition, and this exhibition, at least in its most important buildings, actually demonstrated that victory, and would have demonstrated it internationally if the outbreak of the First World War had not disrupted European unity and held up cultural progress.[220]

220 Pevsner, *Sources of Modern Architecture and Design*, 181 (see note 86).

Would the battle have truly been won once and for all, as Pevsner suggests, had it not been for the First World War and its momentary disruption of industry in the mobilization efforts for war? Schwartz contests Pevsner's analysis on the grounds that Van de Velde was not opposed to the notion of standardization as such, but rather considered it unrealistic given Germany's level of industrialization, which was mediocre at best. Contrary to Pevsner, he considers Van de Velde to be more pragmatic than Muthesius, since the former took into account the reality of the country's productive capacity. Van de Velde asked, "Is anyone really going to let themselves be dazzled by the apparent possibility of thereby achieving quick results?"[221] and suggested that hasty intervention in industry would be a wasted effort for a German economy ill-equipped to carry out such a task.

The complexity of the Werkbund's inner politics was apparent in the exhibition devised by Sonja Gunther and the radical architect Franco Raggi for the 1976 Venice Biennale, "Il Werkbund—1907 alle origini del design" (The Werkbund—1907 to the origins of design). While the curators' stance was resolutely anti-modernist, they offered a conception of design that Pevsner himself would not have contested. They were interested in the intersection represented by Muthesius's position, believing him to be the only figure to have been able to envision "an ethic and an aesthetic of design capable of responding to the growing demand for quality from the new dominant social class and compatible with a young German industry producing consumer goods with a view to economic expansion."[222] Yet

221 Hermann Muthesius and Henry van de Velde, "Werkbund Theses and Antitheses" (1914), in *Programs and Manifestoes on 20th-Century Architecture*, ed. Ulrich Conrads, trans. Michael Bullock (Cambridge, MA: MIT Press, 1975), 30.
222 Franco Raggi and Sonja Gunther, *Il Werkbund—1907 alle origini del design* (Milan: Electa, 1976).

a close reading of Van de Velde's theses shows that he too had toyed with the idea of standardized furniture. In 1897, in "A Chapter on the Design and Construction of Modern Furniture," he expresses support for the idea, on the condition that production be held to a certain moral standard:

> But I could be prouder of the certainly far more individual principle of systematically avoiding designing anything that cannot be mass-produced. My ideal would be to have my projects executed a thousand times, though obviously not without strict supervision, because I know from experience how soon a model can deteriorate through misguided or dishonest handling.[223]

In 1914, Van de Velde had hardened his position, and defended the singularity of the work and the individuality of the artist, insisting that industrial production be approached from the point of the artist rather than the industrialist. Schwartz's analysis resolves this contradiction, as he credits Van de Velde with a form of pragmatism similar to Morris's. He argues that Van de Velde was less opposed to the machine than to the immorality it engendered, and that he rejected not standardization but the discourses that sought to elevate it to an absolute model and a virtue in and of itself, and did so without due consideration of the country's lackluster industrial capacity.

That said, the two approaches set out by Muthesius and Van de Velde's "Werkbund Theses and Antitheses" are not as mutually exclusive as they might first appear.

223 Henry van de Velde, "A Chapter on the Design and Construction of Modern Furniture," in *Architecture and Design, 1890–1939: An International Anthology of Original Articles*, ed. Tim Benton, Charlotte Benton, and Dennis Sharp (New York: Whitney Library of Design, 1975), 18.

Together, they develop a dual concept of design that can accommodate at once the oeuvre and the product, the one-off and the prototype alongside the serially produced item, the bespoke and the standard. They make possible the coexistence of collective and anonymous effort alongside the individual work, of industry and craftsmanship. The history of design ultimately retained just Muthesius's thesis, which Pevsner privileged to the detriment of the ideas of Van de Velde, Taut, and Gropius.

The School, from the Cours supérieur to the Bauhaus

The Bauhaus was founded in 1919 in Weimar, and inherited its principal tenets from the work of Morris. In the first decade of the 1900s, it was prefigured by another, far less well-known school model that was just as innovative: the Cours supérieur at the École d'art publique at La Chaux-de-Fonds, Switzerland, then the world capital of watchmaking. The painter Charles L'Eplattenier, aged just twenty-three, had taken up a teaching post at the school in La Chaux-de-Fonds after having studied at the École des Arts Décoratifs and the École des Beaux-Arts de Paris. There he devised an innovative project of reform in favor of Art Nouveau. Having been inspired by the texts of Ruskin and Morris, he made them mandatory reading for the small group of students he selected to take his class. Though he had only recently begun to teach drawing and decorative composition at the school, he quickly realized that the education it offered relied on an economy that had little hope of survival in the long term: the students dedicated their time to perfecting the meticulous techniques of mechanical watchmaking and pocket-watch engraving, crafts that were the town's lifeblood but which were directly threatened by standardization. L'Eplattenier correctly anticipated that this specialty would soon be swept aside, and indeed in 1910 the success of a new standardized wristwatch provoked an unprecedented economic crisis in the region. With this coming upheaval in mind, beginning in 1905, he had set about reorganizing the school's education, recruiting some of his most promising students, including Charles-Édouard Jeanneret-Gris (later Le Corbusier), to the Nouvelle section, also known as the Cours supérieur. L'Eplattenier reoriented this select group of students toward areas such as building, furniture, architecture, and upholstery; he encouraged them to work as a model community, reminiscent of a guild, where each member was tasked with creating an oeuvre according to their specialty. L'Eplattenier had his students undertake voyages across Europe to discover works of art, gather valuable information and prototypes, meet master craftsmen, and document their experiences and findings on the most innovative practices of the time to share with their classmates. The students were to return to the school at the end of their odysseys to impart what they had learned to their younger peers. The project was original and promising in equal measure, but following a campaign of defamation and a series of conflicts, and despite the support of Peter Behrens and Hector Guimard, on March 18, 1914, L'Eplattenier resigned. The young masters he had recently trained followed him, bringing the Cours supérieur to an end.

Like L'Eplattenier at La Chaux-de-Fonds, Gropius conceived the Bauhaus as a series of workshops that would work highly independently of one another, yet with the techniques taught in each forming part of an intensely collaborative project. With an openly utopian position that aimed to shape the course of the future, the school's organization implied a reconfiguration of the role of both the artist, in the broadest sense of the term, and the industrialist. Gropius sought to foster this change by bringing the knowledge- and technique-sharing system of workshops into contact with experience gleaned from professional world. L'Eplattenier had dreamed of putting technology to work to serve standardization and culture; the Bauhaus worked to make this a reality.

The relationship between the artist and industry was a central question for the Bauhaus. While avant-garde design movements and even Le Corbusier had begun to invoke Morris, his work was particularly significant as a source of inspiration for Gropius as he drew up the Bauhaus's educational model, which would be made public in his April 1919 manifesto, "Program of the Staatliche Bauhaus in Weimar." In four short pages, he set out the intention, the organization, and the content of the classes to be given, as well as the direction he envisaged for the school.[224]

Gropius had begun to outline the key ideas of his project as early as 1914, at the invitation of Van de Velde, who was looking for a successor the School of Arts and Crafts (Grossherzoglich-Sächsische Kunstgewerbeschule) in Weimar. In 1902, Van de Velde had founded a private seminary that would later become said school, but as he became aware that he was being pushed to leave his post, he drew up a list of candidates to replace him, Gropius among them. The two men had known each other for a number of years, both having been members of the Deutscher Werkbund. During the 1914 schism, they had been united in their defense of the artists' interests against the demands of industry, and in their rejection of each of the arguments put forward by Muthesius, Taut, and Scheerbart.

Gropius was eventually appointed by the grand duke of Saxe-Weimar-Eisenach as the school's new director in 1914, and immediately began to reflect on the principles he would later announce in his manifesto. However, his project was interrupted by the outbreak of the First World War, when he was called up as a reservist. Upon his return, the project was approved by the Weimar Republic authorities,

224 See Walter Gropius, "Program of the Staatliche Bauhaus in Weimar," in Hans M. Wingler, *Bauhaus: Weimar, Dessau, Berlin, Chicago*, trans. Wolfgang Jabs and Basil Gilbert, ed. Joseph Stein, 3rd ed. (Cambridge, MA: MIT Press, 1975), 31–33.

and in 1919 he was charged with creating a new school that would promote the unity of art and industry. Gropius felt that it was necessary to take standardization into account, and his leadership of the school reflected this. He encouraged modern artists to abandon the creation of unique and costly pieces reserved for a wealthy clientele in favor of everyday objects accessible to all and adapted to industrialization without compromising on quality. His vision proved difficult to implement: in combining the School of Arts and Crafts with the Academy of Fine Art (Grossherzöglich-Sachsische Hochschule für bildende Kunst) to create the Staatliches Bauhaus Weimar, better known simply as Bauhaus Weimar, Gropius was forced to contend with a rearguard of easel painters who categorically refused to engage with any form of industrial art. He had to act carefully to set his innovative ideas in motion, as they were certain to be met with intense resistance.

Gropius acknowledged a number of influences on his thought, including the utopian dimension of the Aufklärung. The British utopian tradition, initiated in part by Morris, was another source of inspiration, and its influence can be seen in the school's organization and even in the choice of the name Bauhaus, which has been subject to a great deal of speculation since its foundation. I tend to favor the interpretation that links the name etymologically to *Bauhütte*, temporary buildings that housed the various craftsmen participating in the construction of a cathedral, which had inspired Morris's vision of the ideal working community. Gropius in turn references the idea in a letter addressed to Van de Velde in 1916, in which he lauds the spirit of these medieval communities:

> [Within the *Bauhütte*] a prosperous working community could be reborn, similar to the workshops

> of medieval builders, where architects, sculptors, and artisans of all kinds coexisted; each would independently complete their share of the common task, with a deep understanding and respect for a common idea.[225]

While Gropius believed firmly in the virtues of his model for the school, he also saw its potential benefits for industry:

> A working community of the collective artistic disciplines [...] should eventually be capable of producing everything related to building: architecture, sculpture, painting, furnishings, and handicrafts, in closest contact with the existing crafts and industries of the state.[226]

It becomes clear that the Bauhaus model differs from the guild system of which Morris dreamed; by seeking to establish a link between the research and apprenticeship of students and the professional world of industry, Gropius proposed an altogether new vision of utopia. The school borrowed its collegial model from the *Werkstätten*, which were formed from alliances of designers and artists. The most famous was the Wiener Werkstätte, founded in 1903 by Koloman Moser and Josef Hoffmann, which held the autonomy of each craftsman as the ideal. Its ultimate aim was to combine the efforts of artists, craftsmen, and students; pupils who had been trained in the school would refine their projects with their former teachers before

225 Walter Gropius, "Vorschläge zur Gründung einer Lehranstalt als künstlerische Beratungsgestelle für Industrie, Gewerbe und Handwerk" (1916), in *Walter Gropius*, ed. Hartmut Probst and Christian Schädlich, vol. 3, *Ausgewählte Schriften* (Berlin: VEB Verlag für Bauwesen, 1987), 60.

226 Walter Gropius, "Proposed Budget for the Art Academy and the School of Arts and Crafts in Weimar 1919/20," in Wingler, *Bauhaus*, 26.

returning to the factory or the workshop to execute them, ensuring an ongoing exchange between the Bauhaus and the outside world.

Even after he declared that "the Werkbund is dead; no more will come of it,"[227] Gropius remembered the promise that had led to its foundation in 1907 and sought to reanimate it upon his return from the war. As such, he sought to stay abreast of the new circumstances in postwar Germany and joined the Arbeitsrat für Kunst (Workers' council for art). Gropius retained the Werkbund's aim of elevating craftsmanship by combining it with art, industry, and handicraft and adapting organizational principles to the school environment by promoting collaboration between manufacturers and teachers, and balancing the training offered by the school with apprenticeships with craftsmen and industry workers.

Gropius borrowed three of Morris's key ideas in the organization of the Bauhaus: with the artistic workshops, Gropius gave form to his idea of "the modern artist at the service of production" and thus elevated the so-called lesser arts;[228] the Bauhaus's workshop model drew upon the medieval-style guilds that the Arts & Crafts movement had revived; and through the collaboration between workshops, the notion of artistic unity was positioned as the absolute principle of creativity. These guiding ideas were established in Gropius's manifesto and would remain in place until the end of his tenure.

Gropius invited the painter Johannes Itten to leave his teaching post in Vienna to join him in his reshaping of the role of art and the artist in industrial society, a project that

227 Walter Gropius to Karl Ernst Osthaus, December 23, 1918, in *Karl Ernst Osthaus: Leben und Werk*, ed. Herta Hesse-Frielinghaus et al. (Recklinghausen: Verlag Aurel Bongers, 1971), 471.
228 Gropius, "Vorschläge zur Gründung einer Lehranstalt," in *Ausgewählte Schriften*, 60.

also implied a new conception of design. Itten brought with him an innovative and experimental vision that proved to be decisive in the school's history: "Construct the Bauhaus—build—bring together—different forces—unite diverse forces in a single unity—organize diverse forces—hone diverse forces, within a homogenous organism—lead these diverse forces towards a unison—towards a festival."[229] Through Itten's experimental ideas, the Bauhaus drew simultaneously on Morris's project and that of the Deutscher Werkbund to create a unique heritage, a base it would go on to transform entirely. By the same token, Gropius became a figure of reconciliation, proving himself capable of adapting the original project of design to new economic structures and standardization.

In order to give a clear and concise account of the Bauhaus, I will limit myself to the facts of its existence. The school was established in 1919 and would last for fourteen years, until its closure in 1933. Founded in Weimar, it moved first to Dessau in 1925, and then in 1930 to Berlin, where it remained until its closure by the Nazi authorities in 1933. It was Itten who was initially charged with defining the broad strokes of the syllabus and the teaching style, which promoted a mastering of materials and techniques in the style of a *Vorkurs*, or preliminary course. Gropius surrounded himself with strong personalities: in addition to Itten, he invited Lyonel Feininger, Gerhard Marcks, and Adolf Meyer to join the school in 1919, followed by Paul Klee and Oskar Schlemmer in 1921, and Wassily Kandinsky in 1922. Finally, in 1923 László Moholy-Nagy was brought in to replace Itten, and thus do away with easel painting, experimentation, and Expressionism

229 Johannes Itten to Anna Höllering, December 15, 1919, in *Johannes Itten: Werke und Schriften*, ed. Anneliese Itten (Zurich: Orell Füssli, 1978), 69.

in favor of social constructivism. Together, Gropius and Moholy-Nagy would establish a dialogue between art and technology that represented, for them, a communist and anti-bourgeois project. Moholy-Nagy's arrival further signaled a shift away from Morris's influence and toward the Bauhaus's industrialization. The school became a commercial enterprise, entering into business with industrialists to produce manufactured furniture such as Marcel Breuer's tubular-frame chairs and Moholy-Nagy's lamps. In 1928, Hannes Meyer took over the direction of the school and radicalized it according to his utilitarian Marxist principles, where distinctions between art and architecture were subsumed by questions of social utility. Meyer founded the company Bauhaus GmbH, conceiving it in line with Marxist principles, with the goal of offering inexpensive, industrially produced goods. In a context of growing tensions and increasing difficulty, Meyer remained in his role as the school's head until his resignation in 1930. He was replaced by Ludwig Mies van der Rohe, who moved the school to Berlin before he was forced to close its doors in 1933.

The Bauhaus is famous for its creation of an aesthetic of production that was apt to accompany the ascent of a newly industrial society. It has come to be associated with the imagery of standardization, with a design vocabulary that included the innovative use of materials (tubular metal for furniture, for example) and a series of technologies that were little used, if at all, prior to the school's foundation. The Bauhaus aimed to establish a definitive break with the past and create a sustainable avant-garde by giving a material form to its political and social programs. Searching for viable routes for the industrial production of consumer goods, and keen to distance themselves from existing codes, its designers later turned to functionalism. Contrary to the original significance conferred upon it by the architect Louis Sullivan, functionalism was presented by its proponents in the Bauhaus as the formal equivalent of the humanist values essential for democracy, and thus became the instrument of choice for social reform. A close study of the complexity of the Bauhaus ideologies disproves any conception of the history of design, or of the history of the Bauhaus itself, as a continuous and homogenous entity. It shows the inaccuracy of interpretations of the school as a purely modern or a purely functionalist enterprise, and raises the question as to the provenance of such readings, which have gone largely unquestioned to the detriment of other, more nuanced histories.

From its foundation in 1919 until its closure in 1933, the Bauhaus did not follow any single, unalterable course. At first it revisited the ideals of the Deutscher Werkbund, and borrowed Henry van de Velde's experimental and expressionist ideas. Following its move to Dessau, it would take a more functionalist turn. A 1923 lecture given by Gropius entitled "Art and Technics—A New Unity" was emblematic of the school's changing direction.[230] Transforming the school into a commercial enterprise, he developed a new conception of the "ideal unity" in which formal concerns were linked to technological and economic ones. The Bauhaus's aesthetic resulted from a collaboration between industry and art, which it carried out according to the democratic ideals it held dear. Hoping to offer standardized and technological comfort to all, the Bauhaus relied on the notion of a unifying power of design that was destined to improve the entire world. The Bauhaus began to blur between utopian and pragmatic thought, with modern

230 See Walter Gropius and Herbert Bayer, *Bauhaus: 1919–1928* (Boston: Charles T. Branford, 1938), 80. This slogan replaced that of the inaugural 1919 manifesto, "There is no essential difference between the artist and the craftsman."

design, a process that was consolidated by its final incarnation under Mies van der Rohe's direction.

A closer study reveals that the school's history is still more complex. Yet despite this, the Bauhaus is consistently presented as the epitome of industrial design, the founding school of the Modern Movement, and the educational incarnation of functionalism and standardization. The contribution of Pevsner's writing to this perception is clear but cannot alone explain its longevity. The school's founding texts are already intriguing. Gropius's speech at the first exhibition of Bauhaus students' work praises not functionalism but rather spirituality and subjectivity, and critiques the standardization promoted by the Deutscher Werkbund:

> On the strength of his visual gifts, the artist reads the spiritual parallels of his time and represents them in pure form. When such spiritual common property is lacking, there is nothing left for him but to build up his metaphysical element from his own inner resources. [...] We artists therefore need the community spirit of the entire people as much as we need bread.[231]

There is a good deal of supporting evidence for this alternative reading of the Bauhaus as an entity that was not simply functionalist. In a lecture given in Leipzig in 1919, Gropius calls for his peers to unite the spiritual with the mechanical and warns against "the harmful cult of power and the machine which drove [them] from the spiritual to the economic abyss."[232] His choice of illustration for the

231 Walter Gropius, "Address to the Students of the Staatliche Bauhaus, Held on the Occasion of the Yearly Exhibition of Student Work in July 1919," in Wingler, *Bauhaus*, 36.

232 Walter Gropius, "Baugeist oder Kramertum?," *Die Schuhwelt*, October 15, 1919, 819–21.

school's first manifesto—an Expressionist woodcut by Lyonel Feininger—is surely significant. A close reading reveals that, in its early years, the Bauhaus's values were of a spiritual, subjective, and even emotional order, comparable to that of the Expressionist movement. Design history has tended to remember Gropius as the designer of the highly rational Fagus Factory in 1913 or the model factory at the 1914 Werkbund Exhibition, rather than as the sculptor of the *Monument to the March Dead* (1922). This late Expressionist monument contradicts by its very existence the notion of Gropius and his Bauhaus as purely functionalist, and reveals the inaccuracy of a history in which the Expressionist movement gave way to a triumphant functionalism. Even if the wane of Expressionism was undeniable between 1919 and 1929, as the case of Bruno Taut illustrates—having identified as an Expressionist, he later claimed to be a "social functionalist" before describing expressionism as little more than a "mental aberration"[233]—the oscillations between expressionism and functionalism seem to reflect Gropius's own trajectory and interests.

In 1938, shortly after his immigration to the United States, Gropius was invited by MoMA to curate its major exhibition on the Bauhaus, plainly titled "Bauhaus: 1919–1928." Gropius organized the exhibition with Herbert Bayer, a former student at the school who later joined its faculty, and used it as an opportunity to present his vision of modernity. The exhibition's potential to provide the school with a commercial boost may well explain why Gropius placed the emphasis exclusively on the Bauhaus's functionalism and excluded other aspects of its work. Visitors entered the exhibition space beneath a reproduction of Feininger's

233 "An epidemic of mental aberration might be said to have set in, a hopeless obscurantism, which has not been overcome up to the present day." Bruno Taut, *Modern Architecture* (London: The Studio, 1929), 71.

cathedral, which had graced the cover of Gropius's 1919 manifesto. At the gallery's entrance, a series of three-dimensional boards offered a vision of the school's founding principles: "Skill of Hand" was represented by the silhouette of a hand, "Mastery of Form" by an egg, and "Mastery of Space" by a transparent cube. As its title foretells, the exhibition focused exclusively the period from 1919 until 1928, when the school was under Gropius's direction, and glossed over the experiments of its early years prior to 1923. The exhibition implied that the history of the Bauhaus was that of a coherent and flawless modernity—as was typical for Gropius's retrospective presentation of the school—which resisted examination and left little space for contradiction.

Was this a simple question of "selective amnesia" on the part of Gropius?[234] Such is the term that Banham uses to describe Pevsner's total omission of Expressionism from his history of the Bauhaus: *Pioneers of the Modern Movement* includes no mention of the work produced between 1910 and 1926 that did not fit the functionalist mold. By drawing attention to these black spots in the historical memory surrounding the Bauhaus, its "zones of silence,"[235] Banham demonstrates the extent to which the psychological was just as important as the objective in the construction of the modernist project. While Expressionism deserves to be reintegrated into the history of the Bauhaus, it is not a question of placing an excessive importance upon this particular current. Instead, to call upon terms used by Gropius in 1937, it is a question of recalling that the school was more concerned with "exploring the territory that is

234 Reyner Banham, "Stocktaking," *Architectural Review*, February 1960; in *A Critic Writes: Selected Essays by Reyner Banham*, ed. Mary Banham (Berkeley: University of California Press, 1997), 58.
235 Reyner Banham, "History under Revision," in *Design by Choice*, 20–22.

common to the formal and technical spheres, and defining where they cease to coincide" than positioning itself as the apotheosis of rationalism, a perception dismissed as an "erroneous idea," according to Gropius.[236]

These readjustments upset the convention within the history of design that circumscribes the school and its actors in functionalism alone. By returning to its original political position, challenging the notion of its subjugation to capitalism, and studying its inherent ambiguity by way of the contradictory theses of Muthesius and Van de Velde, an examination of the Bauhaus in all its complexity frees the history of design from its commonly accepted functionalist origins, and creates the conditions necessary for a conception of design liberated from the taxonomic constraints retrospectively imposed upon it.

The situation in France was somewhat different from that in Germany. At a time when Art Deco reigned supreme, Le Corbusier began to publish his first texts contesting the dominance of the decorative arts. He had an intimate knowledge of the field, having trained and worked as a watch engraver at the École des Arts Décoratifs in his hometown of La Chaux-de-Fonds. He had studied under L'Eplattenier, and on behalf of the Swiss school's Ateliers d'art réunis he traveled throughout Germany between April 1910 and May 1911 in order to observe the teaching, organization, production, and commerce of the decorative arts in the country. He published his findings in 1912 in a book titled *A Study of the Decorative Art Movement in Germany*, in which he compares the German institutions he had visited with their French counterparts. He despairs at the latter's devotion to Art Deco and the diktats of bourgeois

236 Walter Gropius, *The New Architecture and the Bauhaus* (Cambridge, MA: MIT Press, 1965), 90.

taste, contrasting the French situation with the German one, where promising rationalist experiments had given rise to a dynamic national output. In the course of his research, he attended the 10th Congress of the Deutscher Werkbund, and later met the architect Peter Behrens, whose sober and impersonal style he greatly admired.

While Le Corbusier recognizes the growing importance of design in this study, he considers it only in relation to architecture. He describes this new balance through the image of an airplane whose right and left wings would be design and architecture, respectively. He considered that industrial design had brought civilization to a point of no return, an idea that reappears in his first presentation of his now famous book *The Decorative Art of Today* at the 1925 Exposition internationale des arts décoratifs et industriels modernes in Paris. He used this text to launch an attack on the artistic individualism of the decorative arts and the Art Deco movement. He declares, "The machine has inaugurated the age of the demi-gods. [...] Our confident hearts and thrilled eyes are bent unanimously on this future, which is advancing rapidly, bearing us with it," and praises standardization as the only worthy method of production: "The product of the machine age is a realist object capable of high poetry. We approve so much of this object, we are so fond of it, we would so much like to live with it, that our desire adds to its utility the higher dignity of beauty! The realist object of utility is beautiful. Such is the final conclusion of the spirit forged in the labours of the age."[237] Though he extols the virtues of the rationalist aesthetic, Le Corbusier is at pains to ensure that "no one accuses [him] of wanting to kill feeling."[238] His call to the decorative art of today—"decidedly,

237 Le Corbusier, *Decorative Art of Today*, 192, 188.
238 Ibid., 167.

an inappropriate term!"[239]—far from calling for the exclusion of "feeling" in fact underlines its importance.

Le Corbusier recognized that the furniture and objects that make up the interior were the basis for all "emotive relationships."[240] He proposed the term "equipment" as an alternative that might link these furnishings with standardization. With the notion of equipment, Le Corbusier hoped to shift the focus away from the cult of personality that had built up around decorators and designers. He discusses the term in May 1929, in a letter addressed to Léon Bonifay, the secretary of the Salon d'Automne:

> It seems to me that the term "furniture" [*meuble*] is somewhat vague, disorderly [...] the term equipment, on the other hand, suggests utility, real, and precise functions. It saves time, labor, and money. In a word, it signals the end of meaningless expense. Equipment regroups all everyday functions [...]. In the past, this was the role of tools; from now on, this is the role of equipment.[241]

It was in his October 1920 lecture "L'aventure du mobilier" that Le Corbusier first publicly used the term "equipment": "We ought to have a vast stand at the Salon d'Automne in Paris offering a peremptory demonstration of the principle of the equipment of the modern dwelling with *casiers standards*."[242] He emphasized the adaptability of such an approach: "This equipment can range from the very simple, like the office furniture that is currently available, to the greatest possible refinement. This equipment could

239 Ibid., 85.
240 Ibid., 188.
241 Le Corbusier and Pierre Jeanneret, "New Classification of Town Building, A New Dwelling Unity," in *Œuvre complète de 1924–1934*, ed. W. Boesiger and O. Storonov (Zurich: H. Girsberger, 1935), 121n3.

be installed in the *casiers standard*, and sold at the Bazar de l'Hôtel de Ville or on the Champs-Élysées."[243] With the term "equipment," Le Corbusier appropriated a word usually absent from the vocabulary of design, one that allowed him to better describe the interior fittings of the home in the 1920s at the same time as distancing himself from existing architectural and design traditions. Le Corbusier thus defined a new terrain for design, where its prerogatives blurred with those of architecture; similarly, with the finalized version of the *Casiers standard* in 1924–25, he defined a neutral, standardized, and modular entity, one that could be adapted to the needs of the individual user and to any number of spatial configurations. The references he makes here to industry and elsewhere to automobiles in describing the *Casiers standard* reflect the difficult space, somewhere between industrial production and craftsmanship, in which the designer had until then been forced to work.

242 Le Corbusier, "L'aventure du mobilier" (October 19, 1920), in *Précisions sur un état présent de l'architecture et de l'urbanisme* (Paris: Vincent Fréal, 1930), 107–22. Designed originally for the Pavilion de l'Esprit Nouveau in 1925 at the Exposition des Arts Décoratifs in Paris, the *Casier* is a modular unit in the shape of an open box (in metal or wood) measuring 75 by 150 by 35.5 cm. A standardized element destined for mass production, the *casier* responds to a variety of needs: wardrobe, chair, cupboard, etc., and can be assembled to create partition walls and storage units. "Le Corbusier sought to replace these heterogeneous pieces made for rooms with particular uses with cabinets of a universal form that would function equally well throughout the house. He opted for a regular system of compact, undifferentiated cabinets based on a standard format, which could be combined and superposed in different configurations." George H. Marcus, *Inside Le Corbusier: The Machine for Living* (New York: Monacelli Press, 2000), 33.

243 Ibid., 117.

The Streamline Movement: Designing a New World, Anticipating the Future

Modern design was at once European and American, masculine and feminine, influenced by domestic economy, functionalism, Expressionism, and the dialogue between the individual and the universal. It constantly defied tradition, privileging the idea of a collective progress that was to be attained through the use of powerful technology to serve democratic ends; it promised to liberate the individual in industrial society by providing mastery over technology. In Europe, the Modern Movement's proponents promoted an aesthetic of the machine, while institutions such as MoMA paid tribute to their work in the United States. At the same time, a group of designers in New York began to invoke speed and the laws of aerodynamics to promote their democratic, popular, and technophilic aims. Their work would give rise to America's first industrial design movement: Streamline.

Between Formalism and Functionalism

The designers of the Streamline movement added a new dimension to the debate between formalism and functionalism. This was a movement that, for the first time in the history of design, counted no architects among its ranks. Its proponents originated from a range of fields, including advertising in the case of Egmont Arens and Walter Dorwin Teague, illustration in the case of Raymond Loewy, and even stage design and Broadway in the case of Norman Bel Geddes. It was Bel Geddes who referred to himself as "the first American industrial designer" in 1927, a title to which Loewy also laid claim, citing his creation of the "duplicating angel"[244] for his client Sigmund Gestetner in 1919: "Industrial design was being born and I worked at it frantically."[245]

Apart from this quibble over its origins, the Streamline movement would, as we have already seen, give rise to other, more serious controversies. Its detractors, the Modern Movement's promoters chief among them, believed there was something immoral about the application of aerodynamic forms to immobile objects. Critics railed against the movement for its cosmetic changes that did nothing to alter the function of objects but instead applied superficial, superfluous, and expensive casings and shells. Worse still, they accused the designers of being servants of the market economy. Yet the general public was widely seduced by Streamline design.

It is no coincidence that Streamline was and remains the design movement that prompts the widest range of

244 Loewy, *Never Leave Well Enough Alone*, 81 (see note 32).
245 Ibid., 84.

interpretations. Beneath the most widespread conception of Streamline, which considers it to be somewhere between an elegant form of mise-en-scène and an art of dissimulation, lies an anxiety linked to the ubiquity of ever more complex technology. The era's obsession with technology found a number of different expressions: where modern architects laid bare technology's functions, the designers of the Streamline movement domesticated them. They set in motion an unprecedented technological culture by applying elegant and seductive forms to their creations that aimed to help a generation of interwar Americans adopt these various innovations and assimilate them into their daily lives.

The Streamline movement is often understood to involve a literal application of the physical laws of aerodynamics to various objects. But the attractive profiles it produced were also seen as a necessary and productive form of consumption that harked back to the notion of "creative waste." As the hygienic-aesthetic-organic analysis of Lupton and Miller shows, Streamline can be linked to an American obsession with fusing the mechanic with the organic.[246] They demonstrate the way in which Streamline helped to inculcate the idea of waste as a process necessary for the smooth functioning of American society, which became an incontestable civic belief. They assign a laxative quality to its creations: an "excretory aesthetic, a material celebration of natural and cultural digestive cycles."[247] Cogdell has similarly demonstrated how the rhetoric of the Streamline movement suggested an unsettling parallel between design and the body:

246 Lupton and Miller, *Aesthetics of Waste* (see note 127).
247 Ibid., 2.

> Streamline designers approached products the same way that eugenicists approached bodies. Both considered themselves to be agents of reform, tackling problems of mass (re)production, eliminating "defectiveness" and "parasite drag" that were thought to be slowing forward evolutionary progress. Both were obsessed with increasing efficiency and hygiene and the realization of the "ideal type" as the means to achieve an imminent "civilized" utopia. In short, Streamline design served as a material embodiment of eugenicist ideology.[248]

The movement's vocabulary of forms and their implications—at once social, economic, and political, since consumption had become a civic duty—find troubling but apt metaphors in digestion and excretion, and an even more disturbing double in eugenic ideology.

248 Cogdell, *Eugenic Design*, 4.

The Modern Movement versus Streamline

Where the Modern Movement emphasized the beauty of machinery, technology, and their inner workings, the Streamline movement sought to shield these very things from view. Giedion establishes a potentially fruitful dialogue between the two currents by citing their shared origins in the work of Erich Mendelsohn, Jacobus Johannes Pieter Oud, and Le Corbusier. This apparent symbiosis was rejected by Streamline designers, who sought to establish the independence of their work by distancing themselves from the values of the International Style and aligning themselves instead with American popular culture. A clash of attitudes was clearly visible within the exhibition "Machine Art," organized by Philip Johnson at MoMA in 1934. Everyday tools and implements for industry, home, office, and laboratory were exhibited alongside ball bearings, propellers, and ladles. Each of these objects embodied modernity for Johnson: "Fortunately the functional beauty of most of the objects is not obscure and in any case, so far as this exhibition is concerned, appreciation of their beauty in the platonic sense is the most important."[249] Dentist's tools, X-ray machines, springs, pipes, billiard balls, and other seemingly anodyne objects were treated as masterpieces, exhibited on plinths and in display cases, and accompanied by wall texts. The photograph chosen for the cover of the exhibition catalogue is a black-and-white image of SKF ball bearings. Shown in isolation and with no indication of scale, it demonstrates the high esteem in which the exhibition's organizers held the material and

249 Philip Johnson, *Machine Art* (New York: Museum of Modern Art, 1934).

technological beauty of perfectly functioning objects. The Streamline designers were wholly opposed to this functionalist aesthetic of modernity, and were no more interested in the inner workings of a machine than its nuts and bolts, both of which they firmly believed to be the concern of the engineer rather than the designer.

In 1944, the divergence between the two movements became even starker. Edgar Kaufmann Jr., then director of MoMA's design department, launched the most scathing critique of Streamline to date in the catalogue of the exhibition "Art in Progress," singling out Loewy's pencil sharpener as a particularly distasteful aberration from functionalism. Images of Loewy's creation and an airplane are placed side by side, with a withering caption bemoaning the fact that the "desire to make objects look 'up-to-date' by borrowing forms from unrelated modern machinery often leads to absurdities such as this pencil sharpener streamlined to resemble an airplane."[250] Kaufmann was relentless in his criticism of the Streamline movement; his own Good Design project was clearly aligned with the Modern Movement, and indeed largely synonymous with it. Good Design was instigated in October 1940, when the architect in charge of MoMA's industrial design department, Eliot Fette Noyes, together with Ira Hirschman, launched the "Organic Design" competition. The prize boasted a prestigious jury consisting of Alvar Aalto, Marcel Breuer, Alfred H. Barr Jr., Edward Stone, and Frank T. Parrish.

The first prizes for two of the competition's eight sections—"Seating for a Living Room" and "Other Furniture for a Living Room"—were awarded to Charles Eames and Eero Saarinen, friends and fellow students at Cranbrook Academy:

250 David A. Hanks and Anne H. Hoy, *American Streamlined Design: The World of Tomorrow* (Paris: Flammarion, 2005), 253.

> On the first of October, 1940, the Museum's Department of Industrial Design inaugurated an inter-American competition for the design of furniture, fabrics, and lamps. The purpose of the contest was to discover good designers and engage them in the task of creating a better environment for today's living. [...] A significant innovation was that, in the case of chairs by Saarinen and Eames, a manufacturing method never previously applied to furniture was employed to make a light structural shell consisting of layers of plastic glue and wood veneers molded in three-dimensional forms.[251]

The following year, Noyes organized a traveling exhibition entitled "Organic Design in Home Furnishing," in order to demonstrate the innovative, creative, and functional quality of American design. He hoped to encourage industrialists to work with designers to set the standards of modern design, but his ambitions were stalled by the United States's entry into the Second World War. Kaufmann, one of the two original proponents of the "Organic Design" competition, had similar aims in mind when he launched his own contest—"Good Design"—in partnership with the Merchandise Mart in Chicago and MoMA, from 1950 to 1954. The competition was to become a significant milestone for design in America.

The contest saw a jury gather annually to select a series of objects to be manufactured and sold the following January at the Merchandise Mart, with supplementary products available in a second exhibition and a sale held in July. Following these commercial events, the jury would

251 Eliot Noyes, "A Note on the Competition," in *Organic Design in Home Furnishings* (New York: Museum of Modern Art, 1941), 4.

reconvene to choose the objects, furniture, and utensils they felt to be the most modern, functional, and standardized, whose form best indicated and respected its usage, and whose prices were the most reasonable. Finally, the selected products would feature in an annual exhibition held at the MoMA at the same time as a third sale at the Merchandise Mart.

The first exhibition opened on January 17, 1950, in Chicago. It featured scenography by Charles and Ray Eames that invited the visitor to wander through a world of assorted objects punctuated by images and reproductions, as well as cooking utensils, contemporary furniture, and artworks and historical objects borrowed from the collections of the Art Institute of Chicago. At the entrance to their "Hall of Light," the Eameses included a life-size photo of a Thonet chair, juxtaposed with an enlarged photo of a fork and a Kandinsky canvas. They also included a realistic living space and filled it with the jury's selection of objects. In their trademark style, they mixed genres, disciplines, scales, objects, and representations of objects, thus blurring the codes of design, advertising, and art.

"Good Design" was in part a response to the controversy surrounding Streamline, which took on new proportions following the publication of Kaufmann's essay "Borax, or The Chromium-Plated Calf" in the August 1948 issue of *Architectural Review*. In this article he insisted, in tones reminiscent of Pevsner, that design should "express the spirit of our times" and warned against the dangers of Streamline. He returned to the issue in the catalogue for the exhibition "What Is Modern Design?" with a section emphatically titled "Streamlining Is Not Good Design." The catalogue was a slim booklet whose modest size belied its ambition as a manifesto. Kaufmann outlined the differences between modern design and Streamline movement, and called for the abandonment of the latter, which he saw as a style concerned only with the surfaces of objects and one that produces gratuitous, wasteful, and over-elaborate forms:

> A widespread and superficial kind of design known as streamlining [is] used to style nearly any object from automobiles to toasters. Its theme is the magic of speed, expressed in teardrop shapes, fairings and a curious ornament of parallel lines—sometimes called speed whiskers. The continued misuse of these devices has spoiled them for most designers.[252]

The MoMA curator was unequivocal and unrelenting in his criticism of Streamline, and called for its eradication in favor of modern design, which for Kaufmann was more or less synonymous with Good Design, and whose precepts he summed up in twelve points:

1. Modern design should fulfill the practical needs of modern life.
2. Modern design should express the spirit of our times.
3. Modern design should benefit by contemporary advances in the fine arts and pure sciences.
4. Modern design should take advantage of new materials and techniques and develop familiar ones.
5. Modern design should develop the forms, textures, and colors that spring from the direct fulfillment of requirements in appropriate materials and techniques.

252 Kaufmann, *What Is Modern Design?*, 8 (see note 44).

6. Modern design should express the purpose of an object, never making it seem to be what it is not.
7. Modern design should express the qualities and beauties of the materials used, never making the materials seem to be what they are not.
8. Modern design should express the methods used to make an object, not disguising mass production as handcraft or simulating a technique not used.
9. Modern design should blend the expression of utility, materials, and process into a visually satisfactory whole.
10. Modern design should be simple, its structure evident in its appearance, avoiding extraneous enrichment.
11. Modern design should master the machine for the service of man.
12. Modern design should serve as wide a public as possible, considering modest needs and limited costs no less challenging than the requirements of pomp and luxury.[253]

With these unbreakable tenets in place to promote the "thorough merging of form and function revealing a practical, uncomplicated, sensible beauty" that was the essence of Good Design, Kaufmann demonstrated the difficulty faced by the designer seeking to escape the modernist yoke.[254] In insisting upon the Modern Movement as the valid standard for design as a whole, Kaufmann neglected the Streamline movement's potential for expressing an alternative form of modernity, different to the vision promoted by modern architecture.

253 Ibid., 7.
254 Ibid., 9.

Modernity on the Edge of a Nervous Breakdown: Design Counter-propositions, Design Protest, and Design Criticism

The first blow to the edifice of modern design was dealt by Asger Jorn, the painter, pamphleteer, and former member of COBRA, renowned for its criticism of functionalism and promotion of experimentation. The COBRA group dissolved in 1951, and Jorn, suffering from tuberculosis, withdrew to a sanatorium in Villars-Chésièrs, Switzerland. During his stay, he continued to develop his anti-functionalist ideas, questioning at the same time the role of the artist in industrial society. During the two years he spent recuperating, Jorn honed the future theoretical and critical arms he would later use in his combat against the rationalist aesthetic. Once his recovery was complete, Jorn traveled to Italy to meet the Milanese painter Enrico Baj, cofounder along with Sergio Dangelo of the Movimento di Pittura Nucleare. Joe Cesare Colombo, then a young artist, also joined the group shortly after its creation. Jorn had corresponded with Baj since autumn 1953, and on their first meeting Baj introduced Jorn to Guy Debord's *Potlatch*, an obscure bulletin distributed "to addresses selected by the editors, and to some of those who have requested to receive it."[255] *Potlatch* was free and mailed confidentially, with no more than fifty editions of the first issue.

> The strategic intention of *Potlatch* was to create certain links in order to assemble a new movement,

255 Guy Debord, *Oeuvres* (Paris: Gallimard, 1996), 130.

> which first and foremost aimed to be a gathering of the cultural production of the avant-garde and of the revolutionary critique of society; in 1957, the Situationist International effectively formed around the basis that *Potlatch* had established.[256]

Although Jorn, by his own admission, found the publication's purpose somewhat unclear, he was eager to contact Debord and the two soon joined forces to wage war on functionalism, whose human incarnation they saw in Max Bill, a figure Jorn had previously crossed paths with in 1953 in Switzerland, who had recently taken up the directorship of the Ulm School of Design (Hochschule für Gestaltung Ulm). At the time of Jorn and Debord's meeting, Bill was promising to restore the ideals of the Bauhaus by breathing new life into the functionalism that the pair loathed. On this point and others, Jorn set out to make Bill's life as difficult as possible. To counter the Ulm School and the values it promoted, Jorn founded the International Movement for an Imaginist Bauhaus (MIBI) in 1933, in order to promote an "integral revolutionary cultural attitude."[257] Its objectives were not dissimilar to those of the painters of the Movimento Nucleare, as a letter from Baj to Jorn discussing their respective groups on the January 2, 1954, demonstrates:

> It was precisely to combat purism, abstractism, uselessism, sterilism etc. that I organized our Movimento Nucleare: the sole purpose of many of our manifestations was to combat the presumptuous stupidity of the abstract-concretes and their little geometric finds.[258]

256 Ibid., 8.
257 Asger Jorn, *Pour la forme : Ébauche d'une méthodologie des arts* [1957] (Paris: Éditions Allia, 2001), 28.
258 Asger Jorn to Enrico Baj, January 2, 1954, http://debordiana.chez.com/francais/1954.htm.

In an exchange of letters in January of the previous year, Jorn had spelled out in no uncertain terms his contempt for Bill's project and his proposed strategy for opposing it:

> A Swiss architect, Max Bill, [...] wants to make this academy [the Bauhaus] where Paul Klee and Kandinsky were professors a purely technical one—an academy without painting, without research in the domain of the image, fiction, signs, symbols etc: instruction. I declare war on him in the name of all experimental painters and researchers, and I declare my intention to create an international organization for research in the domain of fiction and image, which will be called: The Imaginary Bauhaus. Would the Movimento di Pittura Nucleare be willing to join such an organization? I have asked the same question to other free-thinking artists in the hope of firmly opposing this oppression of art and of free painting by abstract and functionalist architecture. I wish to create a small journal, *The Imaginary Bauhaus*, and I would like to feature an article by you, attacking purist architecture and setting out the program for a nuclear architecture conceived, like all great architecture, by painter-sculptors. I believe that Michelangelo was the nuclear painter of his age. Please send your article with sketches in Chinese ink for a fantastic architecture. I am counting on you, because the photos of your group's paintings show that you are the only painters of our time to have understood that movement is the basis of all form, that form is the expression or the meaning of movement.[259]

259 Asger Jorn to Enrico Baj, January 1954, in Mirella Bandini, *L'esthétique, le politique: De Cobra à l'Internationale Situationniste 1948–1957* (Arles: Sulliver, 1998), 241–42.

Baj replied immediately, enthusiastically stating, "I am in perfect agreement with you, your convictions are my own. [...] You can be sure of the full support of the Movimento di Pittura Nucleare in your fight against Max Bill's new Bauhaus."[260] The climax came in 1954 at the Triennale di Milano, when Jorn openly attacked Bill, denouncing him as the epitome of the functionalist current of the Bauhaus. For Jorn, industrial production and the equivalence between form, function, and beauty that were together the essence of functionalism could only offer a trite vision of design. He criticized modern design as totalitarian and utopian, and called for its definitive eradication on the grounds that it promoted a disingenuous link between the aesthetic and the moral, between timelessness and universalism, and that it placed a blind faith in the redemptive powers of technology.

Bill effectively insisted that "the guiding principle of good form is moral and aesthetic."[261] Jorn sought to obliterate the "neo-Bauhaus of Ulm," deploring Bill's use of the Bauhaus name and his hackneyed ideas that stemmed from an "uninspired" and "dead" doctrine relying upon the skewed morality of the Modern Movement: "[The moderns] aspired to a humanist analysis of the social and ethical functions of our environment, carried out upon a democratic base and in accordance with a 'concept of urbanism' that would enshrine man's right to a dwelling and ensure him a salubrious and peaceful existence."[262] Jorn hoped to reassert the importance of individual desire in the face of the Modern Movement's insistence on the interdependence of form and function, which it held to be the

260 Enrico Baj to Asger Jorn, in Bandini, *L'esthétique, le politique*, 253.
261 Max Bill, *Form: Eine Bilanz über die Formentwicklung um die Mitte des XX. Jahrhundert* (Basel: Karl Werner, 1952), 11.
262 Asger Jorn, "Image et forme: Contre l'empirisme éclectique," in *Pour la forme*, 10–15.

exclusive condition of beauty. In order to do so, he intended to reverse the modernist equation, calling for artists to appropriate industrial means for their own personal ends, liberated from the shackles of functionalism: "The experimental artist must seize industry and use it to his own non-utilitarian ends."[263]

In 1956, Jorn organized the first Congrès mondiale des artistes libres in Alba as part of the "Incontro internazionale di ceramisti," the first exhibition of the MIBI, at the same time as the first Festival de l'art d'avant-garde was taking place at Le Corbusier's Cité Radieuse in Marseilles. A significant number of artists participated in the Congrès, including Jorn, Baj, Lucio Fontana, Sergio Dangelo, Karel Appel, Corneille, Roberto Matta, John-Franklin Koenig, Roland Giguère, and Édouard Jaguer, as well as a few former members of COBRA. The centerpiece of the event was an exhibition of ceramics created by the Fabbrica Giuseppe Mazzotti under Tullio Mazzotti. It was held between October 22 and November 22, 1956, in Albisola, with Colombo producing the scenography. The collection of handcrafted ceramics formed part of Jorn's strategy to counter the industrial aesthetic of Ulm.

A careful examination of Bill's project reveals that it differed considerably from Jorn's characterization. Though Bill had studied not at the Weimar Bauhaus but its later Dessau incarnation, his vision for Ulm was closer to that of the original school and Van de Velde's model:

> The founders of the Ulm School believe art to be the highest expression of human life and their aim is therefore to help in turning life itself into a work of art. In the words of that memorable

263 Ibid., 28.

> challenge thrown down by Henry van de Velde over fifty years ago, we mean "to wage war on ugliness" [...] As the direct heir to Van de Velde's School at Weimar, the Dessau Bauhaus had set itself precisely the same objects.[264]

Bill also consulted with former professors Josef Albers and Johannes Itten in the planning of its preliminary course, invited Van de Velde to the school's opening in 1955, and had Gropius deliver the inaugural address.[265] Ironically, given the basis of Jorn's vehement attacks, Bill ensured that the school included artist studios, ironworks, and spaces dedicated to nonindustrial production. This disturbed his contemporaries, who aspired to a purely rational and industrial design, to such an extent that Bill was forced to resign in 1958, and was replaced by Tomás Maldonado. Having ousted Bill, Maldonado set about transforming the school into one devoted exclusively to science and technology. It was in this deeply hostile context, at the 9th Congrès des CIAM in Aix-en-Provence in 1953, that Bill set out his vision of the education provided by the school: to train designers who would be capable of immediately entering the cycle of production.

Jorn believed that design—more than art alone—could enable the artist to assume a greater political role in society. He sought to counter the aesthetic value of consumer goods, and the subjection of the designer to the laws of the market and bourgeois functionalism, by offering a vision of a rebellious, antibourgeois, and revolutionary designer—in other words, Morris. At the "Incontro

264 Max Bill, "The Bauhaus Idea: From Weimar to Ulm," trans. P. Morton Shand, in *The Architects' Yearbook*, vol. 5 (London: Elek Books, 1953), 24.
265 Walter Gropius, inaugural speech at the Ulm School of Design (September 1955); published as "Dynamische Tradition in der Architektur," *Perspektiven*, no. 15 (1956): 100–105.

internazionale di ceramisti," Jorn placed the emphasis on craftsmanship—more to reassert its value than for its experimental potential—and avoided any concessions to capitalism, while still underlining the right of the artist to leave behind this kind of craft production in order to explore new terrain through industrial methods.

"Pop Design": Between Popular Culture and Mass Industrialization, a Farewell to Pevsner and Giedion

At the end of the Second World War, British designers reappropriated numerous technological innovations developed by and for the military and applied them to their field. The resulting products made up the "War to Peace" section in the November 1946 exhibition "Britain Can Make It" held at the Victoria & Albert Museum. The exhibition was similar to the Good Design series in its enthusiastic endorsement of innovation and progress. The forms on display broke with the rectilinear shapes of modern design, and reflected postwar hopes for renewal. They paralleled "vital forms" in America,[266] and the *formes libres* of the French artists and architects of the Union des Artistes Modernes, who drew their inspiration from the abstraction of the 1930s. These formal and technological changes threw into question society's relationship with the utopian aspirations of the Modern Movement, and would eventually come to be seen as heralding their downfall. They were replaced by new and more critical visions of utopia, dystopias or "contro-utopias," which aimed to dismantle the hitherto uncontested supremacy of functionalism and industrialization.

In early 1960s Europe, design entered into an unprecedented and long-awaited period of expansion. With a flourishing economy, the age of the machine and the aesthetic of efficiency that had characterized Good Design and been promoted by the Modern Movement gave way

266 See Brooke K. Rapaport and Kevin Stayton, *Vital Forms: American Art and Design in the Atomic Age, 1940–1960* (New York: Brooklyn Museum of Art, 2001).

to a second industrial revolution as technological ideology reached a new stage. It was a revolution that exploited high-performance technology for the benefit of all, answering the call of mass culture and leisure society with its televisions, blenders, and countless other gadgets. Design in the 1960s has often been characterized in terms of a model of bountiful, carefree production. Its most significant feature was, as historian Penny Sparke has shown,[267] a wholly new perspective that turned attention away from matters of production and toward the consumer.

This may explain why some historical analyses of design have suggested that this period saw the bursting forth of a new kind of production, one liberated from all and any political questions. A more sustained analysis reveals that this is far from being the case; design was more than ever the site of cultural and political debate. The 1959 Kitchen Debate is a prominent example; this was the name given by the *New York Times* to the improbable encounter between US Vice President Richard Nixon and Soviet Premier Nikita Khrushchev, which took place at the opening of the American National Exhibition in Moscow. At the height of the Cold War and in front of the cameras of the world's media, the leaders of the world's two superpowers discussed home appliances in front of a model kitchen. Each man extolled the benefits of his country's consumer goods, with the nuclear arms race a thinly veiled subtext. The back and forth quickly turned to challenges: Nixon asked, "Would it not be better to compete in the relative merits of washing machines than in the strengths of rockets? Is this the kind of competition you want?"[268] Khrushchev replied, "Yes that's the kind of competition we

267 Sparke, *Introduction to Design and Culture* (see note 13).
268 "The Kitchen Debate" (1959), transcript reproduced in *The Industrial Design Reader*, ed. Carma Gorman (New York: Allworth Press, 2003), 174.

want. But your generals say: 'Let's compete at rockets. We are strong and we can beat you.' But in this respect we can also show you something."[269] Beyond the sparring, where Nixon set out the virtues of capitalism and Khrushchev those of communism, the kitchen served as an arena for two opposing political and economic visions. That design should come to occupy such an important role from the 1950s onward is unsurprising given the unprecedented scope that it took on throughout this period.

In the 1960s, mass-produced, inexpensive, and widely distributed design became accessible to a far greater proportion of the population than before—would this mean it was finally able to fulfill the democratic promises of its beginnings? The situation proved to be rather more complex. The diktats of good taste made incarnate by bourgeois furniture crumbled as modern values gave way to those of popular culture. This change gave rise to an eclectic kitsch that readily dabbled in bad taste and camp. Susan Sontag defined the latter as a "way of seeing the world as an aesthetic phenomenon," whose ideal is best understood "not in terms of beauty, but in terms of the degree of artifice, of stylization"; camp "discloses innocence, and, when it can, corrupts it."[270] This tendency was enough to deal a fatal blow to the ideals of the Modern Movement. Design, and by extension all objects of consumption, entered into a game of symbols and signs that led them ever further away from functionalism and made them irresistibly appealing to the consumer.

With its ephemeral plastic materials, affordable prices, and incarnation of a new ideology of consumption-as-pleasure, design captured perfectly the spirit and values of

269 Ibid.
270 Susan Sontag, "Notes on 'Camp,'" *Partisan Review* 31, no. 4 (Winter 1964): 515–30.

1960s society. The Pop ideology presented a direct challenge to the Modern Movement, and to the idea of mechanized and timeless creations. Pop also set its sights on technology, which the moderns had previously claimed as their exclusive domain. At the beginning of this trend, which in England first appeared toward the end of the 1950s, Lawrence Alloway set out its implications: "Popular art, as a whole, offers imagery and plots to control the changes in the world; everything in our culture that changes is the material of the popular arts."[271] A culture based on obsolescence, disposability, and taste allowed a new generation to free itself from the clutches of the modern era. Banham celebrated this transformation, which saw Pop design become the mirror of a new society; what it reflected was abundance.

> The aesthetics of Pop depend on a massive initial impact and small sustaining power, and are therefore at their poppiest in products whose sole object is to be consumed, that must be consumed, whether physically, like soft serve ices, or symbolically, like daily papers that can only last twenty-four hours by definition.[272]

The celebration was near universal, with Abraham Moles echoing Banham and reveling in the fact that "all objects are ephemeral."[273] Much more than Streamline, whose influence had been limited to America, pop culture created entirely new conditions and found in design a fitting

271 Lawrence Alloway, "The Arts and the Mass Media," *Architectural Design* 28, no. 2 (February 1958): 84–85.
272 Reyner Banham, "Who Is This 'Pop'?" *Motif*, no. 10 (Winter 1962/63); in *Design by Choice*, 94–97.
273 Abraham Moles, "Vivre avec les choses contre un culture immatérielle," in "A l'heure du design," Art Press Hors Série no. 7, special issue, *Art Press* (1987): 12–16.

expression of industrialization. This transformation was made possible by the rise of the second industrial age within a society that strongly believed in progress and placed enormous faith in the power of technology.

Historians of design have often discussed the dichotomy between Pop as a mass phenomenon consisting of cheap and disposable products within reach of all, and radical architecture as a constellation of international architects who formed groups that sought to break with the market through small-batch, modular products and narratives. The Milanese designer Joe Cesare Colombo was at the crossroads of these two currents—between mass-produced consumer goods and design that critiqued the capitalist system. In the last phase of his short life, he sought to create a new and revolutionary strain of design: *antidesign*.

Part III

Design, Architecture, and Antidesign—The Rise of an Unruly Discipline

As functionalism was reevaluated and reinterpreted throughout the 1960s, the crisis of design's origins led to the collapse of the model associated with the Modern Movement. It was now condemned for its failure to make a reality of the social virtues it claimed to embody: its imagining of aesthetics and forms as the expression of politics, its construction of a deceptive discourse that insisted on the long-term validity of its preferred forms, which were in fact ahistorical and universal. The situation was a complex one for designers, who were torn between a continuing fascination with technology, democratic ideals, and the social program of standardization on the one hand, and a sense of revulsion at their consequences on the other. A small number of designers who considered themselves the heirs to modernist ideas began to investigate the potential ramifications and significance for their own discipline of the failure of the Modern Movement's architectural utopias.

The only country where designers could be said to have really engaged with this question was Italy. Although the majority would nonetheless favor a modernist neo-rationalism, strangely enough, it would be not Italy's designers but rather its architects, critical to the point of questioning the very foundations of their discipline, who would truly consider its consequences. A myriad of small groups of young architects, recent graduates and current students of the architecture department at the University of Florence, opposed through their work the Modern Movement lauded by their professors' generation: UFO, Zziggurat, Archizoom Associati, and Superstudio formed in 1965 in Florence, and were joined in 1970 by Gruppo Strum in Turin. Several years later, these groups were baptized *architettura radicale* (radical architecture) by the art critic Germano Celant.

Opposing the idea of timeless architecture that was at the heart of the modernist project, the radicals privileged the transitory and the ephemeral. They rethought architecture's ends, leaving behind traditional goals of construction and building in favor of a less fixed territory, one of flux and possibility. Like Archigram before them, challenging the absolute values of permanence and durability enabled them to develop a critique of the materiality of architecture. However, unlike their predecessors, the radicals turned their attention to standardization and the objects it produced: the symbols of the speculative-capitalist economy that they intended to dismantle. They began to occupy the terrain of design, which by way of merchandise and consumer goods held sway over the market and allowed them to operate within it. Through this the Italian radicals inadvertently brought about a paradox at the heart of their critique: by appropriating design and integrating it into their architectural practice, they left unchallenged the Modern Movement's assertion of the supremacy of architecture over design. Their experiments with the latter in fact perpetuated this state of affairs and the totality of architecture that it implied.

At the same time as the radical architects were developing their critique, Ettore Sottsass, barely their senior, was establishing his own, more ambivalent position. Meanwhile, Joe Colombo—now an internationally celebrated designer—announced that he was abandoning design, at least in its current form. In the context of an enthusiastic extension of standardization (made evident by the profusion of cheap consumer goods produced by Italian industry) and a critique of such production by the radicals (whose privileging of craftsmanship ensured their output remained the preserve of collectors), he invented antidesign. He disowned his previous work and refused to continue to serve capitalist ends in his capacity as a designer. With antidesign, he initiated a project that sought to hijack the mechanisms of commerce and act as an indictment of industrial society; in doing so he would fundamentally alter the scope, role, and definition of design. Though antidesign has now been assimilated into the contemporary vocabulary and imaginary of design as little more than a protest, I will show here that it was *in fact* the expression of a design capable of asserting its autonomy from—and even its domination of—architecture.

Architectural Maelstrom: Furniture as a New Playground for Radical Architecture

Rejecting the association of architecture to fixed, physical locations, the radicals created a tabula rasa that allowed them to interrogate the legitimacy of their work through the development of an all-encompassing approach that could be applied across terrains such as climate control, consumer goods, or the circulation of individuals within a given space. They thus appropriated all and any items, prostheses, and systems that implied contact with the human body. Gradually the notion of the habitat transgressed its conventional boundaries and ultimately broadened its scope to encompass the environment as a whole. Elements once considered categorically distinct from one another—clothing, cars, telephones, and even air—became architectures in their own right. This position was made explicit by the Austrian Hans Hollein in his 1968 text "Alles ist Architektur."[274] He opens by stating that "architecture is a medium of communication" and one that can be applied to all human activity, since now "everything is architecture." Beyond the literal built environment and construction, architecture is for Hollein an indefinite space of transition, connection of goods, information, meaning, and psychological possibilities, and one that he believes offers humanity a vast range of opportunities and freedoms. In this conception of architecture, the human figures at long last as the central subject: "Man becomes at last the true center and starting point for the definition of an environment, as the limitations [of the built environment] no longer apply."[275]

274 Hollein, "Alles ist Architektur," 138–39 (see note 75).
275 Ibid.

Such a view of architecture is characteristic of the neo-avant-garde of the 1960s, and was shared to a large extent by the Italian radical architects, Austrians Friedensreich Hundertwasser and "Planet Hollein," and the American Peter Eisenman, to cite only its most prolific proponents. All promoted a reinterpretation of traditional architecture and a rupture with the Modern Movement. A key element of their work was an assertion of the existence of architecture beyond the materiality of the built environment, as a site for theoretical hypotheses and conceptual forms. The proponents of paper architecture, in the lineage of Archigram, saw in this approach the only means of creating a viable alternative to bourgeois culture, rationalism, functionalism, and the overconsumption that they believed had come to govern architecture.

Thus began a current of immaterial projects, the only ones viable in the eyes of these architects, since they alone could not be bought, consumed, or assimilated by the mechanisms of the market. These projects invoked the notion of utopia as the only valid site for critique; this position certainly raises complex questions in light of the accusation leveled by the radicals against the Modern Movement and their attack on its tendency toward utopian thinking under the guise of functionalism. The radical utopia differed from the modernist one in that it was not an end but rather a means of critique:

> At a moment when the object is no longer interesting for its formal and visual qualities nor for its functional pragmatic ones, the aesthetic actors—architects and designers—believe that physical creation has become a secondary concern and can be done away with, reabsorbed into the category of the project. In these terms, it has become the equivalent of

> a conceptual idea, an instrument that is no longer practical but rather analytical, critical, semantic or synthetic, according to the emphasis placed on significant concepts or the character of structural relations between the constituent parts of a discourse.[276]

The radicals thus made a distinction between two different kinds of utopia: the first had been inadvertently created by the avant-garde linked to the Modern Movement under the guise of democracy, who were in fact oblivious to the utopian and unreal dimension of their work; the second was the intentionally complex and paradoxical utopia proposed by the neo-avant-garde in order to critique the errors of their predecessors.

The utopia denounced by the radicals was an absolute one, defined by the imposition of order in the form of bourgeois functionalism—a characterization the Modern Movement would doubtless have rejected. Such a totalizing and uncritical utopia was unacceptable to the radical architects.[277] They saw it as one where human needs underwent a reductive generalization, and one that offered only normative and industrial satisfaction. The modern utopia thus promised a false equality to the workers that it condemned to carry out repetitive and hyperspecialized tasks on the production line. The radicals maintained that beyond denying workers a say in the economy and in power more broadly, the market system deluded them into thinking their situation was the result of choice and gave them the illusion of freedom. The radicals analyzed this alienation of the individual through labor, and criticized the role of industrialization in transforming human beings

276 Paola Navone and Bruno Orlandoni, *Architettura "radicale": Documenti di "Casabella"* (Milan: G. Milani, 1974), 55.
277 See Andrea Branzi, "L'architetture sono io," in *Scritti teoretici*, 38 (see note 30).

into little more than tools at the service of production, cogs in the cycle of consumption; they believed that workers had been left with no choice but to collaborate in a society in which they were at once the instrument of production and its ultimate consumers. Such a system could only promise superficial satisfaction, the price of which was the worker's freedom.

With a Marxist analysis of design resembling Morris's critique, the radicals accused the machine and the production apparatus of objectifying, dehumanizing, and commodifying man. They denounced the "manipulation" carried out by the Modern Movement in promising a better future that relied exclusively on greater material comfort. According to the radicals, the error committed by the Modern Movement was twofold: despite the egalitarian values espoused at its inception, by assimilating the values of the industrial bourgeoisie that had been dominant since the Industrial Revolution, it had not only worsened injustice but subjugated humanity. This analysis led the radicals to construct their protest around a kind of utopia *détourné*. Their reappropriation of the utopia was an act of liberation in the context of the moderns' disastrous, ahistorical program. In contrast to the moderns, whose failures they blamed on an inability to engage with the utopian dimensions of their work, the radicals proposed utopias that were acknowledged as such; they described them using the same well-known and codified language, but considered them a kind of "lever" that could help to establish a new relationship between architecture and reality:

> In contrast to the unwitting utopia of modern architecture and town-planning, which proposed an impossible order for the world, avant-garde architecture turned the process on its head: it assumed

> utopia as the given basis of the work and developed it realistically. Once the process was completed, nothing was left out; everything was accomplished in an act that was perfectly executed in itself, as pure creative energy transformed, without loss, into constructive energy. The utopia was not the end but the reality of the situation; there was no allegory in it, just purely natural phenomena. Paraphrasing Flaubert, we were able to say: "l'architecture c'est moi."[278]

Their protest relied upon a strategy based on a "utopia of the real" that both contested the modernist utopia and created space for a critical imaginary. Contrary to traditional definitions of utopia, the radicals' vision remained close to their reality, and played a "double role of imposing a different and demystifying vision, and at the same time of translating, in visual terms, the vigorous conceptual workings developed."[279] This visual dimension, which relied on perceptual shocks, was the end goal of the Italian movement's research. It was first displayed to the public with a series of exhibitions: "Superarchitettura I" at Galleria Jolly 2 in Pistoia, held December 4–7, 1966, followed by "Superarchitettura II" at Galleria Communale in Modena the year after. These "super" exhibitions set out in two stages the manifesto of radical architecture, headed by Archizoom Associati and Superstudio, with the latter group's foundation coinciding with the first exhibition.

The modestly sized exhibitions took place in spaces composed of pieces of wood and undulating forms, clouds, and waves entirely covered with fields of purple, yellow, green, black, and bright red drawn from the palette of Pop

278 Branzi, *Hot House*, 60 (see note 15).
279 Gianni Pettena, "Radical Architecture," in Migayrou, *Architecture radicale*, 297 (see note 31).

art. The prototypes of objects and furniture presented all stemmed from the same principle of the undulating line, an explicit reference to the flooding of the river Arno in Florence in 1962. The deluge caused a number of deaths and deposited colossal quantities of mud in the libraries and museums of the cities, resulting in extensive damage to their collections. This event made the young architects aware of the fragility of their Renaissance artistic heritage. The wavelike shapes referencing the flood became a characteristic form and symbol for Florence's radical architects. They served as a unifying formal principal for "Superarchitettura I," with the exhibition space covered in undulating lines that were echoed in the objects displayed, thus creating a unified whole. The intention was to render impossible the determination of form by function, in defiance of the most fundamental functionalist credo, at the same time as upsetting the modernist insistence on proportion. The radicals played mischievously with history: take for example Archizoom Associati, who mocked Mies van der Rohe's orthogonal forms with the *Mies* lounger, while their *Superonda* sofa sacrilegiously referenced the bathroom seating of the Villa Savoye using the formal vocabulary of Pop art.

The bold wave form enabled the radicals to set their project for a "utopia of the real" in motion. It provided a series of recurring forms that also acted as a parodical *détournement* of the modernist utopias whose contradictory logic they sought to lay bare. These critical forms, which were labeled "dystopias," "abnormal utopias," and "counter-utopias," described intentionally fantastical situations and were intended to dismantle ideological and ostensibly realistic productions of technological progress and its promises of emancipation. They can be found in the descriptions in "Twelve Cautionary Tales for Christmas," a text by Superstudio's architect-anthropologist Gian Piero Frassinelli that perfectly represents the mixture of vitriol and humor that characterized their critique.

Originally written for general interest magazines, Frassinelli's texts failed to rouse interest outside the architectural press and were eventually published in English as "Twelve Cautionary Tales for Christmas," in the December 1971 issue of *Architectural Design*, before appearing the following month in Italian under the title "Le dodici città ideali," in *Casabella*.[280] Each of the twelve apocalyptic descriptions of societies and urban environments is a tale of tragic isolation in a universe that promises a technological freedom which is sooner or later revealed to be illusory. Each city features some form of imprisonment or deprivation, and punishes or even destroys those who fail to submit to the reigning ideology of progress; each is equipped with a system of control that organizes its inhabitants' lives down to the most minute detail. The twelve descriptions are illustrated with color photomontages and aerographic works, and accompanied by a series of slides. The first city, 2,000-Ton City, is a vast cubic structure that houses cells scattered throughout a rural landscape. Imprisoned within them are inhabitants connected permanently to an organic architectural membrane that meets their every physiological and psychological need and affords them eternal life. Yet if the city's sensors detect a repeated desire to rebel, the inhabitant is instantly obliterated: the titular 2,000 tons are revealed to be the weight of the ceiling of each cell, which comes crashing down on dissenters, who are quickly replaced by an embryo—the cell's next inhabitant.

280 Superstudio [Gian Piero Frassinelli], "Twelve Cautionary Tales for Christmas: Premonitions of the Mystical Rebirth of Urbanism," *Architectural Design*, December 1971, 737–42, 785; published in Italian as "Le dodici città ideali: Premonizioni della parusia urbanistica," *Casabella*, no. 361 (January 1972): 45–55.

The tale acts as a magnifying glass, its exaggerations doing nothing to detract from the aptness of its parody of the urban and political organization of contemporary society: 2,000-Ton City describes an apparently benevolent power watching over the well-being of all society that, prompted by even the slightest criticism, reveals itself to be totalitarian and oppressive, and wields the power of life and death over its subjects. The perversity of the system recalls George Orwell's *1984*, where the all-seeing Big Brother monitors every movement of its citizens, or the promise of happiness in Aldous Huxley's *Brave New World*, where psychotropic drugs prevent any seditious thought. Echoing these two dystopias, the first city—a perfect incarnation of the universal planning grid that was the pinnacle of modernism's rational and self-contained aspirations—leaves room for rebellion, but the absolute isolation of its inhabitants means the only possible outcome is an immediate and summary execution. The grid form chosen by Superstudio differs from the programmable matrix of modernism; for the radical group, the grid reflected the immateriality and infinite abstraction of the rest of their work, such as the *Continuous Monument*, the *Misura* series, or the *Istogrammi*, which I will discuss later.

The second city in the series, Temporal Cochlea-City, is governed by a similarly omnipotent technological force, and structured as an immense and endless screw that drills down into the earth. With a propulsion system designed to last for 10,000 years, the city continuously expands itself through a mechanism that ensures permanent growth. Composed of automated cells arranged in concentric rings separated by a spiraling roadway, its inhabitants are first housed in the screw's upper reaches and gradually move downward with its movements as they grow older. They are free to move around as they wish, but any possible exit from the screw is made impossible by the permanent construction site at its upper extremity. Trapped by an illusory freedom and subject to artificial light and air conditioning—characteristics of spaces of production from the factory to the supermarket—this city of cells serves as a metaphor for vast housing projects and skyscrapers that imprison their inhabitants from the cradle to the grave.

The third city, New York of Brains, is constructed on the site formerly occupied by the wealthy residential neighborhoods of New York. New York of course stands as a symbol for modernism and the International Style: the same site would be used by Ettore Sottsass in his 1973 series of drawings *The World as Festival* to illustrate the failure of capitalism. A new city is built upon the ruins of the old, taking the form of a 180-cubic-foot cenotaph filled with 10,000,456 spherical cavities that each contain a physiological solution in which a human brain floats. Powerless and lost in thought or madness, the brains outlive humanity to lead a solitary and eternal existence.

The fourth city, Spaceship City, is modeled on the living capsule. A fifty-meter-wide red wheel is piloted through space by a preprogrammed electronic brain, charged with maintaining its 156 inhabitants in a state of suspended animation. In this deep sleep, they share the same dream for eighty years, before they are killed and replaced. As they slumber, the spacecraft's electronic brain pairs them off to mate mechanically in order to create the next generation, and so on, until the vessel reaches the New Earth. The unconscious cosmonauts thus lead a passive, unconscious existence as they head toward this El Dorado—a utopia?—reproducing and ensuring the survival of the species. This Spaceship City is the last of this series to feature omnipotent and seemingly maternal qualities that manage the life cycles of their apathetic and amorphous inhabitants.

In the City of the Hemispheres, 10,044,900 crystalline sarcophagi are separated by transparent walls, forming a reflective sheet of crystal. Each sarcophagus is inhabited by an immobile individual, who is connected by electrodes to a fully mobile silver hemisphere containing sensory organs that freely roams the exterior world. These perfectly contented minds are wholly disembodied, with their physical existence no more real than the dazzling light reflected by the crystal structure.

In Barnum Jnr.'s Magnificent and Fabulous City, a vast red-and-blue-striped circus tent houses a cylindrical space, which encloses a scaled-down city that in turn plays host to all the world's great monuments. To enter, visitors simply have to purchase a ticket and leave a deposit at the booth, before choosing a famous personality, dead or alive, whose role they will take on during their stay. The visitor can experience the city through a robotic doll to which they are connected, moving around and meeting other characters. They can live out various adventures, from love affairs with movie stars to bloody detective stories, and fulfill their wildest fantasies—including those that end badly. Whatever the outcome, at the end of their visit, they must pass by the cashier in order to settle their bill and pay for any damage caused during their time in the city. The description of this city, delivered in the genial tone of a ringmaster, suggests violence may be common, perhaps even par for the course. In the vicarious existence it offers, this sixth story differs in that its technological system is not imposed, but rather obscured as part of a great spectacle. The title refers to the emperor of artifice, the American Phineas Taylor Barnum, known for his storytelling abilities and as a forerunner of modern-day advertising. His American Museum in New York was a major success, and he went on to found the Barnum Circus, famed for its red-and-blue big tops. This sixth city, where murder is permitted for those who can afford it, is a temple to illusion, a display of P. T. Barnum himself, the self-proclaimed "Prince of Humbugs."

The theatricalization of industry, merchandise, and consumption is thematized in the seventh city, Continuous Production Conveyor Belt City, with a horizontal form that indeed recalls a factory production line. At its head is the Grand Factory, four miles wide and a hundred yards tall, which ensures the continuous movement and expansion of the horizontal city and its eight million inhabitants through the perpetual construction of new districts. The ultimate aspiration of these residents is to move as frequently as possible into newer homes, equipped with the most up-to-date appliances, from which they derive an intense pleasure. Searching for comfort, change, and novelty, the residents are in constant competition with one another for the latest homes next to the Grand Factory.

The eighth city, Conical Terraced City, consists of successive concentric rings, each floor of a smaller size, creating a terraced cone shape. Communication between individuals is impossible, except by way of a "coordinator" brain implant, which allows residents to transmit binding orders to those living directly below them, from the upper levels down to ground level, where the land is farmed and goods are produced. The sole desire of every resident is to reach a higher level, and so they are constantly plotting to gain access to the floor above, often climbing over the bodies of those whose attempts have been foiled by the city dwellers above, fiercely defending their superior position. At the summit of the structure is a cupola, where a solitary man lives, transmitting marvelous dreams once a day to the city below.

The ninth city, "Ville-Machine Habitee," consists of a machine so massive its dimensions are unfathomable. Inhabitants speed along a series of conveyor belts from birth to death, with the machine ensuring their every need is met, but also threatening to crush them in its gears should they stray from the predefined route. Its inner workings are entirely self-sufficient, recycling all dead material and expelling anything superfluous. Typical of the mechanical cities described by science-fiction authors inspired by the Industrial Revolution, the city-machine produces nothing except manure.

The City of Order at first seems unremarkable, closely resembling those in which we live with its squares, streets, and parks. However, its mayor has held office for no less than forty-five years, during which time he has ensured his tenure not by adapting the city to suit its citizens' needs, but rather the other way around. This tenth city is presided over by a council of elected officials—all now deceased—converted into plastic statues whose faces express a gamut of emotions, from anger to joy. If a citizen expresses the slightest objection to how the city is run, they are invited to the town hall and depart again a week later as contented model citizens with mechanisms in place of their brains and plastic beads in place of their innards.

The eleventh city in the series, City of the Splendid Houses, is the most beautiful in the world, since its citizens are encouraged to express their imagination and individualism through the construction of elaborately decorated homes. Each citizen is allotted a five-by-five-meter space, three meters high, with a transparent roof, in which to assemble their creation. Every inhabitant works in the city's factories and receives coupons in place of a monthly salary, which allow them to buy the products necessary for their endless home improvements. Two taps meet all of their material needs, one dispensing a nutritious plasma and the other water. The wealthiest families extend their homes high into the air as they vie to outdo one another, creating tall, narrow towers that overlook the city.

The final city, City of the Book, is governed by the rules listed in a book that hangs around the neck of each citizen. While the book's left-hand pages list a code of ethics and Christian morals, the right-hand pages set out pragmatic behaviors and guidelines for action. The left-hand pages are visible only in daylight, and the right-hand ones can only be read in the dark with infrared night vision; whereas the left-hand pages forbid the taking of a life except in cases of self-defense, the right-hand ones helpfully suggest that bodies be disposed of in the holes provided.

Each of these short tales set out an apocalyptic vision, borrowing from science fiction in order to conjure evocative visions of negative utopia. These texts offered a vision in which architecture ceased to be a "mediation between man and environment translated into a complexity of needs, creating an artificial panorama and a 'second poverty,'" and instead became "a cross-science."[281] The texts also reevaluated the importance of fiction and poetry by showing the role they could play in critiquing and countering the dominant economic system. Frassinelli's stories imitated the typical magazine quiz whose answers feature at the end of the publication, asking readers how many of the cities met their approval; over nine, for example, and you were doubtless a head of state, or at the very least an aspiring one, certainly not a human being. Thanks to the broad circulation of the magazines in which they were published, he reached a readership far wider than radical architecture's small following. In addition to altering the

281 Superstudio, "Superstudio on Mindscapes," *Design Quarterly*, no. 89 (1973): 17–31.

reception of these fictions that pushed the characteristics of the Modern Movement to the point of paroxysm, the scenarios presented disturbed and disturbing utopias revealing the technological horror and inhumanity to which industrial society had given rise. Fiction here acts as a critical vector and a means of liberation from the fallacious ideology of modernism. Superstudio referred to fiction as "invention design and evasion design," defining it as a poetic expression that oscillates between the messianic and the apocalyptic: "We shall build on the ruins of our own wars and those of others, on the smoking ruins of private and public guerilla warfare, on the clouds of numerous mushrooms, atomic ones and those of peyote."[282]

As a powerful tool of dissent and refutation, fiction not only awakens the reader to society's contradictions through supposedly naive subterfuge, but also allows them to identify with characters and experience vicariously the impact of the situation described upon their own life. With this work, in the paper architecture tradition, the radicals denounced the relationship that the Modern Movement sought to promote between form and ideology. The radicals refuted their predecessors' view that form contained symbolic values that could incarnate a fixed and timeless ideology. By taking the ideological and technological consequences of the modernist utopia to their dystopic conclusion, they headed off any potential analogical relationship between form and ideology. The radicals' work thus serves as a warning against the dangers of progress, technology, and the tyranny of industrialization.[283]

282 Superstudio, "Design d'invenzione e design d'evasione," *Domus*, June 1969; published in English as "Evasion Design and Invention Design," in Peter Lang and William Menking, *Superstudio: Life without Objects* (Milan: Skira, 2003), 116–17.

283 See Alessandro Mendini, "The Land of Good Design," in *Italy: The New Domestic Landscape*, ed. Emilio Ambasz (New York: Museum of Modern Art, 1972), 370–79.

Conceptual Art, Radical Architecture

As early as 1962, Pichler and Hollein had refuted functionalist ideas in their "Absolute Architecture" manifesto,[284] promoting at the same time the work of anti-functionalist architects such as Frederick Kiesler and Hundertwasser. From 1961, the Archigram group published its fanzine manifestos. The fourth of these, *Amazing Archigram* (1964), a reference to the first science-fiction magazine, *Amazing Stories*, published by Hugo Gernsback, was reproduced in a number of Italian magazines. The Italian radical architects thus became aware of critical currents opposing rationalism, functionalism, and the values of the Modern Movement. A new generation joined the debate, one infused with Pop art, the ideas of Banham, and the work of Italian and English Brutalist architects. The concept of "Absolute Architecture" signaled the advent of a new level of critical sophistication. Thought and action were placed on an equal footing, a principle that became essential for the neo-avant-garde. The division between the articulation of an idea and its realization was swept away; the idea of a discipline had the same value as the discipline itself and the actual forms that it took on. Far from being a simple tautology, this signaled an opening up of fields that had until then remained the preserve of one discipline or another. This conception underpinned the projects of Archigram, who saw drawing as an end in itself, as drawings did not have to take on physical forms to bring about changes in reality. The radical architects in turn defied the division between discourse and reality, asserting not only that architecture critics ought to be considered architects

284 Hollein and Pichler, *Architektur: Work in Progress*, n.p. (see note 75).

in their own right, but that "the only truly conceptual architecture is that created by the likes of Tafuri, Giedion, and Banham."[285] At the same time, a similar equivalence between concept and creation was also being posited in the art world, particularly by Conceptual artists, who refused any hierarchy between the physical creation and the idea. These artists' position allows for a better understanding of that of the radical architects, who believed that it was possible to alter reality without having to construct buildings or create durable works; the text, the manifesto, the drawing, and even the fanzine were equally valid and viable as expressions of architectural ideas. The hierarchy between different media was thus abolished.

Another more political motivation encouraged their preference for the concept: its immaterial nature allowed them to escape from the reductive systems of consumerism, which had relegated works of artists and architects to little more than simple merchandise. The rejection of material production was an end in itself: in the art world, it robbed public and private institutions of their role as arbiters by creating pieces that could hardly be seen, if at all, and were therefore impossible to consume. Such was the case with Yves Klein's 1950 *Zone de Sensibilité Picturale Immatérielle*, where there was literally nothing to see in the gallery space, or On Kawara's mail-art series *I Got Up*, where the artist sent daily postcards from 1968 until 1979, stamped with the time at which he rose each day. The satisfaction gleaned from an encounter with a complete, finished, material work is denied by these "non-works."

This conceptual turn demonstrates the way in which the crisis in architecture pushed its practitioners to investigate other disciplines and adopt some of their methods.

285 Navone and Orlandoni, *Architettura "radicale"*, 53–54.

This process of questioning would lead to an unprecedented liberty for a new generation of architects who enthusiastically adopted their own "immaterial" architecture. They redefined their discipline in order to go beyond the notion that architecture could only be considered in terms of its built output. They rejected any and all fixed definitions of their discipline and their work, which now benefited from the same freedom they wished to extend to the individual: the freedom to be inconsistent, to change and to adapt, with only the present moment as their frame of reference. This stance expressed their desire to break with convention—and with the history of architecture and the Modern Movement in particular:

> It had been discovered that doing architecture did not just mean making houses, or constructing useful things in general, but signified expressing oneself, communicating, arguing and freely creating one's own cultural habitat, according to the instinctive right that every individual has to create his own environment, but from which the division of labour in society had totally alienated him. Doing architecture became an activity of free expression, just as making love means not just producing children but communicating through sex.[286]

If this combination of architecture and freedom seems bold, it is worth pointing out that the association was bolstered by the collapse of modern architecture, which was brought about by its insistence on the relationship between aesthetic and political values. Modern architecture's downfall was precipitated by its attempt to first define normative

286 Branzi, *Hot House*, 60.

modes of representation for society and then to assert their permanence. Once this program was revealed to be unrealistic, it gave way to two currents of thought, one allied to architecture and the other to design.

> [Modern architecture] embodied the dream of the last beach on which you could lie down. It can be no more than the construction of a social world [...] a bricolage of a thousand different utopias [...] traditional urbanism and architecture operate on the level of absolute utopia. Through their very presence alone they continue to unconsciously appropriate the world, with their architectonic tools and their values of a formal culture which extends to the functions of the home. This is a terminal utopia, an unconscious one, but one which has nonetheless created a crises of social relations within architecture itself.[287]

Branzi thus suggests that it would be *design* that renewed architecture, as proved to be the case with radical architecture. In the next chapter, I will explore the ways in which design attempted to fill the newly vacant terrain left behind by architecture.

287 Branzi, *Introduzione al design italiano*, 11 (see note 30).

Antidesign: A Manifesto for Autonomous Design

It was the Milanese designer Joe Colombo who first took up the gauntlet. In 1968, he began to reformulate design with a new conception that represents a significant episode in the extraordinary strides made in the field in Italy in the second half of twentieth century. Up until this point, almost no designers defined themselves as such; equally rare were those who had received any kind of education outside of architecture and fine art schools, with formal design education no more forthcoming than a clear definition of the discipline. It should thus come as little surprise that at the end of the Second World War, the Congress of Design in Milan in 1954 was attended exclusively by artists and architects. No mention of the profession of designer was made at the conference, and this state of affairs continued until the end of the 1950s, in Italy and in Europe as a whole, before design began to receive representation in the form of various dedicated institutions and associations.

The early stirrings of this shift can be found in 1952. The year saw the publication of "Manifesto per il disegno industriale" (Manifesto for industrial design) in the April issue of *Domus*, and an exhibition explicitly dedicated to design, "Arte e l'estetica industriale" (Art and industrial design) organized at the Fiera Campionaria in Milan. On April 6, 1956, the Associazione per il Disegno Industriale (ADI) was created to define and promote the emerging profession of the designer. Though still the preserve of architects and artists, design gained much recognition from Italian industry, and the period was a promising one for the field. Supported by the government, numerous small- and medium-sized family businesses gave free rein to creators to redesign the everyday goods they produced, from the motorbike to the coffee maker. From this point on, the so-called *progettista* would become an integral part of Italy's industrial production; this term emphasized the project-based nature of designer's work and the individual's approach toward a particular element or style. In the 1960s, the profession of the designer emerged and gained a more coherent structure, attaining greater representation and visibility through various bodies and institutions. However, because the backdrop for this moment was the expansionist and liberal growth of the economy, design—which had already been crudely pegged to principles of standardization and functionalism—came to be envisaged solely in terms of the interaction between production and consumption, as if this had always been the case.

Along with his fellow designers, Colombo believed that design was fast emerging as the means of artistic expression best adapted to the second industrial revolution. He participated in this euphoric wave of production and consumption by creating chairs, kitchens, pipes, and various other items for the era's leading manufacturers, from Riedel to Kartell, Sormani, and Oluce. The numerous possibilities within the design field in the postwar period might explain why Colombo chose to dedicate himself exclusively to the profession. He opened his studio in Milan in 1962, despite holding a diploma from the Accademia di Belle Arti di Brera and an architecture degree from the Politecnico di Milano. Colombo had already gained recognition and exposure in the field of architecture: he had been published on a number of occasions and had constructed a building in Milan between 1956 and 1957, three family homes near Como in 1961, and the Hotel Stelvio near Bormio in the same year. Opting for design was a surprising choice in Italy in the sixties, where, despite the field's growing recognition, it was still considered by architects to be a subordinate part of their profession; Colombo could thus have easily maintained a design practice without having to disavow architecture. In spite of this, from 1962 he defined himself exclusively as a progettista.

In the years that followed, he won a series of awards and titles that included his chosen profession's most prestigious honors, such as the Compasso d'Oro, which he was awarded twice. He was also invited to give lectures, design interiors and furniture, and curate exhibitions the world over. Such widespread acclaim did not lead to satisfaction for Colombo, and six years later he began a fundamental interrogation of his role and practice as a designer. Considering design a deeply political profession rather than a frivolous one, Colombo sought to redefine it along a trio of axes: the collapse of functionalism, the broken promises of industrialization, and the reconfiguration of the prerogatives of architecture, which at the time was undergoing a period of crisis. He made his thoughts public in a version of his widely published polemical text on the notion of antidesign.[288]

288 Colombo's text appeared in different versions; one of the most definitive versions was Joe Colombo, "Sistema programmabile per abitare," *Casabella*, no. 333 (February 1969): 23–33.

The Advent of Antidesign

Colombo quickly left behind the production of goods and dedicated himself to his personal critical project. Inspired by Herbert Marcuse's indictment of industrial society in *One-Dimensional Man*, he began to construct an original conception of design under the banner of antidesign. He drew upon Marcuse's analysis of contemporary industrial society and the dominant "positive thinking"—with repressive forces sapping critical thought and expression in favour of a single ideology of social control—that justified its existence. Colombo set out to counter this process by exploring the traits that characterize industrial society according to Marcuse's analysis: manipulation of workers through alienating factory work, modes of production that were only ostensibly mastered by society, the dominance of and reverence for technology, and the marginalization of the individual. He took up Marcuse's "protest against that which is" and his defense of "negative thinking,"[289] in order to initiate a revolution against the aggressive extension of technology into every cultural sphere.

Antidesign's origins can be traced to Colombo's contribution to the XIV Triennale di Milano, for which he designed a bar and relaxation lounge entitled *Monterelax*. It was on this occasion that he claims to have encountered the Archizoom project *Centro di Cospirazione Eclettica* (Center for eclectic conspiracy). The project so exasperated him that he felt compelled to work toward a conception of design that could offer an alternative to industrial design's blind pursuit of standardization but did not fall into what he

289 Herbert Marcuse, *One-Dimensional Man: Studies in the Ideology of Advanced Industrial Society* (Boston: Beacon Press, 1964), 63, 123–43.

saw as the unproductive experiments of the radical architects. In the February 1969 issue of *Casabella*, Colombo published his first article on the subject. Rather than a written manifesto, he chose to give a concrete example of his approach by way of a detailed and heavily illustrated explanation of his *Sistema Programmabile per Abitare* (Programmable system for living),[290] which he had created for the manufacturer La Rinascente. A "furnishing principle" rather than actual furniture, Colombo's system used a simple geometric shape that could, together with other similar elements, form pieces of furniture to meet a variety of needs. Typical of the modular furniture then in vogue, this project-manifesto was proposed by Colombo as a global solution for space.[291] Though he was not yet employing the term antidesign, his system already opposed the reductive association of design with industry and consumer goods. This tentative criticism was articulated further in the November 1969 issue of *Casabella*, where Colombo used the newly coined term for the first time.

The term was selected to incorporate the notion of negativity. It was a negativity that would prove to be productive in Colombo's analysis. The prefix is neither pejorative nor destructive, and is faithful to Marcuse's vocabulary, which Colombo knew well. Marcuse had denounced the "positive thinking" and "false consciousness" that characterized the one-dimensional man of industrial society, and which he saw as tools of domination and repression. To critique the technological rationalization of the world, he hailed the power of negativity and contradiction, which he believed offered the only valid exit route. In his presentation of antidesign, Colombo refers directly to Marcuse:

290 Colombo, "Sistema programmabile per abitare," 28–33.
291 Ibid., 31.

> In order to emphasize the importance of the concept of the global nature of language, I feel it is useful to refer there to the work of an expert on the subject, contemporary philosopher Herbert Marcuse. In his recent book *One-Dimensional Man*, Marcuse writes that "the analysis is focused on advanced industrial society, in which the technical apparatus of production and distribution (with an increasing sector of automation) functions, not as the sum-total of mere instruments that can be isolated from their social and political effects, but rather as a system that determines *a priori* the product of the apparatus as well as the operations of servicing and extending it."[292]

In order to contest the principles that governed design in the 1960s, Colombo chose as his first target the bourgeois taste that contented itself with recycling historical works. Though it is unclear at times whether he was addressing furniture manufacturers or designers, it is clear that his attack was aimed at both the creations of Italian industrial designers and the reproductions of functionalist pieces from the Dessau era of the Bauhaus. Colombo considered that the latter works, however interesting and appealing they might be, had no place in contemporary production since they were out of step with the needs and desires of the time. The continued exploitation of these designs was, for Colombo, evidence of an industry that was unwilling or unable to take into account the radical changes society had undergone.

Antidesign's apparently negative dimension, justified by Colombo with reference to the power of negation

292 Joe Colombo, "Relazione di Joe Colombo alla tavola rotonda del 5 settembre 1968 alla Fiera di Pordernone," 4; unpublished speech, Studio Joe Colombo Archives, Milan.

in Marcuse's work, allowed him to formulate a counter-proposition against "one-dimensional" design. The omnipresence of a single ideology that allowed no space for contradiction was, he believed, characteristic of a capitalist society grappling with its own renewal. Colombo anchored antidesign in Marxist thought, despite having only a limited understanding of this approach, gleaned from his reading of Marcuse. Despite its rough edges, Colombo's proposition reflected the mood of protest that characterized his generation toward the end of the 1960s across all artistic disciplines. Antidesign was not altogether dissimilar from Joseph Masheck's description of Gianni Pettena as "an architect actively on strike,"[293] nor from the series of artists and architects who declared themselves "anti" around the same time. The most famous of these were the self-proclaimed "anarchitect" Pettena[294] and the "anti-architect" Cedric Price, who labeled his Fun Palace an "anti-building."[295] While these projects shared little in terms of form and content, all acknowledged the constructive power of negation and sought to radically change their respective disciplines by stripping away traditions.

On July 30, 1971, at the age of forty-one, Colombo died of a heart attack, signaling the end of antidesign as he had conceived it. The term was soon recuperated and emptied of its original meaning by the radical architects. During the last three years of his life, Colombo had dedicated himself exclusively to the development of antidesign, and three examples that were his legacy are sufficiently

293 "I imagine Pettena as an architect actively on strike. Like those artists who have No Comment on the life that surrounds us, Pettena is reticent and guarded. But there aren't many people who are 'on strike' now whose artistic response is as constructive as this." Joseph Masheck, "Gianni Pettena, Italian Artist," *Artforum*, June 1972.

294 Gianni Pettena, *L'anarchitetto: Portrait of the Artist as a Young Architect* (Florence: Guaraldi, 1973); republished as "Autorecensione di 'L'anarchitetto,'" *Casabella*, no. 394 (October 1974): 51–53.

295 Mark Wigley, "Cedric Price's Fun Palace," *Domus*, January 2004, 14–23.

emblematic to demonstrate its intention, scope, and variation. Antidesign's first manifestation, *Habitat Futuribile* (Habitat of the future), also known as *Visiona* or *Visiona 1*, dates from 1969. It took the form of a traveling exhibit commissioned by Bayer, the German petrochemical company, which had invited Colombo to promote its upholstery fabrics in furniture expos across Europe. It made its debut at Interzum, a trade fair held June 5–11, 1969, in Cologne. *Visiona 1* later traveled to Switzerland, Belgium, and Italy, where it was presented at the famous Salone del Mobile in Milan. That year, Colombo completed an apartment on via Filippo Argelati, his third private residence, overlooking the *navigli* in Milan. Colombo shared the space with his wife Elda, and although it cannot be visited, the apartment was widely photographed and appeared in a number of magazines, a process overseen by an astute Colombo, who often took the pictures himself. The final manifestation of antidesign, *Total Furnishing Unit*, was completed between 1971 and 1972 by Colombo's assistant, Ignazia Favata. It was created for the 1972 exhibition "Italy: The New Domestic Landscape," curated by the young architect Emilio Ambasz at MoMA and sponsored by the Italian Ministry for Foreign Trade and the oil and gas giant Gruppo ENI.

The high-profile exhibition was conceived as a triumphant display of Italy's dynamism, but was similarly criticized as a swan song for the country's design-industry model. It brought together different current trends from across the field, with Ambasz looking to present an overview of the directions and approaches being pursued at the time. His chosen structure was somewhat problematic in that it divided the exhibition into two distinct parts. The first of these, "Objects," was made up of three subsections: "Objects Selected for Their Formal and Technical Means,"

"Objects Selected for Their Sociocultural Implications," and "Objects Selected for Their Implications of More Flexible Patterns of Use and Arrangement." The second section, "Environments," gathered the work of twelve designers and groups of designers into a trio of equally arbitrary categories: "Design as Postulation," with work by Colombo, Sottsass, Gae Aulenti, Alberto Rosselli, Marco Zanuso, Richard Sapper, and Mario Bellini; "Design as Commentary," which was comprised exclusively of work by Gaetano Pesce; and "Counterdesign as Postulation," with projects from Ugo La Pietra, Archizoom Associati, Superstudio, Gruppo Strum, and Enzo Mari.

Total Furnishing Unit, and antidesign more generally, developed from Colombo's rejection of contemporary design, which he believed could only offer "a chaotic and disordered image [of the home] reduced to a jumble of useless and disparate objects,"[296] with a living space "filled with objects and items of furniture with no coherent role for design."[297] Colombo included his own work in this critique, dismissing it along similar lines. He denounced the dominant model of furniture design and production as complicit with the capitalist system, to which he refused to subscribe. He condemned the proliferation of objects, not as a phenomenon in and of itself, but rather as a vector for the alienation of the working class to which design was originally addressed, and as a means for increasing the wealth of the bourgeoisie at the expense of workers. In a somewhat oversimplified reading of Marcuse's Marxism, Colombo believed that workers were not only dehumanized by the repetitive tasks of factory labor but also compelled, in spite of themselves, to desire the objects they

296 Colombo, "Antidesign," 28 (see note 73).
297 Ibid.

produced; they thus became subject to the whims of the bourgeoisie, whose tastes they could not help but imitate, even in the privacy of their own homes.

This process promoted the idea of material happiness to the detriment of Marx's historical materialism, forcing workers to actively participate in their own subjugation. In order to counteract this fallacy, which had tainted the second industrial revolution, Colombo called for the elimination of objects, which acted as vectors of class symbolism, and proposed to replace them with "an antidesign opposed to the triumphant cult of the object, that is to say a design composed of anonymous elements suited to mass production, personalizable upon assembly, and sold in volume at affordable prices."[298] With this concept, Colombo challenged the dominant understanding of design in Italy. This was a conception that relied on a simplistic interpretation of the relationship between functionalism and design (that had persisted since the Bauhaus) and one overwhelmingly concerned with the production of standardized consumer goods. At the risk of being labeled a naive technophile, Colombo insisted that there was no contradiction in the industrial production of his designs.

With *Visiona 1*, Colombo created a full-scale model of a futuristic apartment using textiles produced by Bayer. Replete with buttons, switches, and joysticks reminiscent of science-fiction gadgets, the project had an air of blissful optimism. With an omnipresent array of technological escamotage, the "Kitchen Box" was a hyper-equipped space for cooking featuring countless hidden devices. The "Night Box," or "Night Cell," was no different; it could be entirely closed off, thanks to an electrical circuit, and incorporated

298 Carlo Guenzi, "Cronache di disegno industriale," *Casabella*, no. 333 (February 1969): 28.

a range of storage spaces that appeared and disappeared at the touch of a button. In the "Central Living" lounge area, the bar could be hidden under cushions. From the kitchen countertop with integrated plate warmers to the clock built into the wall and the calendar incorporated into a speaker, gadgets and ingenious devices abounded in the *Visiona 1* apartment. All the technology was geared toward serving the occupants' desires with temperature control, elegantly fitted appliances whose functions were discretely hidden from view, and a retractable bar in every room.

For his kitchen, Colombo gleefully drew inspiration from the ship's galley and the airplane's cockpit, incorporating a *cruscotto* (control panel) dotted with buttons, dials, taps, controls, and even cigarette lighters; similar devices could be found in the "Central Living" and the "Night Cell." Colombo's wildly enthusiastic use of technology recalls the pathological obsession that Banham labels "gizmology" in his 1965 text "The Great Gizmo,"[299] citing it as a defining feature of the history of the United States. In this sense, and because antidesign placed the motions, needs, and comfort of the user squarely at the center of each project, Colombo and his devices can be said to echo the typical American designer, caricatured by Banham as someone who "changed the face of America [thanks to] a gizmo, a gadget, a gimmick."[300]

Colombo's antidesign was a complex concept, and it is quite reasonable to ask whether the barrage of gadgets in *Visiona 1* was at odds with the standardization and mass production the designer envisaged as antidesign's end goal. Close inspection reveals that it is a question of simple, unpretentious, and often humorous industrialized gadgets

299 Reyner Banham, "The Great Gizmo," *Industrial Design*, no. 12 (September 1965); in *A Critic Writes*, 109 (see note 234).
300 Ibid.

that were often conceived by inventors rather than designers. These gadgets contradict the grand ambitions of the "triumphant cult of the object" that Colombo denounced. A more difficult question might be whether or not the abundance of technology in these antidesign interiors suggests the work of a privileged technophile whose vision lacked perspective. With the desacralization of technology central to his collaborations, first with Jorn, and later with Jorn and Dangelo in the Movimento Nucleare, Colombo went beyond habitual considerations to offer a nuanced vision of the potential of technology.

The joyful profusion of playful gadgets in Colombo's work can be interpreted as an ambivalent antidote to the Modern Movement's reverence for and unwavering belief in the redemptive power of technology. Colombo readily referred to his projects as *macchine* or *attrezzature* (equipment),[301] terms that were very much part of the Modern Movement's vocabulary. For Colombo, however, technology was not heroic; rather, it was presented unpretentiously as demystified, if comically enormous "household appliances."[302]

301 "All the functional objects in the home should be integrated into its space. As such, we should not speak in terms of furniture but rather of equipment." Joe Colombo, quoted in Ignazia Favata, "Joe Colombo, stralci di articoli nel 1970 e 1971," *D'Ars*, no. 60 (1972): 153.
302 Ibid.

Space + Time = Antidesign

By revisiting principles developed from his own experiments, Colombo drew from contemporary critical preoccupations in his reevaluation of the space-time relationship within the home environment. In order to combat modernist inertia, he proposed an adaptation of the living space that responded as fully as possible to the flux of life, introducing the notion of time as a fourth dimension into his work. There was a rich body of work from which Colombo could take inspiration. A number of theories on space were developed at the turn of the twentieth century, and were famously referenced by Marcel Duchamp in his painting *La mariée mise à nu par ses célibataires, même* (*The Bride Stripped Bare by Her Bachelors, Even*, or *The Large Glass*, 1915–23), which sought to incorporate this fourth dimension; Gaston de Pawlowski also invoked this idea in his text *Journey to the Land of the Fourth Dimension*, published in 1912. Perhaps Colombo also drew on Giedion's discussion of the historical dimension of architecture in the fourth chapter of *Space, Time and Architecture*, or on the modularity that characterized mobile design in the 1960s.

In 1951 Colombo joined the Movimento di Pittura Nucleare, and his collaboration with the anti-functionalist Jorn as part of this group would prove decisive in terms of his own stance. Colombo identified strongly with Jorn's belief in the transformation of space as a means of contesting rationalism. According to Jorn, rationalists had "not understood that the only means of avoiding the anarchy of change is to take the laws of transformation into account and to use them to one's own ends."[303]

303 Jorn, *Pour la forme*, 15 (see note 257).

Jorn's influence was particularly visible in the first exhibition of the MIBI. Tasked with designing the scenography, Jorn deployed the kind of dynamic forms he discusses in the articles that make up his book *Pour la forme*, and which find an echo in Colombo's treatment of space in antidesign:

> This concept of a relationship between space and time is the basic parameter of all our research and requires, given the increasingly rapid evolution of the human race, equipment for living that is autonomous and flexible and that can be coordinated, converted, utilized in different ways so that it always adapts itself to its user.[304]

The idea of perpetual change was not solely the preserve of antidesign; it was also key to the thinking of the radical architects. Colombo's position was distinct from theirs, in its combination of a rough idea of Einstein's theory of relativity with the pictorial gestures of the Movimento di Pittura Nucleare. Also key was the notion, which he borrowed from Jorn, that aesthetic form was absolutely incapable of embodying—albeit symbolically—an abstract principle. Colombo was also influenced by Jorn's defense of Giuseppe Pinot-Gallizio's industrial painting and the machine he had assembled in the MIBI experimental laboratory between 1958 and 1959. Colombo firmly believed in the transformative power of industrialization and its capacity to incorporate the fourth dimension into the domestic sphere and everyday life. He sought to demonstrate this incorporation, albeit in a summary fashion, with

304 Ignazia Favata, "Joe Colombo: A Portrait," in *Joe Colombo and Italian Design of the Sixties*, trans. Huw Evans (Cambridge, MA: MIT Press, 1988), 22.

his 1970 *Multi-chair*. The foam armchair's separate elements could be adapted to support the body in any possible position. Accompanying the chair were various diagrams demonstrating its modularity and showing how it could be rearranged to fit the needs and desires of the user on a given day. This was a principle he would later scale up to the entire domestic space in other antidesign projects: the *Mobile Home*, his Milan apartment, and *Total Furnishing Unit*. Colombo's preliminary sketches for "Central Living" make clear his research into and experiments with the synthesis of diurnal and nocturnal space that were the raison d'être of antidesign.

In the paintings from his time in the Movimento di Pittura Nucleare, Colombo envisaged a world in a constant flux, capable of infinite self-regeneration without drawing on external sources. A similar principle underlies his urbanism project, *Città Futurible*, which he conceived in 1952 during his architecture studies and produced in several versions. One of Colombo's sketches features a spherical home, *La casa dell'era nucleare*, whose rooms are scattered around a central staircase, as if to underline the importance of movement and Colombo's lack of interest in assigning a specific function to each space. In another drawing from the same series, which is conserved in the Studio Joe Colombo archives in Milan, a city basks in the rays of a brilliant sun, whose movement and rotation Colombo suggests with a series of arrows; the caption "Sfera = Forma Perfetta" appears beside the sketch. Again it is movement that Colombo emphasizes, this time with the inclusion of a life-giving Sun and the rotation of the Earth itself. Already visible in his student project *Città Futurible*, this insistence on the states of transformation of space and form proved to be a constant motif throughout Colombo's oeuvre.

Colombo's approach differed from that of his peers, as his modular furniture was fully mobile. Antidesign showed that the continuous modifications of usage in space and the use of industrial production methods (which Colombo illustrated, for example, with *Multi-chair*) did not necessarily represent a revisiting of the values of the Modern Movement, as the radical architects claimed. Expanding upon Jorn's ideas on the dynamic nature of man, and in particular his notion that "we must reach a dynamic conception of form, we must confront the truth that human form exists in a perpetual state of transformation,"[305] Colombo saw in movement, both literal and symbolic, the embodiment of antidesign and its adaptability. His architectural drawings show that from the very start of his career, he placed a great deal of importance upon retractability, modularity, transformation, and a desire to create environments that would adapt to rather than simply reflect the desires and needs of their inhabitants and of contemporary society as a whole.

Antidesign's dynamic vision and its reevaluation of space and time can be traced to Colombo's experiments at the start of the 1950s with the Movimento di Pittura Nucleare. This period had a decisive influence on Colombo's nascent thinking on the subject of the interior architecture of the home in Italy, which he had every intention of revolutionizing. Colombo set out to transform the configuration of the living space and, at the same time, to expand design beyond the boundaries that were traditionally imposed up on it. In order to do so within his antidesign project, he developed a series of mobile functional elements: retractable beds, semicircular surfaces that could form both coffee tables and dinner tables, storage that could be extended

305 Jorn, *Pour la forme*, 15.

to form room dividers, sliding screen wardrobes, canopies that could be opened both manually and automatically, and magnetic lamps that could be suspended or attached to a given surface, to name but a few. However, Colombo's work went beyond these mobile objects, which considered in isolation were not so different from the kind of maneuverability and modularity that underlay many of the transformations of domestic space in the 1960s; Colombo's creations allowed for transformations over the course of a day, a decade, or even an entire lifespan.

With its new conception of the spatiotemporal relationship, antidesign promised a softening of the line between the diurnal and the nocturnal. With the execution of particular tasks no longer circumscribed in space—whether in terms of its configuration, location, or segmentation—it fell to antidesign to adapt to the evolution of human activities. The case studies in antidesign offered by *Visiona 1*, *Total Furnishing Unit*, and Colombo's Milan apartment articulate a new vision of domestic space according to these ideas. While all three feature a near-identical principle, which sees various different functions gathered in a dynamic volume, the concentration of functions is inversely proportional to the available space in each project. *Visiona 1* covered some one hundred square meters, while *Total Furnishing Unit* was no larger than twenty-eight square meters, yet both spaces were deftly utilized by Colombo so that even the smaller project would be capable of offering the same level of comfort as a much larger dwelling.

Colombo was particularly adept in his use of media, and he skilfully used a relatively broad circulation of magazines to promote his ideas. He consistently photographed his own work, and his pictures often appeared alongside commentaries, captions, and texts that were also his own. Such is the case for the four-page spread "Una casa V.I.P.

per un designer V.I.P.," which appeared in *Domus* in January 1971.[306] Complete with diagrams demonstrating their various functions, the article presents two complimentary furnishing units. The first, *Roto Living*, formed the living room and the dining room, and the second, the *Cabriolet Bed*, consisted of a bedroom complete with a kind of hooded bed-car hybrid.[307] As well as integrating a variety of modular elements, each of the units was fully mobile. The seventy-square-meter apartment could be easily transformed from a living room, with *Roto Living* at its center and the *Cabriolet Bed* against a wall, to a bedroom, once the *Roto Living* was stowed away and the *Cabriolet Bed* extended.

Colombo's restructuring of domestic space was developed from his analysis of the growing need for housing, the overcrowding of cities, and the lack of available construction space in city centers. From 1967, Colombo prophesized that developments in audiovisual technology would eliminate the need to travel to work as tasks would be accomplished remotely from home.[308] His enthusiasm was such that he wrote,

> By referring in particular to the most far-reaching hypotheses and those most likely to come to fruition, the rise of audiovisual communications, remote controls and videotapes, we predict the negation of distances and as a result the transformation of the living spaces in urban centers, their dispersion in nature or a preference for nomadic homes.[309]

306 Joe Colombo, "Una casa V.I.P. per un designer V.I.P.," *Domus*, January 1971, 21–25.
307 Ibid., 20; and Arturo Belloni, "Dynamisches wohnen, J. C. Colombo," *MD: Möbel Interior Design*, no. 2 (February 1971): 26.
308 Favata, "Joe Colombo: A Portrait," in *Joe Colombo*, 16.
309 Joe Colombo, "Proposta per il Museo d'arte," 1; Studio Joe Colombo Archives, Milan.

The shift of work from the school and office to the home necessarily entailed a transformation of the domestic space; yet Colombo observed that housing as it was currently being designed by architects seemed to fail to account for this trend, and even go against it. He worked with futurologists and attempted to anticipate the transformations to come; according to one anecdote, Colombo once cleared all the books from his house, certain that they would soon be replaced by new means of acquiring knowledge.

In order to better adapt to imminent changes in lifestyle, Colombo felt it was essential to go beyond separate rooms, each with a specific function, which currently governed the organization of domestic space. He identified a contradiction between the architecture of standardized homes that codified and divided space according to particular functions on the one hand, and the changing needs and activities of their inhabitants according to their personality or the time of day on the other. Colombo opposed this dynamic that saw architects impose particular configurations upon the home, and sought to conceive a better way of using available interior space. Rather than designing larger apartments, Colombo proposed the application of antidesign to any home in order to endow it not with a fixed number of predefined configurations but with a capacity for adapting to the unknown. The designer's own apartment was a prime example of the application of these ideas: with the space utilized in different ways according to his and his wife's activities, the apartment seemed far larger that it was.

With antidesign, Colombo thus sought to disrupt conventional relationships between function and space:

> In the past space was static; this has been the classic notion for millenia. Our century is characterized by dynamism instead ... there is a fourth dimension:

> time. It is necessary to introduce this fourth dimension into space [...] For the home this means that, instead of using a space divided up into sub-spaces with precise functions (living-room, kitchen, etc.) one can imagine a space that an be altered according to the needs of the moment ... one can be satisfied with a smaller overall volume. In reality, with more room for living in.[310]

Antidesign thus replaced an organized and rational vision of the home, like that proposed by Existenzminimum, with one capable of accommodating the unexpected, the playful, and the chance occurrence. It opposed modernist rigor and its logic of efficiency, instead focusing on the psychological dimension of the home, which Colombo reevaluated continually: "Every effort is made to give man in his limited living space the sensation of freedom, total comfort (physical and psychological), rest and privacy."[311] Dynamism was a key concept for Colombo and formed antidesign's guiding principle. It was a means of transgressing the rigid limits traditionally imposed by homes upon their occupants, and a tool for creating more personal and individualized situations.

Colombo's project developed from the idea that architecture was, in its current state, incapable of comprehending and accounting for human nature. To bring antidesign to fruition however, he would first need to articulate and differentiate the respective roles of architecture and design. With the dissociation of exterior and interior

310 Joe Colombo, "Joe Colombo, patron de la casa nostra," interview by Pierre Buhler, *H*, no. 3 (August–September 1971); quoted in Favata, "Joe Colombo: A Portrait," in *Joe Colombo*, 12.

311 Extract from notes for a lecture given in connection with the Joe Colombo exhibition organized by *Design Research* magazine in San Francisco and New York, 1966; Studio Joe Colombo Archives, Milan.

space as his starting point, Colombo revisited the ideas of Marc-Antoine Laugier, who outlined his conception of architecture in terms of a response to mankind's primitive need for shelter, beginning with the most primitive hut—"[The architect] then introduced the necessary products and through this same process, the container almost always conditioned the contained"[312]—and refigured this in terms of the work of the designer. This observation led him to pursue his project further still, by entirely reevaluating the interaction between the container and the contained:

> Since it is now possible to program the elements and equipment necessary for the dwelling according to criteria of maneuverability, flexibility and control of every parameter, we can create a livable system that can adapt perfectly to any given temporal and spatial situation. Starting with a contained that adapts comprehensively to a given space, and proceding according to a more rational methodology, we will be able to lay the foundations of a conception of the container.[313]

Without further hesitation Colombo proclaims: "Furniture will disappear; the habitat will be everywhere,"[314] a prediction that neatly summed up the disciplinary opposition he envisaged between architecture and design.

The integration of furniture into architecture is far from specific to antidesign; it is in fact a reference point for modernism; Roberto Matta, Frederick Kiesler, and Adolf Loos had all carried out similar projects. Loos explicitly

312 Joe Colombo, "Une architecture différente pour un mode d'habiter différent: Le système programmable pour habiter," in *Qu'est-ce que le design?*, n.p. (see note 43).
313 Ibid.
314 Favata, "Joe Colombo: A Portrait," in *Joe Colombo*, 17.

discussed the process in his 1924 essay "Die Abschaffung der Möbel" (The Abolition of Furniture), in which he extolled the architectural virtues of integrating furniture into walls and structures, and outlined a distinction between equipment and mobile furniture.[315] Colombo's perspective is somewhat different: rather than promoting a total fusion, he differentiates structure from furniture in favor of standardized fittings. To underline the importance of this distinction, he rejects the term "furniture" in favor of "equipment" (*attrezzatura*).[316] This choice of terminology allows him to exclude decoration, style, furniture, ornaments, and objects, and to center his analysis exclusively on antidesign's spatial dimension. He was in no doubt that "the terminology of 'furnishing,' 'decoration,' 'furniture,' etc. is today outdated. All objects which play a role in the home must be integrated into the spaces at our disposal. As a result, they should no longer be considered as decoration but rather as 'equipment.'"[317] What remains uncertain, however, is whether or not Colombo was aware of the historical baggage of his chosen terminology, which had been employed previously by Le Corbusier and Alison and Peter Smithson.

I have discussed how, for Le Corbusier, the term "equipment" was a means of distancing himself from the habitual vocabulary of decorative arts of the 1920s. After the Second World War, Alison and Peter Smithson revisited the concept in their 1956 *House of the Future*, which they conceived and presented as belonging to the field of consumer goods, further strengthening the links between structure

315 Adolf Loos, "Die Abschaffung der Möbel," in *Die Schriften von Adolf Loos in zwei Bänden*, ed. Franz Glück, vol. 2, *Trotzdem: 1900–1930*, 2nd ed. (Vienna: Herold Verlag, 1962), 388–90.

316 This fascination with equipment was shared by Reyner Banham: see "A Home Is Not a House," in *Design by Choice*, 56–60 (see note 4); and *Los Angeles: The Architecture of Four Ecologies* (New York: Harper & Row, 1971).

317 Colombo, quoted in Favata, "Joe Colombo, stralci di articoli nel 1970 e 1971," 153.

and furnishing. The Smithsons frequently employed this notion as the point of origin for a new architectural vision that was clearly distinct from the discipline's heroic past. In their 1958 article "The Appliance House," they described the impact of this phenomenon, asserting that "the concept of domestic architecture could be changed by accepting the logical implications of the use of household appliances."[318] The following year, they returned to the idea, comparing a caravan to "a big piece of equipment."[319] For the couple, equipment promised to radically transform the role of the architect, who "had little control over these rooms whose walls are lined with appliances which would, over the years, so fundamentally change as to leave none of the original (architect-devised) space. The appliance industry fixed the dimensions and styling."[320] By redistributing various functions within a unified space, architects could redefine their own role and therefore challenge the established frontiers between architecture and design. While Helena Webster, in her introduction to *Modernism without Rhetoric: Essays on the Work of Alison and Peter Smithson,* suggests that in doing so they "had reduced architecture to product design,"[321] others, including Banham, saw their work as an attempt to reassert the unconditional supremacy of architecture.

318 Alison Smithson and Peter Smithson, "The Appliance House," *Design*, no. 113 (May 1958): 43.
319 Alison Smithson, "Caravan, Embryo, Appliance House," *Architectural Design* (September 1959): 348.
320 Alison Smithson and Peter Smithson, *Changing the Art of Inhabitation* (London: Artemis, 1994), 111.
321 Helena Webster, "Modernism without Rhetoric," in *Modernism without Rhetoric: Essays on the Work of Alison and Peter Smithson*, ed. Helena Webster (London: Academy Editions, 1997), 41.

Design as Architecture: Micro-architecture or Macro-design?

Each instance of the term "equipment," whether in the work of Le Corbusier, the Smithsons, or Colombo, contributed to a redrawing of disciplinary boundaries, a phenomenon that was particularly marked toward the end of the 1960s. Colombo, and designers like Olivier Mourgue and Verner Panton who followed in his footsteps with subsequent installments of "Visiona," used furniture as a means of exerting their influence over domestic space. This caused some consternation among architects.

> Design, *le mot à la mode*. After environment, *aménagement*, planning, is to promote a better world by way of the rational integration of all-consuming technology. In design, architecture, marketing, aesthetics and industrial production, psychoanalysis and functionalism, come together to modify old practices. In design, some see the total negation of architecture, others its renewal. The architect fancies himself to be a designer, but the designer rejects "architecture." Both strive, using similar means, for a comprehensive command of space. Both suffer from the same misconceptions as to the ends of their work and their role in a changing society. Each object to which they turn their attention has, by definition, its "architecture" or its "design"; yet architecture and design have yet to find their own objects.[322]

322 Emery, intro to "Le design," 2 (see note 49).

These were editor in chief Marc Emery's opening lines to the April–May 1971 issue of *L'Architecture d'Aujourd'hui* dedicated to design. The radical architects developed their critique around a rejection of the Modern Movement and of design, which they judged as at best ineffective and at worst an agent of the dominant capitalist system. Colombo, meanwhile, set out the principles of antidesign that would redefine the role of designers such that they were in a position to oversee architecture's renewal. Previous attempts to consider home and furniture as a single entity had always come at the expense of design and its standing as a discipline, but Colombo believed that the designer alone was capable of creating a home suitable for the era. He thus led a frontal attack on the history and authority of architecture, which, since the time of the Modern Movement, had viewed furniture as a "reduction" or "concentration" of architecture—to borrow Saarinen's terms. Yet the work of the radical architects, despite their critique of the Modern Movement, was very much part of this tradition, in that they approached furniture as a means of renewing the architectural discipline as a whole.

Colombo distanced himself from chairs and from furniture more generally, believing these to be an ideological paradigm of architecture, a notion concisely described elsewhere by Branzi.[323] Antidesign gave Colombo the opportunity to reconsider the living space, the city, and the relationship between them, a goal he pursued through the concept of expansion.[324] In order to mark a point of no return in the relationship between design and architecture, Colombo went on the attack by relieving the architect of his traditional functions:

323 Andrea Branzi, "La sedia come modello ideologico," in *Scritti teoretici*, 66–67 (see note 30).

324 See Joe Colombo, "Habitat umano, dalla sedia alla città: Idee e proposte per soluzioni globali," in *Il milione – Libro dell'anno* (Novara: Istituto Geografico de Agostini, 1971), 64–65; and "Dal microcosmo al macrocosmo," *Casa arredamento giardino*, January 1971, 23.

> The architect will cease to be the creator of houses and become an urbanist or a designer. In fact, the solution to overarching problems implies the deployment of instruments capable of offering the necessary solutions, and thus the deployment of prefabrication, serial production, and the institution of a specialized category of creators and operators of homes.[325]

For Colombo, the domestic space was the exclusive preserve of the designer. Taken seriously, such a declaration throws into question the relationship between architects and designs and the role of each, as well as the living space in general. Among the various issues raised by Colombo's position, the most important was the affirmation of a new role for the designer, one that reversed the long-standing hierarchy that saw architecture dominate design. Colombo's assertion, "It is now clear that architects will become planners or else designers of prefabricated elements and integrated equipment,"[326] is emblematic of this era in which architecture and design were shaken to their foundations and frequently placed in opposition. Had antidesign endured, could it perhaps have led to the disappearance of the architect?

Colombo's position could easily be interpreted as a provocation, and architects unsurprisingly wasted little time reacting. While there was little protest from the radicals, for reasons I will address, Claude Parent, cofounder with Paul Virilio of Architecture Principe, responded explosively to his ideas in the same issue of *L'Architecture d'Aujourd'hui* in which Colombo's polemic on antidesign appeared. Parent

325 Colombo, "Habitat umano," 64–65.
326 Colombo, "Dal microcosmo al macrocosmo," 23.

saw designers' interventions into domestic and retail spaces alike as an illegitimate incursion into architecture's rightful territory, accusing them of a totalitarian annexation. He railed against designers' "putsch," maintaining that as a group they ought to be grateful to architecture for having liberated them just a short while ago from the straitjacket of decorative arts:

> Architects carry the heavy responsibility and the tragic glory to have fought for and promoted design, to have mounted this warhorse with which, in order to win architecture's right to modernity; for this, they would lose for many years the Ariadne's thread of the architectural endeavor.[327]

Parent's analysis is certainly accurate in its description of the manipulation of design by architecture; yet the surprise he expresses at design having taken the opportunity to re-define and expand into the spatial conception of the dwelling seems naive to the point of being tendentious:

> Design [...] moved out of the shadows and away from its decorative obsession thanks to the creative and theoretical actions of architects [...] design's own actions are now developing; they show a tendency toward a total occupation of the built environment, based on the two social condtions that are the confusion of values and the weakness of architecture in our era. This takeover of the environment relies on industry which, after having inadvertently birthed design, used

327 Claude Parent, "Face à face: Architecture et design," in "Le design," 20.

> it as a means of subjugating the world of creation. Just a few years after its birth, design became imperialist and universal. This attempted putsch is unacceptable. A healthy (and extremely necessary) questioning of the environment must involve the appropriate division of territories between the different disciplines.[328]

Such a position reveals Parent's lack of awareness as to the battles design had already fought. However, this is surely to be expected when, as I have attempted to show, design has benefited from neither the history nor the recognition that it deserved.

Design was only really able to profit from the possibilities offered by industrialization from the Second World War onward; twenty years later, at the end of the 1960s, designers had begun to investigate the rewards and the dangers of standardization and to explore design's potential for transforming both humanity and its environment. Design now asserted itself, for the first time in its history, in its own terms, and refused to be defined in terms of architecture or art. This situation prepared the groundwork for design's revolution: Colombo would soon redefine design, the designer, architecture, and urbanism in one fell swoop. Design was no longer a question of producing objects nor of creating furniture as a kind of concentrated architecture, but rather one of radically questioning the status quo.

In order to do so, Colombo invoked the "microcosm," a notion through which he sought to redefine the private sphere according to a dilatory principle. The microcosm became the starting point for design and expanded outward

328 Ibid., 20.

to encompass the immediate urban area and ultimately the entire community: "Everything which makes up man's microcosm, in which he lives and dies, represents a terrain for research that aims to create a new habitat more in sync with the contemporary world, more coherent, structured and coordinated."[329] Design was to be redefined by linking the microcosm to the macrocosm. Colombo envisaged the individual as the representative of the wider community; similarly, he considered the domestic territory as an exemplary environment for the wider city, which in turn ought to restore dignity to the individual. The microcosm was thus antidesign's central concept, one that allowed Colombo to formulate a specific approach to the habitat: the private sphere and all its constituent parts became the operational territory of the antidesigner, and the starting point from which the city was to be understood, imagined, and inspired. As a result, the living space and everything within it was no longer under the aegis of comfort or functionalism, but rather played a strategic and ideological role in the transformation of a society in which everything was to be interconnected. It was along these lines that Colombo articulated a theory of design capable of asserting its disciplinary independence, and of refusing to be subject to decorative and aesthetic categories or to act as architecture's alibi. If the solutions offered by design had been sufficiently well devised to be used by architects, then designers, like architects, could assert ownership over their creations. For Colombo, antidesign was the only project with the potential to set in motion the reform made necessary by the crisis of the modernist model, the only means of replacing the discipline of architecture that many architects now judged to be in a state of terminal decline.

329 Colombo, "Antidesign," 28.

However, because antidesign was often peremptory in tone, expressed through mantras—as though Colombo was attempting to convince himself—it was thus destined to be mired in naivety.

In reality, architecture did not wait for Colombo to emerge from the shadow of modernism's failure. Since Alison and Peter Smithson's defiant break from the CIAM in 1956, the Italian neo-avant-garde, in particular the radical architects, had already announced the death of their discipline and turned their revolutionary attention toward territories such as the output of design. Their trajectory was the inverted mirror image of Colombo's expansion of design into the territory of architecture. Colombo's project was also hampered by the solitary nature of his combat, particularly in an era of countless groups and groupuscules. Colombo's proclamation of the death of architecture suggests that he failed to recognize the existing self-critical dimension present in the work of many architects, perhaps due to his training as an architect and self-identification as a designer. He instead positioned himself as something of an unwanted savior; but the salvation he offered implied a generalized redistribution of roles as well as the eradication of the profession of the architect and its replacement with that of the designer.

Not one to shy away from contradiction, Colombo at once condemned architecture and outlined the conditions for its survival. He prescribed a violent transformation, of the kind that he himself had already experienced in his early break with architecture. Colombo reasoned that, in light of its failings, architecture could no longer be entrusted with the construction of homes, particularly given that the organization of space it proposed constrained the movement of individuals. Colombo accused architecture of neglecting to consider the changes to man brought about by his social conditions, his needs—in short, what he considered to be reality. Having brought about its own downfall, Colombo believed that architecture ought to limit itself to urbanism and leave the conception of the new habitat to the designer. Architecture would not be sidelined entirely, but its role was conditional on a radical change in its methods: it needed to adopt those of the designer. Colombo redrew the disciplinary map in order to assert the methodological supremacy of design over architecture. Ultimately, the architect was faced with a drastic but simple choice: become a designer, or disappear.

> The architect's position (as one offering global solutions) must change. Rather than planning homes, the architect must become either an urbanist or a designer. In fact, the solutions to overarching questions implies the use of instruments offered by solutions such as prefabrication and serial production. [...] It is now clear that architects will become planners or else designers of prefabricated elements and integrated equipment.[330]

From the point of view of the architect, design was bound up with industrial production. During the war and immediately afterward, designers worked with industry in highly pragmatic and concrete endeavors, escaping from the theoretical relationship dreamed of by the Deutscher Werkbund and the Bauhaus. This episode proved at once vital and fatal—finally affording design the coherence and legitimacy it had lacked but also giving rise to protests such as antidesign.

330 Colombo, "Habitat umano," 65.

In the past design had insisted upon the necessity of industrialization, which had led to the demise of craftsmanship. It was now incumbent upon designers to test the validity of the theories underlying their discipline. Industrial production had allowed design to prove its worth, acting as a model that allowed for the kind of dynamism architecture sought to attain through prefabrication. Architecture's newfound interest in standardization led logically toward one in design; as such design went from its longstanding second-rung position of decorator to a model for architecture. Unsurprisingly, design readily encouraged the mother of all arts in its transition.

> The solutions of a complete future habitat that we have already tested, that open up the question of renewal, tend to a coordinated, planned and organized habitat-structure which would have the entire technological and scientific process at its disposal and would eliminate the existing superstructures which serve no function. These structures that are internal to the habitat must be arranged with respect to a new and different architecture which presupposes prefabrication and an urban system [that would govern] the organization and the distribution of new habitats.[331]

Architects came to the realization that design was no longer limited to the conception of consumer goods, and that the space they had vacated had allowed design to expand its field. Design's preexisting familiarity with prefabrication meant that it was apt to both promote and critique the

331 Colombo, quoted in Favata, "Joe Colombo, stralci di articoli nel 1970 e 1971," 153.

new articulation of living space: "The notion of design, at first limited to the shaping of goods of mass consumption, expands necessarily to the domain of architectural production as architecture becomes further integrated into automated industrial production."[332] This redefinition of the scope of design reveals a new dimension to the discipline, introducing the idea that design cannot be reduced solely to the production of goods.

332 Klaus Zillich and Jasper Halfmann, "Transformer la science en un moyen de libération," in "Le design," 14.

Design as an Industrial Model

Beyond the example of the Great Exhibition's Crystal Palace, numerous architects and designers had investigated the potential of buildings constructed using industrially produced elements, from Jean Prouvé and Ionel Schein in France, to Buckminster Fuller and the Eameses in the United States, to Alison and Peter Smithson and their *House of the Future* in Britain.[333] The Smithsons in particular examined the limits of functionalism, combining their critical distance from the history of prefabrication with their familiarity with mass-produced consumer goods to formulate alternative propositions. A stark disconnect emerged between the ideas set out and put into practice by the Bauhaus on the one hand, and the fantasy underlying the standardization of domestic goods on the other. Working at the limits, overlaps, and contradictions between these two currents, the Smithsons highlighted the incoherence of the ideas of those who had set out the theoretical terrain of architectural design.

The question of industrialization remained a bone of contention between architects and designers, as demonstrated by Alberto Rosselli's text in the winter 1966/67 issue of *Lotus* magazine, in which he evaluated the architect's relationship with other disciplines from a psychological point of view.[334] Rosselli's article focuses on this particular model of industrialization and whether it can and should be adopted by architecture, and, if so, to what extent. According to Rosselli, the architect is by their very nature receptive to other disciplines, yet rather than imitating them in their entirety, the architect closely examines their methods

333 "Thus the caravan is the nearest to an 'Appliance House' that the market has to offer." Smithson, "Caravan, Embryo, Appliance House," 348.
334 Alberto Rosselli, "L'architettura ricerca nuove relazioni," *Lotus*, no. 3 (1966).

and tools, without ever losing sight of the goal of architecture, which is, of course, architecture itself. His article argues that architecture should be invested in new technological processes, on the condition that they be considered means rather than ends. In a context where, for the first time in the history of Italian design, creativity and industrialization could be considered compatible, architects had an obligation to redefine their profession accordingly. As industrial production methods failed to keep up with an enormous demand for construction, Rosselli believed that it was essential for architects to adapt: It was now impossible to consider the city and the domestic space as static, immobile elements. The construction industry had no choice but to adopt these new methods of production:

> One of the most debatable points of today's architecture is its tendency to follow, imitate, and confuse itself with other disciplines, to ultimately forget its true nature and vocation. This may be a reflection of the uncertainty that mires the culture and thought of architecture today, or evidence of the influence of other collateral disciplines that are playing an ever more important role in its constitution.[335]

Unsurprisingly, not all architects were comfortable with the increased profile design had acquired through its proximity to industry. Some shared Rosselli's belief that the industrialization of construction could only be achieved through significant changes to the architectural profession and its processes, others scorned the industrial model altogether, while another perspective held it as a necessary if dangerous boon for architecture's survival.

335 Ibid.

The Capsule: A New Form for an Autonomous Design

With antidesign, Colombo sought to demonstrate that it was altogether legitimate for design to engage with issues that had traditionally been the exclusive preserve of architecture. At the same time, he laid the foundations for design's disciplinary independence. In order to accomplish this, in the context of the recent achievement of space travel, he appropriated the forms and principles of space capsules to give visual form to the disciplinary autonomy heralded by antidesign. While there was nothing new in formal terms about capsules and cells, their popularity and widespread application in living spaces toward the end of the 1960s was indicative of the new purposes and status they acquired around this time. They acted as case studies for architects in search of a language appropriate for prefabrication and industrialization. For Colombo, moreover, the capsule represented a singular form, central to his entire oeuvre, that embodied the new role he envisaged for the whole of design. References to the capsule recur across his texts and lectures, and Colombo cultivated an unprecedented symbolic, and perhaps even metaphorical, equivalence between the autonomy of his design practice and that of the discipline as a whole. In the 1960s, with the space race between the Cold War's opposing superpowers in the background, the capsule was a highly evocative concept that suggested, among other things, intergalactic travel. Such was the case with the playful experiments with capsule forms that comprised a central part of Archigram member Warren Chalk's research:

> From every point of view the space capsule was an inspiration: how different in concept and in

> efficiency from the tradition of buildings! The statement was a capsule dwelling, with the ergonomy and the sophistication of a space capsule. The parts would be tailored and able to be updated as technology moved forward, and as the dweller changed his needs [...] it soon became obvious that the capsule dwelling would be a preferred type within a Plug-in City. It also became obvious that the wedge-shaped unit sitting into a tower was a limitation of the concept.[336]

While references to the capsule were omnipresent in the work of designers and architects at the time, the concept was perhaps most fundamental to the Japanese architects Kiyonori Kikutake, Kisho Kurokawa, Fumihiko Maki, and Masato Otaka, designers Kenji Ekuan and Kiyoshi Awazu, and the critic Noboru Kawazoe, who together formed the Metabolist movement. For them, the capsule represented a protective envelope in which hidden or unknown activities could happen. Inspired by the serial production of homes in the work of Jean Prouvé, the Smithsons, Yona Friedman, and Aldo van Eyck, as well as science fiction, the Metabolists developed structures that could multiply and expand to form towers and even megalopolises. In 1969, Kurokawa published his manifesto, "Capsule Declaration," in which he argued for the capsule as a nomadic, prosthetic, and hybrid living space that would unite man with his environment:

> The capsule is cyborg architecture. Man, machine and space build a new organic body which transcends confrontation. As a human being equipped with a

336 Peter Cook, *Archigram* (New York: Princeton Architectural Press, 1999), 44.

> man-made internal organ becomes a new species which is neither machine nor human, so the capsule transcends man and equipment.[337]

On the occasion of the 1970 World Exposition in Osaka, Kurokawa built a prototype capsule habitat for a prefabricated community center in Sapporo, as well as the Nakagin Capsule Tower in Tokyo. He described them as fully self-sufficient and standardized technological universes:

> Variations of entrance and window positions produce four capsule types. Working equipment may be either on the left or the right side of the capsule; this increases the number of varieties to eight. [...] The designers resolved to amplify the apartment nature of the capsules by including in them moderate facilities for office work and by providing services of the kinds afforded by hotels. These considerations formed the basis of the design of the individual capsules. They contain a bed and bedding, storage space for clothing, a desk for office work, a bathroom that includes all sanitary facilities, telephone, audio equipment, and even sheets and toothbrushes.[338]

In contrast to these technophile applications, in the hands of the radical architects the capsule played an important role in the critique of the Modern Movement. This is particularly evident in Superstudio's "Twelve Cautionary Tales," and in Ugo La Pietra's *La cellula abitativa* (The cellular society), which was presented in "Italy: The New

337 Kisho Kurokawa, "Capsule Declaration," *Space Design*, no. 3 (March 1969); in *Metabolism in Architecture* (London: Studio Vista, 1977), 75.
338 Ibid., 105.

Domestic Landscape" and an issue of the magazine *In* dedicated to "the death of the object."[339] La Pietra proposed a series of "semantic" cells that could counter and subvert the logic of the industrial production of the living environment by creating personalized spaces of freedom for the individual within the existing social order. La Pietra was keenly interested in the new possibilities of audiovisual technology, and used the living cell as a kind of spatial filter for information. His capsule offered an escape from bourgeois conformity: "The concept of the private living cell constitutes one of the points where information and communication are regrouped, constructed, and put into circulation. As such it goes beyond the principle according to which the private home is an 'information terminal.'"[340] The same principle underlies the capsule of "La storia dell'albero e della capsula" (The story of the tree and the capsule) by Zziggurat, a lesser-known group within the radical movement.[341] The project consisted of a story told through images in which trees were literally encapsulated to form spatial structures that could be placed everywhere. These orthogonal capsules at first appear strikingly similar, at least in formal terms, to the illustrations in "Twelve Cautionary Tales," yet the message they deliver is quite the opposite. The radicals' position on living spaces is at its most explicit in the description of the series' second city, Temporal Cochlea-City:

> The city is composed of living-cells arranged in a double row of concentric circles. Between the two

339 Ugo La Pietra, "La cellula abitativa: Una microstruttura all'interno dei sistemi di communicazioni," *In*, no. 6 (June–July 1972): 18–31.
340 Ibid.
341 Zziggurat, "Storia dell'albero e della capsula," *Domus*, April 1972, 42. "The group proposes design as an activity which anyone can engage in as a method of liberating the hidden potentialities in people and things." Global Tools, *Global Tools Bulletin*, no. 1 (Milan: Edizioni L'uomo e l'arte, June 1974), n.p.

> contiguous circles of cells runs a roadway. Each cell has a single opening, a door giving on to the circular roadway, the other three walls backing onto other cells are totally opaque and soundproof.[342]

Superstudio's tale dramatizes the consequences of rationalism taken to its logical extreme. The capsule represents a closed-off and entirely automated space, reproduced en masse and placed alongside countless identical capsules in concentric circles to form a city. Through standardized units, the city ensures that every parameter of its inhabitants' lives remains the same:

> The floor of the cells is soft, all apparatus required for the satisfaction of individual living needs are hidden in the ceiling and are tele-controlled. The entire city is climatized at a constant 25°C, with 60% humidity. Each cell is constantly lit to an intensity of 150 lux; the roads are illuminated to an intensity of 500 lux; this light contains all the wavelengths of the visible spectrum; that of the roads also contains small quantities of ultra-violet light.
>
> The cells have no system for closing or screening.
>
> Inhabitants live one to a cell, and possess no clothes or other objects because the city provides for their every need. They are absolutely free to act and organize their lives, both as individuals and as a community; to be alone; to gather in groups; to create laws or regulations; the only restriction is that they cannot go outside of the city because the upper ends of the circular roads are closed by the automatic building site.[343]

342 Superstudio, "Twelve Cautionary Tales," 737.
343 Ibid.

The capsule is entirely self-contained, and like a human organism, interdependent with its inhabitant. Superstudio author Frassinelli sets out in precise detail the invariable predetermined program that determines existence from birth to death:

> Each cell contains an "automatic obstetrician" which, applied to the abdomen of the future mother, extracts the foetus painlessly. The baby is transported by pipeline to a cell in the newly-built section, where it is fed and looked after automatically. Only in this phase is the door of the cell sealed by a steel panel. For four years the child remains in his cell, during which time he learns the ethics and working of his city. Thereafter the metal door slides away and disappears forever into the wall.[344]

Like a living being the capsule has a limited lifespan, and self-destructs once its materials have expired. Each inhabitant spends the first four years of their life enclosed in their cell by a steel door, learning the codes of the city in which they are to spend their entire life. Some may try to imagine the exterior world, but leaving the city is impossible, and so they know nothing beyond their sterilized capsules and the ruins at the city's farthest reaches.

> Often, placing their hands and ears against the warm, vibrating metal walls of the building-site, they try to penetrate the mystery of the outside world. But it is rare for someone to go down the road beyond the zone of extreme old age, into

344 Ibid.

> the spirals of decay and putrefaction of things and men, and yet further into the uncertain light and the heat, into the spirals scattered with detritus, dust, bones, until they reach the dark, suffocating and vibrant zones spiralling towards indefinite depths.[345]

This inescapable prison—with the contrast between order and geometric form on one hand, and the vast, rotting spiral on the other—is a purposefully appalling prospect. The capsule thus embodied for Superstudio all the characteristics associated with modernity. Their twelve cities were only ideal in the sense that they pushed standardization, hygiene, industrialization, and other phenomena that the Modern Movement held dear to their absolute limit. The "Twelve Cautionary Tales" were clearly not bedtime stories for architecturally inclined children, but instead meant to terrorize readers; as Branzi put it: "Criticism of the Modern Movement was also and above all expressed by taking Rationalism to an extreme, with the intention of exposing the underlying contradictions of the movement, along with the fragile nature of its apparent unity of research."[346] By pushing utopia to the point of paroxysm, the tales take aim at both the values of technological progress and their supposedly emancipating, moral dimension, and at the ostensible virtues of the *Continuous Monument*, Superstudio's previous project. Even within Italy's architectural neo-avant-garde, then, the capsule took on a multiplicity of meanings, equally useful as both a dystopian example of rationalism's limits and a space offering a wealth of new possibilities.

345 Ibid.
346 Branzi, *Hot House*, 73.

For Colombo, the capsule offered a means of giving form to his arguments for design's disciplinary autonomy. Emilio Ambasz, the curator of "Italy: The New Domestic Landscape," gave Colombo carte blanche to produce a work for the exhibition, which would eventually take the form of the *Total Furnishing Unit*. However, Colombo's archives reveal that he had initially proposed a caravan, and had provided the MoMA with a detailed description of the project in fifteen or so typed pages, before abandoning the project for reasons that remain unknown. In a statement of intent dated May 28, 1971, Colombo sets out the epistemological basis for his project and mentions having collaborated with physiologists, psychologists, and ergonomists from the outset of his preliminary research. Colombo begins his text by outlining a series of critical elements that allow him to justify his proposed project: "Typically, the caravan is considered as a limited volume which ought to accommodate not only all conventional items of furniture, but, worse still, a considerable number of devices."[347] His choice of a caravan adds new emphasis to antidesign's characteristic movement and autonomy.[348]

Indeed, antidesign revisited the idea of the autonomous capsule in various ways, incorporating independent functions and bringing together the container and the contained. For example, photographs of *Visiona 1* demonstrate Colombo's desire to illustrate his capsules' autonomy, often showing them cropped, in isolation and without context, as if they are somehow separate from the spaces in which they are situated. This emphasis on autonomy can be found in every realization of antidesign, and would prove decisive for Colombo's work. Each capsule exhibits a similar

347 Ibid., 2.
348 Joe Colombo, "Museo d'Arte Moderne di New York, proposta di una roulotte," Studio Joe Colombo Archives, Milan.

indifference to its immediate surroundings, which, in any case, are kept as neutral as possible. This is visible even in Colombo's earlier work, such as the 1964 *Minikitchen*: a kitchenette, produced by Boffi, mounted on casters and comprising a mobile and highly compact block that incorporated a multitude of functions that were, for the most part, hidden by an ingenious system of sliding screens, drawers, and cupboards. The *Minikitchen* was not a space, but an independent unit, with a volume of no more than a half cubic meter that contained all the functions that conventionally occupied an entire room in an apartment. The unit thus challenged the traditional idea of an apartment by offering a credible alternative to the idea that each room should have a specific function. In addition to offering the same level of functionality as a kitchen, its theoretical mobility, although limited in practice by cables and piping, served as a declaration of independence to function outside of the wider architectonic structure. Rather than proposing to combine the kitchen and living room in a single continuous space, as was then in vogue, the *Minikitchen* challenged the idea that functions should be assigned to particular spaces. This decoupling of function and space made it possible to relocate according to the user's needs and whims. The *Minikitchen* was thus more of a service than an object, able to extricate itself from the bounds of a given space to create new, temporary ones defined only by the user's activities—in this case the preparation and consumption of food. Drawing too upon a renewed conception of standardization, the *Minikitchen* was imagined as an industrial product that would overcome the tyranny of the fixed floorplan which had until then governed the hierarchy between design, architecture, and urbanism.

Colombo's subsequent caravan proposal for the MoMA followed in the *Minikitchen*'s steps toward standardization.

The sketches that accompany his statement of intent show a simple volume that is almost rectangular, save for its rounded angles and large, oblong window and elliptical doorway, which bring to mind space shuttles and submarines, marking the boundary between interior and exterior. The combination of orthogonal and rounded forms is typical of Colombo, and can be seen both in his furniture, such as the 1965 *Spider* lamp and the 1970 *Boby* trolley, and in his larger projects, such as the bar he designed for the Triennale di Milano or the pod containing both bedroom and bathroom in his *Visiona 1* project. Colombo's use of standardized, movable blocks with rounded edges suggests, in formal terms, the disciplinary autonomy that he sought to attain through antidesign: these oblong and hermetic unities recall the spherical volumes that Colombo had already explored in his nuclear paintings.

Clearly, Colombo's caravan was connected to the automobile, which had become a major reference point for home design since the beginning of the twentieth century. The automobile connected movement and domestic comfort, its homelike interiors eventually giving rise to veritable houses on wheels. At first the automobile was associated with speed, comfort, and a form of luxurious leisure travel that protected its occupants from the hostile outside world; then its connotations shifted toward a programmatic model for the Modern Movement and its values. The assembly line production of cars in factories was viewed as the crowning achievement of industry and the most visible example of the application of standardization in everyday life. Inspired by this success, architects like Gropius and Le Corbusier would in turn conceive cars of their own. However, the caravan should not be viewed as a prosthetic add-on for the automobile; since Raymond Roussel and his famous house on wheels, or Buckminster

Fuller's Dymaxion House, they could be considered fully autonomous mobile homes.

Although the final years of the 1950s saw a number of architects attempt to distance themselves from the modernist period, one of its favored incarnations, the automobile, persisted as a shining example of standardization. Peter and Alison Smithson followed this current, developing an innovative practice based on new forms and materials such as plastic that had until then been underutilized, if at all, in architecture, as well as new construction methods similar to those of standardization.

The automobile was an attractive model for architects and designers alike. In 1956, as part of the annual Daily Mail Ideal Home Exhibition, the Smithsons presented their *House of the Future*. The house's temporary structure had striking similarities, in terms of the questions it posed and the solutions it offered, with Ionel Schein's *Maison tout en plastiques*, exhibited the previous year at the Salon des arts ménagers in Paris. The *House of the Future* was conceived specifically for the exhibition as a model for a mass-produced home in which each and every element could be modified and replaced, like the side-view mirrors or tires of a car. The house's constituent parts could similarly be upgraded in line with the latest technology and innovations. The analogy with the automobile is fundamental to the Smithsons' project in that their highly visible and widely publicized *House of the Future* represented both a conclusive and an experimental example of standardization. The result of collaborative research between designers and engineers, the house was set to be produced industrially, it was conceived as a consumer good, and the buyer had the option of replacing and adapting every component part to suit their taste, down to the house's color. The *House of the Future* vaunted its industrial origin, and demonstrated that the mass production of homes and their interiors was indeed possible. This argument partially relied upon the precedent set by the car, which, as discussed above, encapsulated and incorporated all the comforts of the home into a space equipped with windows that allowed for contact with the outside world. The car represented the new freedoms of movement and travel, while its technology was admired for its clear lead over other industrial sectors, which "like the home [...] are immobile, or move at a snail's pace, or else plumb the depths of bad taste. So surely it is the time for this burst of new, authentic design, incarnated by Joe."[349] For Colombo, whose ideas on standardization were far more advanced than those currently circulating in the architectural sphere, the "ideal model" of the automobile embodied technological innovation and a perfect mastery of the conditions of industrialization and the market, in stark contrast to the gloomy and reactionary furniture industry.[350] The car was a paragon of high technology and prefabrication, and a paradigm for designers and architects alike; what's more, it was clearly the work of design rather than architecture, and promised, therefore, to place designers at the top of the disciplinary pyramid.

Admiration for cars was far from universal among architects: Claude Parent saw them as unbearably degrading, the symbol of a new propaganda of incarceration that even led him to allude to concentration camps. For Parent, to collaborate with industry was to make a deal with the

349 "Una nuova concezione dell'arredamento: Joe Cesare Colombo," *Lotus*, no. 3 (1966).

350 M. Pia Valota, "Joe C. Colombo," *Casabella*, no. 358 (November 1971): 47. Daniele Baroni also makes this connection: "Oggetti [...] che nella forma si ponevano in stretta connessione con le carrozzerie delle spider fuoriserie della grande tradizione automobilistica: gusci aerodinamici in materiale plastico, grossi cuscini rivestiti in pelle nera, radio e luci ni incorporate" (The shapes of these objects [...] are linked to the bodies of the limited edition Spider cars of the great automobile tradition: aerodynamic plastic shells, ample black leather cushions, radios and built-in lighting). Daniele Baroni, "Joe Colombo," *Interni*, June 1971, 56.

devil, one that would see creativity obliterated in favor of technology and that represented the fatal flaw of design:

> Industrialize the building. How? Certainly not with architects, or else, with architects who are ready to bend to the "doctrine" of industry, that is to say to obediently copy and reproduce the methods of its crowning achievement: the construction of the automobile. Hence the new propaganda slogan. Let us build homes as we build automobiles, and let us start to follow its chain of compromises and concessions from the home (symbolically called Citroën) to the caravan, without forgetting the mobile home. The latest incarnation of this concession, the utopian action of the Archigram group in London which hails through science-fiction the technological frenzy of current industry. And what if architects, by some extraordinary chance, were not so supple, so numerous, if they had the scruples, a sense of remorse before these first manifestations of their talent forced into the mould of industry? Well, others would be there to take up the gauntlet... designers.[351]

In their article "The Appliance House," Alison and Peter Smithson outline the contradictions inherent to industrialization and discuss possible solutions. The automobile represents a benchmark in terms of publicity for the architects: "The present concept of what a house should be is being sold by advertisers on the basis of cars and domestic appliances."[352]

351 Parent, "Face à face," in "Le design," 20.

The mobile, nomadic concepts embodied by the capsule anticipate the autonomy that Colombo would later fix as the goal of antidesign. The capsule—a term that, it bears mentioning, has been confused with the word "cell," particularly in the work of the Metabolists, who used the two interchangeably—was very much present in the formal vocabulary of the 1960s, yet Colombo endowed it with an altogether different significance: he considered it the best form to represent the disciplinary autonomy of design at a time when architecture dominated the home environment. With the capsule home, Colombo drew upon the space capsule as a metaphor for absolute autonomy, transposing its independent, self-contained character to architecture, where it was further amplified by the use of plastic, Colombo's favored material, which enabled surfaces that were, at least in visual terms, smooth and continuous,[353] and with which he initiated a new discourse of cohesion, unity, and coordination.[354]

352 Smithson and Smithson, "Appliance House," 47.
353 Hoffenberg and Lapidus, *La société du design*, 67–72 (see note 38).
354 Colombo, "Antidesign," 28.

Plastic: Chemistry and Alchemy

Colombo's projects were realized almost entirely using plastic, which gave form to everything from bathroom pods to beds. The omnipresence of plastic in his work is unsurprising given its unique characteristics in comparison to other materials available at the time. Although the better part of Colombo's plastic creations predate antidesign, the material was nonetheless the designer's weapon of choice as he contested the status quo. In the field of design in the 1960s, plastic embodied the euphoric mass production that was enthusiastically promoted by technophiles, architects, and Pop designers. However, it had also been deployed by Ionel Schein, the Smithsons, and the radical architects as a means of differentiating their work from the wood and metal furniture so characteristic of functionalism. Without dwelling on the production of plastic itself, it is worth mentioning the analysis of Ezio Manzini, who has focused on the relationships between design and materials in his work. For Manzini, the sheer artificiality of plastic defined its relationship with man; in the hands of the designer, it became a means of creating an interface between humans and technology. Artificiality, design, plastic, and antidesign all depended entirely on industrial production, which for Colombo represented the only means of addressing the needs of a collective humanity as opposed to those of the individual:

> Through the introduction of the notion of anti-design [...] and through pure research, we will perhaps attain a new image of production, one which will allow us to go beyond all the compromises that the machinery of advanced industrial civilization seeks

> to impose. The distribution of products will be the exclusive territory of large retail operations; the customer will have disappeared to be replaced by the consumer, who is not an individual but a collective. Fairly quickly, design, production, and distribution will come to exist for the collective alone.[355]

Antidesign was the result of a joint endeavor between designers and industrial manufacturers, with capsules imagined not as limited editions, but for mass production and distribution. Colombo aspired to an affordable price that would put the capsule within reach of most, envisaging standardized pieces that could be adapted, customized, and combined according to the needs and desires of the owner, who could thus create a coordinated and unified space. As such, there is nothing surprising about Colombo's choice of plastic: cheap and easily produced, it was antidesign's perfect medium. Plastic also offered another means of breaking down the conventional disciplinary hierarchy; its smooth and flawless aspect struck critics from Barthes to Banham,[356] for whom the cheap and cheerful artificiality and malleability of plastic signaled a clear break with the Modern Movement and a literal incarnation of the architectural body. The flexibility of plastic represented an intentional usurpation of modernist orthodoxy with regard to materials, and would in turn be reflected in the architectural field. Sylvia Lavin retraces this process in her text "Plasticity at Work," analyzing and comparing three emblematic cases: Claes Oldenburg's *Bedroom Ensemble* (1963–69),

355 Colombo, *Qu'est-ce que le design?*, n.p. This was his answer to question 26, "What is the future of design?"

356 "But *Barbarella* is the first post-hardware SF movie of any consequence. [...] Responsive environments in the sense of not being rigid and unyielding; articulated only by hinges between disparate rigid parts: an ambience of curved, pliable, continuous, breathing, adaptable surfaces." Banham, "Triumph of Software," *New Society*, October 31, 1968; in *Design by Choice*, 134.

Cushicle (1966–67) by Michael Webb, and Colombo's *Total Furnishing Unit*.[357] Lavin emphasizes the importance of the exhibition environment for these three works, and first distances them from the respective fields of their authors—visual art, architecture, and design—before returning them to these disciplinary contexts.

She justifies her selection on the grounds that all three projects deal in domesticity: though they were not conceived for actual occupation, these spaces offered or suggested a number of possible usages. All utilized plastic, albeit to different ends: for Oldenburg, it was an industrial canvas; for Webb, a skin; and for Colombo, a means of designing a semi-solid module. Having examined the presence and role of plastic in the first two case studies, whose authors had attempted to initiate plastic architecture, Lavin goes on to chart Colombo's trajectory from designing individual objects to more complex ones, part of wider spaces and environments. The homogeneity of plastic would play a prominent role in the establishment of antidesign and Colombo's struggle against architecture:

> And indeed the individual components of the *Total Furnishing Unit* are deployed with such density that they suggest almost a homogenous mass squeezing out any functional space except the basic ergonomic, envelope of the body. But more than just their density produces this effect: the almost seamless surfaces of their thermoset plastic repress any indication of joinery and disconnection. Furthermore, while Oldenburg and Webb relied on distinctions between surface and depth, between

357 Sylvia Lavin, "Plasticity at Work," in *Mood River*, ed. Jeffrey Kipnis and Annetta Massie (Colombus, OH: Wexner Center for the Arts, 2002).

> skin and structure, Colombo's house is almost an uninterrupted piece of plastic, a smooth and semi-solid zone perforated only by the movements of domestic activity.[358]

Lavin thus aims to demonstrate that Colombo's use of plastic was motivated not only by its inherent plasticity, but also by the possibility that it offered to erase the opposition, long established by architecture, between structure and surface—a key aim of antidesign. With this homogeneous, unified space Colombo created an instantly recognizable formal echo of the autonomy of antidesign. As far as Colombo was concerned, then, "plastic [...] alone provided the means needed to eliminate the disciplinary hierarchies on which architecture had thrived."[359] Colombo fused architecture and plastic, "seemingly absorbing the discipline itself into this macromolecular structure."[360] With its seamless, smooth, and massive volumes, the *Total Furnishing Unit* abolished the opposition between architecture and design to align itself firmly with the latter.

358 Ibid., 80.
359 Ibid., 79–80.
360 Ibid.

Antidesign versus Controdesign: The Furniture of Radical Architecture and the Architectural Space of Joe Colombo

Before they gained widespread recognition in the 1980s through New Design, the radicals had not considered design as a discipline in its own right, but simply as an activity that fell within their purview as architects. When they did address design, they did so in terms of *controdesign*; the radicals' terminology was clearly reminiscent of antidesign, yet they never seriously engaged with Colombo's ideas.

Ettore Sottsass produced the first text on controdesign, but this offers only a vague definition of the term.[361] More concretely, it refers to the furniture produced by the various members of the radical architecture movement, including the *Passiflora* (1967) and *Excelsior* (1969) lamps and the *Misura* series (1969–70) by Superstudio, and the *Superonda* (1967) and *Safari* (1968) sofas, the *Mies* lounge chair (1969), and the *OLook* (1968) and *San Remo* (1970) lamps by Archizoom Associati.[362] The radicals chose to explore the possibilities offered by the field of furniture in the belief that it was design that governed the relationships between individuals. They believed that design not only instituted certain postures and relationships of the body, but also reflected relations of power, whether in terms of property, economy, aesthetics, good taste, or social hierarchy. They considered that relationships and exchanges between individuals could be transformed by modifying the codes already in circulation within the home.

361 Ettore Sottsass, "Il controdesign" (1972), in *Sottsass's Scrap-Book: Disegni e note di Ettore Sottsass Jr.*, ed. Federica di Castro (Milan: Casabella, 1976), 130–31.
362 This is far from an exhaustive list of their output, which ran from furniture to vases.

Superstudio's Furniture

Beginning with "Superarchitettura I," their 1966 exhibition at the Galleria Jolly 2 in Pistoia, Superstudio's members sought to put their theories into practice. Readily imitating society's codified image of the architect, they went as far as donning the coats traditionally associated with the profession in their building on via di Bellosguardo in Florence. While waiting for commissions, they set about designing objects and furniture. The first works they presented—the *Sofo* armchair and the *Passiflora* lamp—were produced the following year by the Italian manufacturer Poltronova, with Superstudio's founder Adolfo Natalini creating the prototypes. Shortly before beginning their major 1968 work *Continuous Monument* Superstudio published "Un viaggio nelle regioni della ragione" (A voyage into the regions of reason) in *Domus*. This consisted of a series of twenty images, recalling a storyboard or comic book, followed by a story in which the forms, waves, clouds, and ziggurats lose all their functionality as they transform into immense, abstract, autonomous geometric forms. After this first salvo on functionalism, Superstudio developed a system with the plastic laminates company Abet Print, which they presented at the exhibition "L'invenzione della superficie neutra" (The invention of neutral surfaces) in 1970. The isotropic, homogeneous, and totalizing laminated surfaces of their *Istogrammi* simultaneously reference Conceptual art, Land art, the Minimalism of Sol LeWitt and Walter De Maria, as well as the perspectival grid that had been a mainstay of urban planning since Roman times.[363]

363 The term *istogrammi* was the suggestion of physicist Edoardo Boncinelli; see his "Dai cataloghi del Superstudio: Istogrammi," *Domus*, April 1971, 46–49.

Superstudio explored systems on a human scale that could be applied to everything from small objects to mobile furniture to entire cities. For "L'invenzione della superficie neutra" they designed a series of wooden furniture—tables, chairs, mirrors, beds, wardrobes, and sideboards—covered in laminate no. 6, a three-by-three-centimeter, black-on-white grid specially produced for the collection by Abet Print. The series was produced by Zanotta as the *Misura M* line, a title Superstudio would also apply to their next project *Misura L*, a collection of Volterra alabaster and chrome lamps and vases, produced by the Florentine company Misura, which was also the project's namesake.

> But seeing that you cannot go backwards, and that the process is irreversible (and revivals confirm this) and seeing that the system offers us transparent or nonexistent objects (the sales system sells only one product itself), and seeing also that we need something in order to live (utensils, signs, totems) we put the process of design back into motion. [...] We then come to propose "invention design" as an alternative or variant to "product design" or "industrial design" as currently conceived. But any valid design is always invention design (and in this connection think back to the meaning of the terms "design" and "invention" in Renaissance tracts).
>
> The term to use, then, may well be "evasion design." [...] What we want to do is lay the foundations for an existence that is one long protest: a "be-in."[364]

364 Superstudio, "Evasion Design and Invention Design," in Lang and Menking, *Life without Objects*, 116–17.

The same year, Superstudio designed a series of six lamps, *Lumi alti*, for a nationwide competition held by the Japanese company Yamagiwa. Modeled on the solar system, the six floor lamps were envisaged as planets, as this description of one of the series, the *Falling Star*, suggests: "Like a meteorite, a star or a heavenly planet (Saturn, for example), the lamp brings color to colorless rooms; it is a falling star in your home, placed with love and care on a glossy black box; it is a magical mandala for interior lighting."[365] With their flexible and rigid tentacles, and circular and spherical fluorescent tubes, the lamps abound with metaphors, from the pink, transparent, fanlike *Gherpe* lamp to the *OLook* lamp, whose two adjustable purple or white shells lend it the appearance of an enormous eye that watches over the room's inhabitants.

This series of lamps was soon followed by the group's first theoretical text on design, published in the June 1969 issue of *Domus* under the title "Design d'invenzione e design d'evasione" (Invention Design and Evasion Design).[366] The text describes a space that demands the involvement of its users, one which allows them to act in the moment by escaping from the pervading apathy of modern life. The chromatic and sensory properties of objects gave them a central significance for Superstudio's transformation of the environment:

> Every object has a practical function and a contemplative one: and it is the latter that evasion design is seeking to potentiate. Thus there is an end to the 19th-century myths of reason as the explanation of everything, the thousand

365 Unpublished document, Superstudio Archives, Florence.
366 Superstudio, "Evasion Design and Invention Design," in Lang and Menking, *Life without Objects*, 116–117.

> variations on the theme of the four-legged chair, aerodynamic shapes, and the sterilization of dreams. [...]
>
> [The "be-in"] means involving all the users of our products and creating an operative area.
>
> Such total involvement may be achieved in two ways: by supplying products that are poetically functional or by supplying patterns of behaviour.
>
> In the first case you supply multi-significant (ambiguous) products, objects of universal use, and each user puts them to the use he thinks fit.
>
> In the second case you supply the rules of a game to be played with all kinds of objects, or containers that can be filled with all kinds of things.[367]

"Evasion Design and Invention Design" set out Superstudio's refusal to conceive of objects and furniture in terms of functionalist standards; rather, their intention was to occupy the user's private life. In this sense, their work was similar to the deliberately imposing and massive furniture created by Archizoom Associati. With oversized objects such as Archizoom's *Bazaar* chair and *Safari* sofa, and Superstudio's *Luxor* series, the radical architects used furniture as a kind of Trojan horse.[368] With these appealing, even seductive objects, which were accompanied by ironic and provocative advertisements, Superstudio aimed to smuggle their ideas into the home to destroy its bourgeois symbolism from within.

The *Superonda* sofa was one such example: doing away with the wooden structure and foam padding of

367 Ibid., 116–17.
368 See Laura Barile, "Architettura e gioia di vivere: Le esperienze di un gruppo di neolaureti fiorentini; Un cavallo di Troia nella civilta dei superconsumi," *Corriere delle Sera*, April 5, 1967.

conventional furniture, it consisted of a single polyurethane block that served as both structure and filling, covered in imitation leather. Once the seductive, shiny, soft, and sensual sofa was installed in the bourgeois buyer's home, it could set about changing the interior through the uses and postures that it pushed its new owners to adopt. With its parallelepipedal form, wave-shaped indentations, and two interchangeable tessellating elements, Archizoom Associati's *Superonda* sofa was radically different from a conventional couch and precluded all traditional ways of sitting—and being. Their immense *Safari* sofa employed a similar tactic, persuading its users into less than comfortable positions in order to encourage them to invent novel and more pleasant situations.

Archizoom Associati were explicit in their use of such a "Trojan horse" strategy, which they applied through cumbersome, massive items of furniture. "Why this interest in furniture?" was the rhetorical question posed in 1967 after the "Superarchitettura" exhibitions; the answer being that it offered a means of hijacking the mechanisms of mass production, distribution, and consumption:

> This is an attempt (as the definition "superarchitecture" demonstrates) to introduce architecture into channels of consumption capable of influencing mass behaviors. This operation marks the beginning of the end of a certain kind of enlightened design, the fruit of an intellectual elite who believed in the mythical power of intelligence and good taste to save the world.[369]

369 Archizoom Associati, handwritten note to Marco Fini, late 1967, Paolo Deganello Archives, Milan.

The young architects' demystification of modernist myths thus began to take form. By designing base units of furniture with forms and structures that were almost architectural, they offered a fresh way to concieve of seating and intervened in the spheres of both designer and consumer. Their furniture therefore not only transformed architecture, but also had an impact upon design.

The same could be said for the *Centro di Cospirazione Eclettica*, a hybrid space presented by Archizoom at the XIV Triennale di Milano, which opened on May 30, 1968. It consisted of a space enclosed by a black curtain, within which the visitor was confronted with a plethora of symbols: funerary objects reminiscent of ancient Egypt, a tombstone, a photograph of Malcolm X, fake and real plants, furniture from a modernist bedroom, a large gym mat surrounded by colored ropes suggestive of a boxing ring, upon which a narrow table had been placed, seemingly at random, as well as a stuffed eagle representing American imperialism. The space was lit by the fluorescent tubes that would become the group's signature. With its multiple references to Islamic art, such as the black curtain of the Kaaba at Mecca, the construction of the tomb, the palm leaves, and to the fight against racism—Malcolm X's portrait, surrounded by palm leaves, facing down the stuffed American eagle—Archizoom Associati's *cospirazione* emphasized those cultures forgotten by the Modern Movement.

While the *Centro di Cospirazione Eclettica* expressed the political dimension of Archizoom Associati and its members, its titular conspiracy also alluded to the one they were concocting against design: by envisaging an allegorical and functional design, they sought to restore meaning to objects that had come to be considered in purely functional terms. However, as Roberto Gargiani has pointed out, Archizoom Associati were out of step with the revolution of May 1968.[370] The platform they had chosen for their protest belonged to the very culture they were criticizing: the Triennale building, a highly prestigious Milanese design institution. Though there is certainly a coherence to their "conspiring" at the heart of the most important design event worldwide, as international sales were being made, orders placed, and the next year's trends decided, they were alone; the student and youth movements rejected the fair, preferring more overtly political fields of activity. Archizoom Associati's call for "terrorism" and the formation of "cults" was limited to the domain of design, and so ultimately addressed only a narrow audience and failed to connect with a wider movement.

Following the two "Superarchitettura" exhibitions in Pistoia and Modena, Archizoom Associati would reject all rationalism in favor of poetry, kitsch, and eclecticism. From 1967, they began to create models for the *Rosa imperiale* series of "Letti di sogno," or dream beds,[371] featuring bedroom suites complete with walls, beds, wardrobes, rugs, lamps, and bedside tables. Gathering together and combining symbols from Middle Eastern cultures, Pop art, and the Modern Movement with a gleeful disregard for coherence, the dream beds—*Rosa d'Arabia*, *Presagio di rose*, *Naufragio di rose*, and *Elettro rosa*—were produced at the invitation of Sottsass and *Domus*. Archizoom Associati imagined these bedrooms as a revolt against the placid ideal of the coquettish bourgeois interior:

> The problem for us [...] is how to serve up an ice cream in such a way that he [the customer] loses the

370 Roberto Gargiani, *Archizoom Associati 1966–1974: Dall'onda pop alla superficie neutra* (Milan: Mondadori Electa, 2007), 78.

371 This title was an homage to Mario Tronti's declaration that "so long as the field is occupied by the enemy we must spray it with bullets, without tears for the roses." See Mario Tronti, *Operai e capitale* (Turin: Einaudi, 1966), 14.

> desire to eat it for the rest of his life. Or an ice cream that, once it has been bought, grows bigger than him and humiliates him. Or that becomes a piece of the world surrounding him and frightens him [...]. In short, an ice cream with no alternatives: either you eat it or it eats you. Or rather: it starts to eat you as soon as you have finished it. And then we think: apple-bombs, poisonous sweets, false information, in short Trojan blankets, beds, or horses that are brought into the house and destroy everything in it. We want to let in everything that stays outside the door: careful contstructed banality, deliberate vulgarity, urban fittings, dogs that bite.[372]

Behind a pretense of eclecticism, the bad taste of the dream beds contained a viciously subversive dimension, and as such they confirm the importance of design for the group. Whether as a Trojan horse or a parasite, it was design alone that proved capable of infiltrating the home thanks to its habitual association with the domestic interior.

However, readily dealing in contradictions, Archizoom Associati and Superstudio also pronounced the death of the object.[373] Superstudio's break with furniture was particularly swift, as the group began to simplify and reduce their work in order to develop a "neutral" language capable of restoring a semantic dimension to everyday and functional objects. The notion of the disappearance of the object extended well beyond the field of design, paralleling similar developments in Conceptual and Pop art. While Pop

372 Archizoom Associati, in *Domus*, October 1967, 41; published in English in Branzi, *Complete Works*, 38 (see note 30).

373 Archizoom Associati and Superstudio, "Distruzione, metamorfosi e ricostruzione degli oggetti," *In*, nos. 2–3 (1971); published in English as "Destruction, Metamorphoses and Reconstruction of the Object," in Lang and Menking, *Life without Objects*, 120–21.

artists played with the significance of objects to glorify them, Conceptual artists dematerialized the art object by reducing it to a simple referent. Both movements therefore tended toward the destruction of the object.[374] Echoing Colombo's stance, Natalini observed, "If design is merely an inducement to consume, then we must reject design [...] design must disappear."[375] It was in this tension between the disappearance and the presence of the object that controdesign operated:

> [Controdesign] has found the indispensable condition for its own survival in the trends and internal structures of the market. And in fact it is altogether possible to read this phenomenon—as has already been the case for interior organization and furnishing—in terms of a vast and precise publicity and promotional operation internal to a moment of expansion for consumer goods, or of the organization of this expansion.[376]

In order to offset handmade avant-garde items that were necessarily limited to small production runs and a bourgeois clientele, controdesign's proponents proposed "neutral" furniture such as the *Misura* series:

> The laminate is a continuous abstract grid of lines which intersect at 3 centimeter intervals. These lines are marked out on a neutral white or pale background. The specificity of the chosen design creates a homogeneity and an isotrope of the surface in its

374 This theory is developed by Paola Navone and Bruno Orlandoni in "Il disagio delle avanguardie," *Casabella*, nos. 404–5 (August–September 1975): 76.
375 Adolfo Natalini, "AA School of Architecture Lecture," March 3, 1971; quoted in Lang and Menking, *Life without Objects*, 20–21.
376 Navone and Orlandoni, "Il disagio delle avanguardie," 76.

> totality. It can also be used in the three major directions of the Cartesian system [...]. Every solid element present is defined by the totality of the surfaces, and each surface is defined in turn by the self-generating lines: in this case, both are strictly orthogonal. This is a conscious choice to reduce the operations of design to their bare minimum and to facilitate as much as possible the circulation of information between these operations.[377]

Superstudio believed that designers had a responsibility to reconsider their role in the nightmarish situation they had actively contributed to. In order to do so, they adopted the grid as their weapon of choice and a means of infinitely scaling up their operation. The grid represented a kind of neutrality through its rejection of traditional codes of representation and perspective. Their entirely original conception of the grid approached it as a self-perpetuating productive instrument that abolished all hierarchies[378]—even those of scale—in favor of a systematic universality, one capable of monopolizing space in its entirety: "Between the abstract grid, which structures the universality of the system, and the detail of an object, there is no longer any hierarchy, everything is part of the same unity of the immediate physical experience of the environment."[379] Whether in terms of concrete production, forward-looking thinking, or disciplinary classification, space becomes uniform; as such, although it wanted to abolish codes of representation, divisions, and hierarchies, controdesign's unilateral conception of furniture maintained an architectural

377 Roberto Gargiani and Beatrice Lampariello, *Superstudio* (Rome: Laterza, 2010), 114.
378 Frédéric Migayrou, "Extensions de la grille," *Les Cahiers du Musée national d'art moderne*, no. 82 (Winter 2002/3): 4–23.
379 Ibid., 11.

approach. The equalization it promoted left no room for other approaches, such as Colombo's belief that the anthropocentric logic of urban space necessarily began with an outward extension of domestic space.

Design Reborn as a Discipline against the Market

The radicals' critique centered on the economic and productive status quo. Controdesign's revolutionary stance was part of a long-standing tension between politics and design, and emphasized the power of the imagination as opposed to pure rationalism. The radicals' sustained attacks on capitalism sought to problematize and question design's relationship with liberalism, and the determinedly political and revolutionary nature of their work reveals a dimension of design history that is often minimized. Denouncing modernity, they offered an alternative a series of "non-objects," and justified their production by discussing them as signs:

> The meaning of these "non-objects" exhibited in New York by the members of controdesign is quite explicit: how can one believe in the rationalist conception of architecture, the myths of methodology and typology, the concept of the minimum living space and the house as a cell? Technology is blind, the game of forms is reactionary: both are servile followers of production. We cannot draw up pleasant things as a response to this singular spirit of oppression and the frenzied race of consumption. There is no possible way out—neither inside nor outside the boundaries or design.[380]

However, the radicals' protest proved questionable, for in the end they did indeed produce a collection of furniture.

380 Alessandro Mendini, "Radical Design," *Casabella*, no. 367 (July 1972): 5.

Nonetheless, all those who attempted to imagine an existence outside the dominant capitalist system through their work—Conceptual artists, radical architects, and Colombo—questioned the materiality of the object as a vehicle of symbolic power as well as its place in society and its role in the economic system.

Each of these approaches would, in their own way, explore the conditions necessary for a way of life free from the profit-driven contingencies of capitalism. By rejecting tangible production in favor of abstract proposals, texts, and projects, radical architects aimed to escape commercial constraints, though their work would ultimately remain confined to the experimental field and hence be familiar only to a small group of connoisseurs. Controdesign's limited runs of furniture, which its proponents justified in terms of a rejection of standardized production, were in opposition to the more democratic mass production that Colombo envisaged for antidesign, which he aimed to distribute through major Italian chain stores such as La Rinascente. The radicals hesitated between an industrial production that promised to facilitate the entry of their "Trojan horses" into bourgeois homes, and the craft production that they ultimately chose for more pragmatic reasons.[381] Controdesign insisted that its protest could only be coherent if it refused to participate in the existing system of industrial production, even if this meant small production runs or craft manufacture and thus a narrow, elite audience. But Colombo's democratic discourse and promotion of inexpensive design should also be questioned, since none of his antidesign projects went into production.

381 Industrial enterprises proved to be more skeptical than art galleries and Italian furniture houses such as Poltronova, even though the latter could only offer a modest output. Only a few models of the *Safari* sofa were produced, for example, with one being sold to actor Vittorio Gassman.

Though they were featured in exhibitions and magazine articles, Colombo remained intransigent in his rejection of exclusive production; the radicals, meanwhile, readily took advantage of the experimental potential of the gallery and the opportunities offered by the collectors' market. Colombo's designs utilized innovative technologies and methods such as the polymerization of plastics, while Archizoom Associati and Superstudio extolled the simple virtues of bricolage and non-technological processes—though in order to produce the *Safari* sofa, the group's assistant Sergio Cammilli made use of polyurethanes and imitation-leather upholstery to make the suite relatively light and comfortable. For the dream beds, they collaborated, like Sottsass and Superstudio, with Abet Print.

Wealthy collectors were the only audience aware of the designers' activity and the only ones with the financial means of acquiring their work. Controdesign thus rejected one problematic system of production for another. Antidesign faced a similar fate despite Colombo's attempt to operate beyond the gallery by developing links with businesses and producers, such as the furniture manufacturer Sormani, which he approached to produce his *Cabriolet Bed*. The question remains a point of controversy even today. Branzi, who participated in the original debate, maintained that any critique of the relationship between the economy and modernity necessarily involves an infiltration of the same imperialist system that is its target, which can only be accomplished by design:

> Archizoom Associati warned: "We should not be deceived by the turbine of consumption and its capactiy for absorption, since behind it stands a marble dog-in-the-manger that will neither eat nor move." Imperialism was the hidden factor

> underlying this worldwide prosperity; it had to be defeated by its own weapons and not by the reformist morality of the bourgeoisie.[382]

Because of design's interdependence with political economy and industry, Branzi believed that it is the only discipline offering viable strategies of protest:

> We see design, therefore, as a site for the rebuilding of architecture: not in the sense of mere additional growth, "from the spoon to the city" as Ernesto Rogers would have it, but rather as an attempt to find, amidst the dramatic epistemological crisis in modern architecture—a crisis which has threatened the very existence of the modern world—a point from which a real link between man and the system of his objects could be forged.[383]

The political transformation of society and its new modes of production from the second industrial revolution onward were key factors in the decision of architects to experiment with controdesign. The primary strategy of controdesign reflected changes in design production and incorporated notions previously distant from or even alien to the discipline: the abstract, chance, kitsch, unexpected, and imperfect that were present in various alternative savoir faire. Another of their tactics was to employ fictional and literary methods, and in particular the notion of dystopia, pushing the inconsistencies and dangers of a given situation to their extremes. With these visions of a latent apocalypse, they

382 Branzi, *Hot House*, 55.
383 Ibid., 8.

sought to encourage a critical interrogation of the present. Controdesign's third strategy echoed that of Conceptual art—effacing the object entirely in order to operate outside the dominion of the market and of capitalism:

> Objects and also ideas, especially good ones, are accessories of capitalism which have wrongly been considered irreplaceable expressions of human activity. [...] The vacuum that has been opened up allows much space for the recreation of one's own behavior, for the invention of new forms of communication, for love.[384]

However, their work ran the risk of reflecting Baudrillard's stark warning in *The Consumer Society* that capitalism was sustained by contradiction, and thus to criticize it was to consolidate its power: "Just as medieval society was balanced on God and the Devil, so ours is balanced on consumption *and* its denunciation."[385] Germano Celant, meanwhile, denounced design as by definition an element of the capitalist system that it purports to criticize: "The idea of giving design a new ideological and operational dimension, so that it would no longer be available to serve as an instrument for neocapitalist infiltration, has been transformed into a populist 'socialization' of the same idea."[386] The most vicious critique came from Manfredo Tafuri, who denounced architecture's turn toward design, a move that he saw as replacing a modernist ideology with a radical one. Controdesign's choice to co-opt design in order to operate inside the market is indeed problematic—particularly

384 Lapo Binazzi, "Non-design: Dall'oggetto alla sopravvivenza," *Casabella*, no. 386 (February 1974): 22; published in English as "Non-design: From the Object to Survival," in Migayrou, *Architecture radicale*, 310.
385 Baudrillard, *Consumer Society*, 196 (see note 38).
386 Germano Celant, "Radical Architecture," in Ambasz, *Italy*, 380.

since the assumption that design is somehow inextricably linked to liberalism fails to account for the way it was envisaged and utilized by figures such as Morris. Tafuri considered controdesign's attempt to infiltrate the domestic sphere as invalid, believing that architecture's experiments with design were only a hollow success, made possible through a politically compromising flirtation with consumer goods.

In "Design and Technological Utopia," his contribution to the catalogue for "Italy: The New Domestic Landscape," Tafuri despairs that radical architecture's potential to effect change appears rather limited faced with the might of the dominant capitalist system: "All the intellectual anti-consumer utopias that seek to redress the ethical 'distortions' of the technological world by modifying the system of production or the channels of distribution only reveal the complete inadequacy of their theories, in the face of the actual structure of the capitalist economic cycle."[387] Echoing Baudrillard, Tafuri considered the Italian radicals' attempt to surreptitiously undermine capitalism through design to be nostalgic and doomed to fail, since it refused to confront capitalism directly, resulting in its inevitable recuperation by the very system it opposed. The critiques of these two theorists demonstrate the difficulty of political engagement within the sphere of commercial arts. However problematic it was, controdesign's protest nonetheless attests to the shift of anti-capitalist debates from architecture toward design in the turbulent early years of the 1970s, despite the scathing critiques leveled at the latter.

However, design was still struggling to obtain recognition, and the architects who experimented in the field

387 Manfredo Tafuri, "Design and Technological Utopia," in Ambasz, *Italy*, 388–404.

tended to treat it as a kind of instrument or accessory for their own discipline. The radicals further hampered the definitive establishment of design as a discipline by using the terms "controdesign" and "antidesign" interchangeably, severely undermining Colombo's project. Antidesign's fate was sealed with Colombo's death, and it quickly became synonymous with controdesign, designating all and any productions by the radical architects. The indiscriminate use of the two prefixes reflected the radicals' tendency to minimize differences within the field, and as early as 1971 the radical critic Almerico de Angelis was using Colombo's term as a synonym for controdesign. Sottsass further confused matters by framing controdesign as a term that "is used everywhere [...] and if the housewives aren't yet using it, it's only a matter of time."[388] He struggled to offer a definition, instead suggesting controdesign designates a type of behavior and a "way of being aware," before ultimately claiming that

> [controdesign] is a rage, or better, a boredom,
> or maybe desperation, or maybe a joke,
> or maybe simply the result of the awareness of
> what is happening in the field of design,
> given that this design business is becoming
> increasingly demanding and applied and
> consumed, exaggerated and sought after, and
> above all used by everyone, actors and
> audiences, designers and manufacturers, sellers
> and buyers.[389]

388 Sottsass, "Il controdesign," 130–31. In the French version of this article, which appears in the exhibition catalogue *Ettore Sottsass*, ed. Thierry Grillet and Marie-Laure Jousset (Paris: Éditions du Centre Pompidou, 1994), *controdesign* is translated as "antidesign," further demonstrating (and adding to) the confusion surrounding these terms.
389 Ibid., 131.

If Sottsass discussed design as an invasive force, for Colombo there was nothing parasitic about it. He believed that furniture could effect positive change in the domestic environment and that if there was to be a revolution, it would originate from the field of design. While this position seems somewhat naive and significantly less critical than those of the radical architects, this is largely because Colombo was seeking to transform design, his own discipline, from within; whereas for the radicals, design was just one tool in their arsenal for reshaping architecture according to their revolutionary ideas. It is important to highlight the differences in the aims, discourses, and actions of the proponents of controdesign and antidesign, which were often determined not only by their intentions but also by the reality of the markets for and the histories of their respective disciplines. Indeed, it is in disciplinary terms that antidesign and controdesign can truly be distinguished from one another. The radicals considered design to be the natural terrain upon which to oppose the Modern Movement and the unacceptable state of affairs; the shift toward this discipline was also a means of compensating for the crisis that architecture was then facing. Colombo, on the other hand, conceived of design as unquestionably superior for domestic space, outweighing architecture and, for that matter, any other discipline.

Ultimately, the two strategies both sought to politicize the relationship between creation and the economy, thus emphasizing the value of individuality—even if, as previously discussed, Colombo initiated antidesign in opposition to the radicals' *Centro di Cospirazione Eclettica*, which he felt to be a somewhat redundant experiment. Branzi, who had met Colombo at the presentation of *Visiona 1* in 1969 together with radical designers Massimo Morozzi and Paolo Deganello and industrial designer Mario Bellini, would retrospectively acknowledge the importance of anti-design for controdesign and for the *No-Stop City* project in particular.[390] But this shared ground cannot entirely dissimulate the substantial differences between the two positions along disciplinary lines, with the radicals fierce defense of architecture remaining at odds with Colombo's project and its assertion of the supremacy of design.

390 Andrea Branzi, interview by the author, December 3, 2004.

After Antidesign: The End of History or the Beginning of Redefinition?

Though at the moment of its emergence in England, design had been shaped according to progressive socialist thinking, it was in the economic effervescence of the 1960s and the mass production, distribution, and consumption that came with it that design at last began to take on its current dimension and enjoy widespread popular awareness. However, just as it seemed that design's original democratic promise had come to fruition, designers themselves were torn between two opposing positions. Far from being resolved, the questions raised by Morris became more relevant than ever. It was this situation that pushed Colombo to develop a self-critical stance that interrogated the role of design and of the designer in relation to the system of production. His project, antidesign, proved to be a uniquely productive one that would renew the discipline as a whole, as he sought to reconcile concrete, industrial production with a critical and anti-capitalist perspective.

The three short years of antidesign's existence, before it disappeared along with its creator, played a central role in the construction of the history of design. They effected an irreversible epistemological rupture, one that demanded a rereading of design's history beyond the boundaries defined by Pevsner and Giedion's work, and represented nothing less than the assertion of design's status as an independent and autonomous discipline. The break caused by antidesign also demanded a reevaluation of the conventional hierarchy between the arts, and made it possible to understand the extent to which, from design's complex origins through to the present day, the question of its autonomy has consistently been present as an underlying issue. So while antidesign was prevented from fulfilling its potential by Colombo's sudden death, and even if the conventional history of design has largely drawn on other sources as I have discussed, its existence alone is enough reason to reopen the field of design and begin an exploration of the possibilities of a parallel history: that of an autonomous discipline.

Part IV

Total Design—From Autonomy to Expansion

> In some ways, design has never had an independent history of its own; it has always been seen either as industrial culture or as social décor, if not merely as a curious chapter in the history of customs. Currently the design project is credited with the role of a minor, applicative part of modern architectural culture—a disciplinary setting for the final steps of a more ambitious project taking its cue from the metropolis. It is expected to confine its attention to the utilitarian object and to realize that unity of human technologies within the "project" so dear to the Modern Movement. But this type of operative unity between design, architecture and town-planning, based on a rigid hierarchy of decision-making, broke down some time ago, giving way to a common antagonism among the three disciplines, each one of which now claims not only its own total autonomy but even the need to set itself up as a complete alternative to the others.[391]

It is in these terms that Andrea Branzi introduces the reader to his first history of Italian design, *The Hot House*. Branzi's history belongs to the tradition that imagines a unity between the arts, echoing the idea of the total work, a notion close to the Wagnerian Gesamtkunstwerk. Wagner's idea promoted a harmony between knowledge and skill, a transhistorical notion that he put forward in his 1849 text "The Artwork of the Future," which can also be found in the work of Schiller, Novalis, and the German Romantics. This idea, which had already held a central importance for Art Nouveau,[392] gave way to what Branzi terms in his

391 Branzi, *Hot House*, 9 (see note 15).
392 See Debora L. Silverman, *Art Nouveau in Fin-de-Siècle France: Politics, Psychology, and Style* (Berkeley: University of California Press, 1989).

introduction a "common antagonism" between the different disciplines. This deceptively simple statement in fact raises a question that is essential to our understanding of the history of design. The notion of artistic unity re-emerged in avant-garde design and architecture, in guises as varied as Gropius's concept of "total architecture" and Le Corbusier's "synthesis of the arts," and would give rise to important differences and unexpected but significant changes. Wagner's project belongs to the speculation of another era, and its contemporary relevance is debatable; yet the persistence of the concept and terminology of the total work of art in the field of architecture, and particularly in the work of the Modern Movement, merits an investigation into why it has seen such longevity and what it might eventually reveal about the debates that formed the backdrop to antidesign and controdesign. The easiest way of going about this would be to demonstrate the flaws in Branzi's assessments, to argue that his writings, necessarily biased by his role in Archizoom Associati, are not to be taken seriously.[393] While Branzi himself readily acknowledges the bias of his work, it is nonetheless important to analyze his affirmations of design's disciplinary autonomy, and examine whether this is a question of absolute or relative independence.

Branzi suggests that design—though it remained a minor question of ornamentation or the finishing touches to the architectural project—overturned the hierarchical structure that had relegated it to the bottom of the disciplinary pyramid. The very fact of design's minimization had fostered the creation of new, interdisciplinary relationships that escaped the control of traditional structures in

393 Branzi's histories of design include *Hot House*; *Il design italiano 1964–1990*; *Introduzione al design italiano*; and *Learning from Milan: Design and the Second Modernity* (Cambridge, MA: MIT Press, 1988).

order to redraw the disciplinary map. By raising design to the same level as architecture and urbanism, Branzi would legitimize Colombo's work with antidesign, which had redefined not only design itself, but the role and characteristics of the designer. By enshrining design as a discipline, Colombo afforded it autonomy. Given antidesign's role as the central vector for the changes in the definition and scope of design, I will here demonstrate that the twin questions of disciplinary autonomy and superiority have been essential to the history of design, from its inception and throughout its evolution, and would eventually allow it to gain its independence.

Design Deploys Its Trojan Horses

That Pevsner chose to emphasize the artist's environment as a decisive factor for Morris's project in *Pioneers of the Modern Movement* is highly significant:

> But when, in 1857, he had to furnish his first studio in London, the thought struck him that before one can settle down to paint elevating pictures, one must be able to live in appropriate surroundings, must have a decent house, and decent chairs and tables. Nothing was obtainable that could possibly satisfy him. This was the situation which all of a sudden awakened his own personal genius.[394]

Pevsner thus locates the origins of modern architecture in the consequences of a dialogue between space and its occupants. Occupied space is (or can be) a cohesive unity in which all elements contribute to a single, overall meaning—a total work, then. However, with this principle of coherence and interrelation, the history that Pevsner was looking to write was, as I have discussed at length, not that of design but architecture. It is worth returning to Pevsner's text—with its curious position as the first and foremost history of design—not only because it is evidence of design's difficulty to articulate an autonomous set of origins, but because it reveals that the myth of unity promoted by the idea of the total work hides a new hierarchical order.

Taking on numerous forms, from the Middle Ages, to Victor Hugo's *Hunchback of Notre-Dame*, to Morris's London workshop and Gropius's Bauhütte, the total work recurs

394 Pevsner, *Pioneers of the Modern Movement*, 22–23 (see note 1).

constantly as a concept embodying notions of collaboration and unity between the arts; it evokes the arts' cohesive potential by establishing a dialectic opposition between the construction of cathedrals in the Middle Ages on the one hand, and the atomization of man in modern society on the other. Such was the basis for Morris's arguments. He despaired at the decay of British society, which he believed resulted from the artificial separation between greater and lesser arts. Morris hoped that a reconsideration of the roles of each and every form of artistic expression and their accompanying values could encourage vital social reforms. He believed that this redeployment of the arts was a necessary step toward society's salvation. In his famous 1877 speech "The Lesser Arts," he sought to promote this new perspective using fiery language to denounce the conventional distinction between the lesser and greater arts as outdated; Pevsner attributes this division's origins to the crisis of the eighteenth century, when the categories of artist and craftsman first emerged and gave rise to a hierarchy presided over by liberal arts that were seen as superior to all others.

> Apart from the difference between a great master and a scholar, apart from the differences of the natural bent of men's minds, which would make one man an imitative, and another an architectural or decorative artist, there should be no difference between those employed on strictly ornamental work; and the body of artists dealing with this should quicken with their art all makers of things into artists also, in proportion to the necessities and uses of the things they would make.[395]

395 Morris, "The Lesser Arts," in *Political Writings*, 42 (see note 79).

Morris believed that man's relationship to the world could be modified only through the daily use of beautiful objects; in turn, the resulting happiness would create an art that was decorative, noble, and popular.[396] For Morris, the origin of design coincides with a desire to overturn the existing hierarchy that structures the different arts, in order to affirm the value of the decorative arts—though he does not challenge the predominance of architecture, the "foundation of all the arts" and "an all-embracing art."[397] Taking as his model the workshops of the Middle Ages, where a number of different craftsmen collaborated on a single work, Morris called for a return of unity between the arts where the "consciousness of each one that he belongs to a corporate body, working harmoniously, each for all, and all for each, will bring about real and happy equality."[398] Resonating far beyond Morris and his work, the idea of design and the values associated with it initiated a period that saw diverse expressions not limited to the production of useful items, but instead aimed to renew the domestic environment and society as whole. This notion was central to Muthesius's interpretation of Morris's work. He would continue the total project initiated by Morris and the Arts & Crafts movement by creating the Deutscher Werkbund, and his vision for the industrial production of quality goods that would be the expression of his nation's power and the civilizing potential of standardization. However, by separating the arts once more, and making them submit to architecture, he betrayed a fundamental tenet of Morris's original program. Muthesius's decision seems to have been

396 Ibid., 42.
397 William Morris, speech to the National Association for the Advancement of Art in Edinburgh (October 30, 1899); in *Art and Its Producers, and The Arts and Crafts of To-day: Two Addresses Delivered Before the National Association for the Advancement of Art* (London: Longmans, 1901).
398 Ibid.

motivated by a desire to see architecture secure control over industrial production, as evidenced by his plan for the restoration of the German economy:

> Our movement is in the process of creating what we might call a new style of life. This is the true objective of the modern applied arts. The creation of a new interior is only one step towards the transformation of the design of the apartment and the home which contains this interior. [...] This reestablishment of an architectural culture is the first condition of all the arts.[399]

His comments seem indisputable. At this time in France, Henri Cazalis, neither an architect nor a designer nor a painter but a poet and doctor, observed the disastrous repercussions of industrialization and the rural exodus on the health of city dwellers. He concluded that Morris's propositions for interior decoration ought to be applied as quickly and widely as possible. After demonstrating a causal link between disease and unsanitary living conditions in Paris, he drew up a series of precepts and treaties on the fittings, organization, and decoration of interior space. Like Morris before him, Cazalis decried the separation and lack of coherence between the arts:

> Our major and our minor arts, our artists who work in too great a solitude, too distant from one another; there must be a unity that we lack at

399 Hermann Muthesius, inaugural lecture of a cycle on the state of the applied arts at the Berlin Commercial College, Spring 1907; published as "Die Bedeutung des Kunstgewerbes," in Julius Posner, *Anfänge des Funktionalismus: Von Arts and Crafts zum Deutschen Werkbund* (Berlin: Verlag Ullstein, 1964), 176–87. This lecture caused much consternation among the audience and eventually led to the foundation of the Deutscher Werkbund in October that year.

> present, a direction, a leadership even, rather than the present anarchy; we must have a Morris, a man of genius who could provide this, yet at present we are lacking this man.[400]

Again echoing Morris's beliefs, the broad reforms that he proposed necessitated the unity of different arts and a comprehensive approach wherein even seemingly trivial decorative elements would receive due attention: "W. Morris [...] began his great artistic reform with the transformation of wallpaper."[401] For Cazalis, each aspect of decoration and the interior had a role to play in the reforms to public health and social organization that he envisaged:

> Art [is] in everything [is] everywhere, art [is] for all [...] art everywhere means first and foremost art at home, and throughout the home, and art in the village, and in the town, in every street and on every square; it means art in each public building, and most of all those buildings destined for the working classes, the crowds, what I call "houses of the people," from the school to the station, from the barracks to the hospital.[402]

For Cazalis, decoration, nature, and architecture were linked in a harmonious continuum that emanated outward from art to encompass all aspects of existence. Fifty years before, Morris had expressed his hope that "art will make our streets as beautiful as the woods, as elevating as the mountain-sides."[403] Cazalis similarly imagined decoration

400 Lahor, *William Morris*, 51 (see note 198).
401 Lahor, *L'art pour le peuple*, 10 (see note 208).
402 Lahor, *Les habitations au bon marché*, 64 (see note 192).
403 Morris, "The Lesser Arts," in *Political Writings*, 55.

and the home as a totality that would "commencer à la maison, et la continuer partout."[404] This perspective, passed down from Morris to Cazalis, gave a decisive role to the unity of the arts, one that promised to overturn the hierarchy and divisions that had allowed architecture to assert its dominance.

The aesthetic of the unified whole can be found across the work and thought of European avant-gardists from Wassily Kandinsky to the Futurists. It is one that can also account for Jugendstil and the Viennese Modernstyl, as well as Art Nouveau. It demands that each and every production be an aesthetic expression and concentration of the greater, all-encompassing total work. This was also the goal of L'Eplattenier's Cours supérieur and the Bauhaus: both aimed to redraw the disciplinary map. However, Gropius's program at once continued and inverted Morris's vision by proposing an entirely new model for the relationships between the disciplines based on fusing the total work of art with total art. This was how Gropius, echoing Morris, proposed to elevate the lesser arts to the level of the beaux arts. In a speech made to students at the first exhibition of their work in July 1919, he made clear his intentions:

> No large spiritual organizations, but small, secret, self-contained societies, lodges. Conspiracies will form which will want to watch over and artistically shape a secret, a nucleus of belief, until from the individual groups a universally great, enduring, spiritual-religious idea will rise again, which finally must find its crystalline expression in a great Gesamtkunstwerk. And this great total work of art, this cathedral of the future, will then

404 "Begin in the home, and continue far beyond it." Lahor, *L'art pour le peuple*, 77.

> shine its abundance of light into the smallest objects of everyday life.[405]

In his 1919 manifesto, published for the school's inauguration, Gropius raised the question once again, insisting that he aimed to put an end to the divisions between the various arts, stating that the goal of the school would be "to reunify all the disciplines of practical art—sculpture, painting, handicrafts, and the crafts" while underlining the importance of the total work of art.[406] Gropius perpetuated and expanded upon Morris's belief that objects ought to contribute to the unity of the home, but with an important difference: unlike Morris, the founder of the Bauhaus believed that they ought to correspond to a higher aesthetic ideal that broke with the past and pointed toward a better future. He aimed to make the Bauhaus aesthetic an expression of the political rupture he envisaged and a means of disseminating its new, democratic values.

In fact, a letter sent to the painter Fritz Mackensen in 1915 shows that even before the foundation of the Bauhaus, Gropius had a clear vision of its educational mission and communal structure; he set out his ideas and belief that architecture ought to act as the cornerstone of the other artistic disciplines to be taught in the school:

> In your last letter you spoke of a small, independent architecture school... I am not able to conceive my position as holding the lecturer's chair of an architecture class, and could never view the teaching of architecture as a subdivision, since it is all-encompassing.[407]

405 Gropius, "Address to the Students," in Wingler, *Bauhaus*, 36 (see note 224).
406 Gropius, "Program of the Staatliche Bauhaus," in Wingler, *Bauhaus*, 31.
407 Walter Gropius to Fritz Mackensen, October 19, 1915, in Wingler, *Bauhaus*, 22.

Gropius was equally explicit in his belief in the superiority of architecture in his 1919 inaugural program for the school, where he stated, "The ultimate aim of all visual arts is the complete building,"[408] positioning his own discipline as the culmination of a totality that encompassed both the new man and his work. He further stated, with regard to the school, "The new structure of the future, [...] will embrace architecture and sculpture and painting in one unity and [...] will one day rise toward heaven from the hands of a million workers like the crystal symbol of a new faith."[409] Gropius thus inverted the role that Morris had set out for design by denying its autonomy and reasserting its subjection to architecture. The artist and designer Bruno Munari later offered an analysis of this decisive moment: "The misunderstanding was likely due to the fact that the legendary teachers of the first school of design [...] were for the most part architects, painters, and sculptors. They nonetheless gave rise to a new aesthetic figure: the designer."[410]

Gropius insisted in his 1919 speech that the role of the new school was not to create practical, everyday objects:

> [During the period before the war] we designed artistic ashtrays and beer mugs, and in that way hoped to work up to the great building. All that by smooth organization. That was an incredible presumption on which we were shipwrecked, and now things will be reversed.[411]

By employing the homogenizing model of the total work of art, Gropius clearly reaffirmed the architect's superiority:

408 Gropius, "Program of the Staatliche Bauhaus," in Wingler, *Bauhaus*, 31.
409 Ibid.
410 Bruno Munari, preface to *Artista e designer* (Bari: Laterza, 1971), 9.
411 Gropius, "Address to the Students," in Wingler, *Bauhaus*, 36.

"This great total work of art, this cathedral of the future, will then shine its abundance of light into the smallest objects of everyday life."[412] Gropius's totalizing vision is characteristic of the broad educational program that he defined for the Bauhaus. In the school's first Expressionist incarnation, he sought to unify art and life, frequently using the metaphor of the "cathedral of the future" to describe the fusion of architecture, painting, and sculpture in a single form. But throughout the expressionist stage, and indeed its subsequent constructivist and functionalist incarnations, the unity of the arts promoted by the Bauhaus always conferred upon them a secondary role, while architecture's hegemony was reinforced. However, whether historical irony or simply a sign of the times, the fact remains that it was not until Hannes Meyer took over as the school's director in 1926 that architecture was taught as a discipline.

Before 1926, the context of the total work of art gave rise to an unintentional paradox. Gropius's desire to carry out his unifying project under the aegis of architecture clearly detracted from the principle of harmony and equality between the arts that he and his fellow teachers extolled. The situation was at odds with Kandinsky's notion that each work ought to be created according to its own rules and specificities. Despite the risks of compromising his initial project, Gropius would prevail with his architectural interpretation of the total work of art at the Bauhaus. In 1922, he was forced to reorient his program, and in order to raise its profile and reiterate the school's totalizing project he announced a new slogan: "Art and Technics: A New Unity."[413] To this end he removed Johannes Itten, who had defined much of the school's teaching, from his post. Itten was replaced by

412 Ibid.
413 See Gropius and Bayer, *Bauhaus: 1919–1928*, 80 (see note 230).

László Moholy-Nagy, who substituted Gropius's total work of art for a "total work" that he believed stemmed from a collective "biological necessity" that draws all of humanity toward a universality or the "totality of life."[414]

The question of unity was far from settled. In his 1923 article "Bauhaus Week in Weimar," Giedion described the extraordinary creativity he had witnessed at the school's exhibition in August, including an impassioned plea for architecture. After stressing his admiration for Oskar Schlemmer's *Triadic Ballet*, he discussed the hierarchy of the various disciplines and the supremacy of painting before despairing at the state of architecture within the Bauhaus. To illustrate his concern, he described the model *Am Horn*, a small, single-family home that had been on display at the exhibition, and suggested that it was "doubtful that this plan—designed by a painter—will come to very much."[415] When the painter, the architect, and the designer *all* appear to be qualified to draw up plans for the house as they would an item of furniture, the distinction between design, art, and architecture is called into question.

The paradigm for this approach comes from the idea of a collaboration between different art forms, before it manifests as a hegemonic orchestration by a single architect. It is well known that the Bauhaus was explicitly conceived as a total work of art where all artistic disciplines were organized under the broader umbrella of "architecture." Less obviously, this original model extended its prerogatives to the second generation of modern architects across the globe. This is what Mark Wigley signals with the concept of design as "totalizing agent" in his essay "Whatever Happened to Total Design?":

414 László Moholy-Nagy, *Vision in Motion* (Chicago: Paul Theobald, 1947), 28.
415 Sigfried Giedion, "Bauhaus und Bauhaus-Woche zu Weimar," *Das Werk*, no. 9 (1923): 232–34.

> Clearly, the dream of the total work of art did not fade in modernism's wake. On the contrary, all of the issues raised by architects and theorists of recent generations that seem, at first, to signal the end of the idea of the total work of art turn out to be, on closer look, a thin disguise of the traditional totalizing ambitions of the architect.[416]

The will for collaboration seems to become compromised by the drive for the supremacy of architects, and for an expansionist movement that blurs the limits between interior and exterior.

Curiously, such totalizing ambitions have found a singular expression in the production of furniture pieces. Furniture was not generally considered by modernist architects to be a discipline per se, but it proved to be a playground and an equivalent for architectural construction, different only in terms of scale, with the idea that a chair, for instance, was a reduction of architecture. This came at the expense of design, with architects from Saarinen to the Smithsons seeking to consolidate their discipline's control over furniture by discussing furnishing as a "concentrate" of architecture. This conception of the relationship between architecture and design became more entrenched with Charles and Ray Eames and the position they occupied within the field: given their industrial output, the majority of which was items of furniture, are they to be thought of as architects or as designers? The Eameses do not fit neatly into the latter category, and often refused the label of designer: Charles trained as an architect at Washington University in Saint Louis, although he did not complete his studies, while his future wife, Ray Hoffman, studied

416 Wigley, "Whatever Happened to Total Design?," 5 (see note 60).

painting for eight years before collaborating with him. Thanks to production runs with the likes of Herman Miller, the couple won international acclaim as furniture designers, while numerous films and exhibitions attest to their promotional skills. Yet Charles Eames situated his work firmly within the field of architecture, which in his eyes encompassed everything from "the setting of a breakfast table to a circus performance."[417]

The couple produced the first sketches for their *Case Study House No. 8* in Santa Monica in 1945, and construction was completed toward the end of 1949. The building, created as part of a series of architects' homes sponsored by the American magazine *Arts & Architecture* under editor John Entenza, represents a particularly significant moment in the shifting relationship between architecture and furniture. In both formal and structural terms it bears a strong resemblance to the *Eames Storage Unit*, a bookcase designed by the couple between 1950 and 1952 and produced by Herman Miller. The home and bookcase share the same structures, standardized materials, color palette, and approach to the use of space. The bookcase could pass for a scaled-down model for the house:

> After the construction of their "Case Study House No. 8" in 1949, Charles and Ray Eames reworked the concept of modular wall units from the ground up. In keeping with the construction and design pattern of their house, they developed a form of freestanding shelves which is assembled according to the principles of industrial mass production [...]. Although the reasonably priced building set was suitable for homes

417 Beatriz Colomina, "Reflections on the Eames House in the Work of Charles and Ray Eames," in *The Work of Charles and Ray Eames: A Legacy of Invention*, ed. Donald Albrecht (New York: Harry N. Abrams, 1997), 129.

> as well as offices and went on display in 1950 in six different variations at the influential exhibit "Good Design" cosponsored by the Museum of Modern Art, it was still difficult to sell [...] because of the complicated assembly involved.[418]

The storage unit was, of course, modeled on the house and reinterpreted its modularity and key motifs. However, unlike the house it offered an original interpretation of the functionalist principles of the early twentieth century, in particular those of the Wiener Werkstätte, De Stijl, and the Bauhaus, as evidenced by its standardized elements, largely geometric forms, and primary color blocking.[419] The case of the Eameses shows that no matter how important a role design might have played in a given project, its creators still tended to minimize its significance based on their preference for architecture. Far from being specific to the Eameses or the United States, this attitude was equally prevalent in Europe. France offers a number of similar examples, such as that of Charlotte Perriand, who trained at the École de l'Union centrale des arts décoratifs in Paris and exhibited with the Société des artistes décorateurs before becoming one of the founding members of the Union des Artistes Modernes in 1929. Despite an education and career that would appear to point toward the decorative arts, or else design, Perriand always considered herself to be an architect.

The prevalence of architects in the field of furniture production can in part be explained by the awareness of spatial issues that is integral to their profession; often architects' prolonged and extensive involvement in projects

418 Mathias Schwartz-Clauss et al., eds., *100 Masterpieces from the Vitra Design Museum Collection* (Weil-am-Rhein: Vitra, 1996), 84.
419 Ibid.

suggests a difficulty conceiving of the life of the spaces they create that begins once the project is completed and moves beyond their control. The presence of objects and furniture is often considered incompatible with the work of the architect.[420] The conflict between Mies van der Rohe and Edith Farnsworth is a particularly telling example. At the origin of their quarrel was Farnsworth's refusal to accept Mies's furniture for the home she had commissioned him to design. This episode was anticipated by a poster created by Willi Baumeister for the 1927 exhibition in Stuttgart entitled "Die Wohnung" (The dwelling) that Mies had overseen: in response to the question posed by the poster "Wie wohnen?" (How should we live?), a large red cross was scrawled across a bourgeois interior. Little wonder that he was unable to accept Farnsworth's desire to furnish her new house with traditional furniture. While this clearly evidenced a lack of understanding on Farnsworth's part as to the nature of the modernist project that her new home embodied, Mies's indignation points toward a reversal in the power relations between client and architect. Though rarely acknowledged, it seems that architects often felt that it was more coherent to create spaces that could not be modified in line with the tastes of their future inhabitants.

The situation was by no means a new one, with Baillie Scott, a disciple of Morris, describing a similar dynamic as early as 1895:

> It is difficult for the architect to draw a fixed line between the architecture of house and the furniture. The conception of an interior must necessarily include the furniture which is to be used in it, and

420 Alice T. Friedman, "Domestic Differences," in *Not at Home: The Suppression of Domesticity in Modern Art and Architecture*, ed. Christopher Reed (London: Thames & Hudson, 1996), 190.

> this naturally leads to the conclusion that the architect should design the chairs and table as well as the house itself.[421]

The Modern Movement developed this notion on a more theoretical level, but also continued to perpetuate the underlying idea of unity between the interior and exterior, and between space and furniture: "The inside and the outside of a modern structure are regarded as one thanks to the technological development of building with large sheets of glass, and the aesthetic development of sensing objects simultaneously from many vantage points."[422] Giedion explores the emergence of this relationship between architecture and furniture through his historical study of furniture in *Mechanization Takes Command*, suggesting that it resulted from the reorganization of elements previously thought of as distinct into a new unity. Giedion dates the tendency toward totalizing conceptions of space to the 1920s, linking trends in America to the corresponding decline in the standing of the decorative artist in Europe. In this context, he maintains, the architect gradually rose to prominence as the only figure capable of overseeing the synthesis of the arts with space:

> Around 1920 the architect superseded the decorative artist as the author of new furniture types [...]. By the new standards, the decorative artist, superficially changing forms, had failed. The initiative passed into the hands of architects. Architect and designer merged into one person.

421 M. H. Baillie Scott, "The Ideal Suburban House," *The Studio*, no. 16 (January 1899): 127–32.
422 Peter Blake, *The Master Builders* (New York: Knopf, 1960); quoted in Marian Page, *Furniture Designed by Architects* (New York: Watson-Guptill, 1984), 7.

> And many who began as designers later revealed themselves as architects [...]. "Looking at present-day trends" we commented in 1931, "one sees that the decorator has lost all prestige as a designer of furniture. Almost every important inspiration comes from architects now setting standards for the future. Today the slightest item of furniture must participate in the new architectural spirit—a fusion that the architect takes quite for granted."[423]

Giedion points to what he sees as the weaknesses of the decorator, who was limited to "superficially changing forms," which left the field clear for the architect, the only figure apparently capable of carrying out a comprehensive work. Giedion's reductive view of the decorator is surprising given that he witnessed firsthand the particularities of the profession, having founded a furniture company, Wohnbedarf, in Zurich in 1931. How should we read his assertion of architecture's superiority as a unifying force if not in terms of the Modern Movement's bias in favor of the discipline? When Giedion discusses the America of the 1920s, he observes a transformation in the role of the architect and a tendency to assert ownership over the idea of the totality, before describing the spread of this trend to Europe in the 1930s. The harmony promised by the total work of art, wherein each individual would work as part of a wider whole toward a unified project, thus gave way to a new vision—although it stemmed from the same notion of the total work of art. Here was a totalitarian approach—a new disciplinary order in which modern architecture was to

423 *Die Bauwelt*, no. 33 (1933); quoted in Giedion, *Mechanization Takes Command*, 484 (see note 1).

reign supreme—which was all the more striking given that the modern myth of the totality was in direct opposition to the idea of a fragmented and uneasy modernity suggested by Loos. Such a concept of totality proves to be equally distant from the ideas of Gropius and his Bauhaus colleagues, who held modernity to be a universal concept, but considered the total work of art to be a vestige of Romanticism.

The total work of art was, however, a concept that proved to be vague enough to survive its inconsistencies, and to mutate into a "synthesis of the arts" in the hands of Le Corbusier, who set out the broad principles of his vision in the 1935 text "La sainte alliance des arts majeurs."[424] Perriand would in turn deploy the idea to describe her work and collaborations: "As always I promoted integration: architecture-equipment-environment, to accentuate an interior made of harmonious volumes."[425] While the synthesis of the arts tended toward the expression of a totality, any unity it offered was provisional: this conception held architecture to be a self-reliant entity that only occasionally, and only under specific conditions, entered into contact with other fine arts. Unlike previous conceptualizations of the total work of art, here architecture was preserved from "contamination" by other disciplines, and its absolute autonomy was the precondition of any synthesis with other arts. Thus Le Corbusier's vision marked the completion of a process, initiated by Gropius, that broke entirely with Morris's ideas. Perpetuating an already suspect model of unity, the synthesis of the arts revived once more a system of clear distinctions between the arts in which there was an irrefutable hierarchy. Consistently used as a model for

424 Le Corbusier, "La sainte alliance des arts majeurs ou le grand art en gésine," *La bête noire,* no. 4 (July 1935); and *L'Architecture d'Aujourd'hui* 6, nos. 5–7 (May–July 1935): 86.
425 Perriand, *Une vie de création*, 231 (see note 32).

the other disciplines by the Bauhaus, architecture eclipsed the other arts, whose value its proponents no longer sought to affirm, and thus the founding principles of architecture's unifying project were abandoned, even while architects themselves denied accusations of hegemony.

Futurama: The Spectacular, Streamlined Future

The totalizing vision of antidesign was almost without precedent. Perhaps the only significant exception was the Streamline movement, which predated antidesign by some forty years. Its proponents—Raymond Loewy, Norman Bel Geddes, Egmont Arens, and Henry Dreyfuss, to name only the most well-known designers—sought to demonstrate the all-encompassing nature of their discipline. The values of these designers were clearly in opposition to those of the Modern Movement and its supporters at the MoMA and in the architectural profession. The fierce criticism faced by Streamlining was at least in part an offensive led by modern architects against a younger generation of industrial designers who, in going beyond the creation of industrially produced consumer goods, threatened to overstep the bounds of their profession.

Characterized by its simplified, smooth, and slender forms, Streamlining offered a vision of design that was efficient, seductive, and most importantly all-encompassing. Streamlining promised to reshape the entire world, and while there was a certain naivety in its approach to transformation, the movement was also subversive in its brazen redefinition of the designer's prerogatives—as per Loewy's famous aphorism, the discipline now dealt in everything from lipstick to locomotives.[426] By disregarding the production of useful goods and the consumer satisfaction that conventionally defined the industrial designer's work, Streamline challenged the validity of architecture and

426 Raymond Loewy, "Raymond Loewy, Designer of Locomotives and Lipsticks, Creates a Future Travel Dress," *Vogue*, February 1939, 141.

urbanism's monopoly over other fields. Loewy's position signaled the beginning of design's annexation of adjacent territories, as he and his fellow designers set out to show that everything could be streamlined.

The most striking example of this expansionist bent, which saw design upset conventions established by greats such as Gropius and Le Corbusier, took form in New York at the 1939 World's Fair. The event celebrated the future with an all-American vision of modernity: the first talking robot was presented to the public alongside stands displaying everything from the latest industrial packaging to the fantastic pastry creations of the Wonder Bakery. This was a showcase of the urban and political future. Invited to exhibit their work, Bel Geddes offered a vision of the America of tomorrow, Loewy a journey into outer space, and Dreyfuss a democratic urban utopia; together, they staged a spectacular vision of the city of the future to the general public.

Bel Geddes's "Futurama" was by far the most ambitious of the works, and the most popular. General Motors commissioned him to imagine the world of the 1960s for a display in the company's pavilion. The work occupied 3,120 square meters, with 500,000 models of buildings, including an all-glass skyscraper city. These were connected by motorways and surrounded by countryside dotted with experimental farms. "Futurama" was an elaborate demonstration of the new order that design proposed to establish and lead.

The installation was a major highlight for the exhibition's 70,000 daily visitors, with 2,000 per hour braving the long queues to take in Bel Geddes's vision of the future.[427]

427 See Olivier Lugon, "Des cheminements de pensée: La gestion de la circulation dans les expositions didactiques," in "Oublier l'exposition," ed. Pierre Leguillon, special issue, *Art Press*, no. 21 (2000): 21.

Visitors entered in pairs and were seated in comfortable chairs that moved them slowly along a conveyor belt encircling a diorama on two levels. From this moving vantage point, they were treated to a spectacle of the future in all its glory: motorways filled with 50,000 miniature cars, gravity-defying skyscraper cities, and high-tech factories, farms, and dairies. Each seat was fitted with an earpiece, and a narrator guided visitors through the "many wonders that may develop in the not-too-distant future."[428] Removed from the present day, they became temporary citizens of this futuristic world:

> Futurama culminated in a life-size intersection of a city of tomorrow, complete with advanced-model autos (and an auto showroom), an apartment house, a theater, and a department store in which visitors could buy souvenirs—virutal proof of their time travel. If the first part of Futurama resembled a kind of 3-D cinematic experience, this final element must have left visitors feeling as if they had actually entered into a science fiction movie, stepped into an essentially cinematic vision of the future.[429]

All in all, the tour of the future lasted sixteen euphoric minutes. The pavilion attested to Bel Geddes's background as a stage designer, here magnified to an immersive, cinematic scale. The design on show was characterized by the exhilaration of constant movement and speed associated with Streamline. At its heart was a desire to see design go beyond the creation of everyday commodities, and to

428 D. J. Bush, *The Streamlined Decade* (New York: George Braziller, 1975).
429 J. P. Telotte, "'I Have Seen the Future': The New York World's Fair as Science Fiction," in *A Distant Technology: Science Fiction Film and the Machine Age* (Hanover, NH: Wesleyan University Press, 1999), 162.

extend the domestic space to encompass city and countryside, with the style applied to skyscrapers and dairy trucks alike.

The 1939 World's Fair marked the advent of a generation of designers ready to reshape their country in the present as well as in a near future that promised happiness, democracy, and progress. Given its spectacular scale and use of technology, it is hardly surprising that "Futurama" would become a model for subsequent exhibitions that sought to offer a vision of the future. The dialogue between the present and the future, the linear projection forward in time, and a speculative approach were the tools of choice for the Streamline movement as a whole. Its expansionist version of design thus implied not only the occupation of new disciplinary territories but also temporal ones, as evidenced by the badge each visitor received at the end of their voyage through the "Futurama" installation, which proudly proclaimed, "I have seen the future." Bel Geddes's visionary project embodied an audacious aspiration, one enthusiastically related by fellow designer Harold Van Doren, who considered him to be nothing short of genius:

> The real popularizer of the Streamline idea was a genius of the theater—who put his talent and enthusiasm into the visualization of a world of the future [...]. It was in the air. What Geddes did was dramatize it, well before it had really arrived, and so convincingly as to crystallize the scattered forces already tending in that direction, and bring reality to a tendency which up to then had consisted of theory and tentative experiment.[430]

430 Harold Van Doren, *Industrial Design: A Practical Guide* (New York: McGraw-Hill, 1940), 152.

The power of "Futurama" lay in the exhibition's ability to give form to a continuous and limitless process of expansion and production that transgressed the boundaries of industrial and product design and thus reshaped the very space in which these objects existed. Van Doren praised Bel Geddes's ability to extrapolate parallel tendencies in different fields to form a coherent anticipation of the future. In Bel Geddes's work, the world became a vast interior space that fell within his discipline's purview and could therefore be reshaped as he saw fit. This was the underlying principle of "Futurama," wherein Bel Geddes, a designer, gave form to an entire world without the help of the urbanists, planners, architects, and countless other professionals who would have conventionally had a role to play. Here, the interior and the exterior fall within an exponential, outward movement from everyday objects, and are treated as one and the same. With "Futurama," Bel Geddes thus asserted design's ability to offer an all-encompassing, comprehensive worldview. It was a notion reinforced by fellow designer Dreyfuss, who created the 190-meter-tall *Trylon* obelisk and the 65-meter-wide *Perisphere*, the two monumental emblems of the World's Fair. Inside the *Perisphere*, visitors could discover another diorama of a futuristic metropolis, the *Democracity*. In the Chrysler pavilion, meanwhile, Loewy devised the *Astroport*, a spectacular installation featuring a space-ready rocket on a launchpad. Once on board, the public were plunged into darkness and treated to a thunderous take-off simulation:

> Every twenty minutes a batch of visitors was admitted to a huge half-cylindrical area, in total darkness except for the spotlighted rocket in its launch pad installed in a shallow pit on one side of the space. The launch area showed all kinds

> of lights, white and colored, blinking and conveying a feeling of activity and suspense. A deep rhythmic sound, the whirling of powerful motors, compressors, and high-frequency sound waves made the whole area vibrate and pulse [...] the rocket seemed made ready for lift-off and the audience were on edge. Then at the sound of sirens Lift off! In a moment, a blinding flash of hundreds of strobe lights and the roar of compressed air suddenly released—the rocket, through optical illusion, seemed to disappear overhead in the blackness of space. Then total silence while a gradually diminishing point of light faded away to the stars.[431]

With the *Astroport*, Loewy had created, perhaps unintentionally, a stunning metaphor for design, giving literal form to its ambition to conquer the universe.

431 Raymond Loewy, *Industrial Design* (Woodstock, NY: Overlook Press, 1979), 108.

Architecture as Furniture

Following the Second World War, the idea of unity remained omnipresent, albeit in a slightly different form. The relationship between architecture and design reemerged as a central question, with Ernesto Nathan Rogers offering one interpretation in 1946, with his famous expression "Dal cucchiaio alla città" (From the spoon to the city).[432] Rogers's formula evidences the notion inherited from modern architecture's golden age, that the relationship was merely a question of scale. Whether at a small (design) or large (urbanism) scale, it held that the disciplines of design and architecture were ultimately one, and that their approaches were also identical: "The architect's role is to transform into poetry all formal representation: from the spoon to the city."[433]

In 1967, the radical architects began their series of theoretical projects. Their production of furniture around this time attests to the survival of this conception of the relationship between architecture and design well beyond the crisis of the Modern Movement. The furniture that they created was first exhibited as a series of prototypes, before being produced by furniture houses such as Gufram, founded by the Guglielminetti brothers in Turin in 1968, and Poltronova, founded in 1957 by Sergio Cammilli following a meeting with Sottsass. Once the radicals' furniture had gone into production, it was advertised in interior design and architecture magazines such as *Domus* and *Casabella*. This was the case for Archizoom Associati's

432 This expression is sometimes attributed to Walter Gropius or Max Bill; see François Burckhardt et al., eds., *L'école d'Ulm: Textes et manifestes* (Paris: Éditions du Centre Pompidou, 1988), 5. However, I have been unable to find any trace of this expression in texts by Gropius and Bill.

433 See Anty Pansera and Alfonso Grassi, *L'Italia del design, trent'anni di dibattito* (Casale Monferrato: Marietti, 1986), 16. The origin of this phrase remains uncertain.

Safari sofa, designed in 1968 and manufactured that same year by Poltronova. The advertisement's copy featured a characteristic mix of humor and aggression:

> An imperial piece
> in the dreariness of your domestic walls.
> A piece that is finer than you.
> A very beautiful piece
> that you would not deserve.
> Clear your sitting-room!
> Clear also your life![434]

The sofa consisted of four plastic modules, which, seen from the outside, formed a square. With its imposing scale, it would take up most of the available space in an average living room. Each element was hollowed out to form a quarter of a circle, and combined they formed a comfortable seating unit. They were upholstered in colorful or leopard-print fabric, while the exterior shell was white plastic. The leopard print can be seen as a nod to English Pop art, in particular the bodybuilder clad in a Tarzan-style singlet in Richard Hamilton's 1957 collage *Just what is it that makes today's homes so different, so appealing?*[435] The *Safari* sofa's leopard motif combined the symbolism of Pop art with that of exoticism; these multiple levels of interpretation were intentional and indeed an important part of Archizoom Associati's work. The group always worked by adding complexity, for, as Paola Navone and Bruno Orlandoni explain, "in the image, [they] found the means of passing judgment on the society of the image."[436]

434 This advertisement was printed in a number of publications, including the October 1971 issue of *Domus*.
435 Richard Hamilton, *Just what is it that makes today's homes so different, so appealing?*, 1956, collage, 25 × 26 cm, Kunsthalle Tübingen, Zundel Collection.
436 Navone and Orlandoni, *Architettura "radicale"*, 27 (see note 276).

Beyond the work of the radicals, Italian furniture production in 1968 and '69 primarily consisted of furniture houses re-editioning the classic modernist furniture pieces they had acquired the rights to, such as those by Breuer and Le Corbusier. Faced with this conservatism, in 1969 Archizoom Associati created the *Mies* lounge chair, a geometric steel structure consisting of two separate elements. The seat was made of light-brown rubber, with a cowhide pillow referencing Le Corbusier and Perriand's *LC4* chaise longue. Although at first its function appears enigmatic, the lounger's apparent rigidity is offset by the obvious suppleness of its latex seat, whose flexibility is further emphasized once it is occupied. Neither a homage to Mies himself, who had died that year, nor to the Bauhaus, and less still to functionalism, the lounger was typical of Archizoom Associati's furniture in that it represented an antidote to the reheated modernism then in vogue. The target was less the Modern Movement itself than those who sought to sustain it at all costs rather than allowing it to pass away with its dignity intact.

The *Mies* project anticipated the intentionally artificial, autonomous urban project proposed by Archizoom Associati the following year: *No-Stop City*.[437] Drawing on the industrial logic of the supermarket and the factory, *No-Stop City* appropriated and adapted utopian models to offer a critical representation of the state of the contemporary metropolis. The result was an urban environment governed by overconsumption, whose seemingly infinite interior drew on the "supermarket typology" as the only space in which "the logic of the industrial system" is expressed.[438] The homogenizing rationale of the

437 See "The Radical Movement" in Branzi, *Hot House*, 63–72; Andrea Branzi, ed., *No-Stop City: Archizoom Associati* (Orléans: HYX, 2006); and Gargiani, *Archizoom Associati 1966–1974*, 169–225 (see note 370).

438 Branzi, *Hot House*, 69.

supermarket, with its artificial lighting and air conditioning, its absence of windows, and its constant advertising messages, recalls Isaac Asimov's 1953 novels *The Caves of Steel* and *The Naked Sun.*[439] These works of science fiction feature what the author defines as architectural "hardware," traditional and modern constructions, and "software," temporary and inflatable ones. Asimov provides extended descriptions of two very different planets, and emphasizes their cultural differences, partly by exploring their different architectures and the impact of each on the respective planets' inhabitants. Solaria is a relatively sparsely populated planet in comparison to the megalopolises of Earth. Its 20,000 occupants and their countless robot servants inhabit vast open-air estates, with windows opening onto nature and the sky above. On Earth, meanwhile, cities are artificial, subterranean, overcrowded, and entirely dependent on technology.

No-Stop City was founded upon a new conception of the links between architecture and design; the latter was taken as a model by the radical architects due to its association with commerce, the market, and the circulation of commodities. They believed that design's ostensible exchange with consumerism and the market could offer an example for their own discipline, and a means of renewing it. Design had, in their eyes, begun to take into account relationships and interactions between humans in modern society; it now fell to architecture to do the same. Archizoom Associati believed that the metropolis was only just becoming conscious of a revolution that was already well underway: the city had ceased to be a place, and was now better considered a system of relationships

439 Reyner Banham cites these two texts in "Triumph of Software," in *Design by Choice*, 133–37 (see note 4).

and behaviors. The city dweller was no longer a resident but a participant involved in a non-stop network of evolving relations.

The new metropolis consisted, above all, of information and images transmitted by media. The disappearance of geography, places, and sites allowed for a new idea of the city and, through this, a new conception of the role of the architect. *No-Stop City* upset the hierarchical structure in which architecture outweighed design, and was in turn itself trumped by urbanism. Archizoom Associati applied design and its capacity to deal in real and economic terms to the city, as underlined by Branzi: "The *No-Stop City* struck a direct channel between the metropolis and its furnishings. The city became a collection of beds, tables, chairs and cupboards; domestic furniture and urban fittings were made one."[440] *No-Stop City* thus represented an unexpected upturn in design's standing, coinciding with a new view of architecture that was no longer representative of a particular kind of politics, but rather of society as a whole, down to its smallest elements. This was nothing less than a head-on attack on the foundations and ideals of the Modern Movement: architecture represented neither power nor political or social authority, but rather encompassed all of these.

Archizoom Associati's appropriation of design is a complex case for historians. It sheds light upon the failure of architecture to account for the transformations taking place in postindustrial society, while simultaneously evidencing architecture's incredible capacity for criticism and transformation. Perhaps unintentionally, *No-Stop City* also bolstered design by redefining its role and conferring upon it unprecedented importance as a model and example for

440 Branzi, *Hot House*, 72.

other disciplines. Italy's architectural crisis had prevented a young generation of architects from proving their worth, thus they had turned toward furniture for the simple reason that it was easier to produce and sell than buildings. Archizoom Associati's interest in design stemmed from the possibilities offered by the industrial production of furniture and its promise to improve the lives of all.

The members of Superstudio viewed the discipline in very different terms. Superstudio had been producing furniture since their inaugural exhibition, "Superarchitettura I," and collaborated regularly with Gufram. Though it is difficult to see how the objects and furniture they produced with Gufram ought to be considered if not in terms of design, these pieces were representative of their critical stance toward the discipline. Superstudio's members worked from the same starting point as Archizoom Associati, and echoed their unequivocal condemnation of rationalism and functionalism. However, Superstudio's critical stance was accompanied by an interrogation of industrial production, which they compared to the quality of craft techniques and expertise. This was to be the basis for a dialectic, which rapidly became more complex, between craftsmanship and its tendency to seek salvation "in a primitive Arcadia or even in Alice's wonderland" on the one hand, and the formless, alienated commodities of industrialization on the other.[441] Between these two equally unsatisfactory propositions, the only winner was consumption. In order to disengage from this system, Superstudio announced in the pages of *Casabella*—the group's mouthpiece after Alessandro Mendini became its editor—its dedication to "invention design and evasion design," and act as the irrational and

441 Superstudio, "Evasion Design and Invention Design," in Lang and Menking, *Life without Objects*, 116 (see note 282).

poetic counter-proposition. It is worth returning to the counter-position to examine how Superstudio used this new approach to escape from the false dialectic outlined above. To escape the situation of postindustrial craftsmanship versus capitalist standardization, Superstudio imported the epicenter of design from functionality to poetry: "The activity of planning and operating in the field of industrial production assuming poetry and the irrational as its method, and trying to institutionalize continuous evasion of everyday dreariness created by equivocations of rationalism and functionality."[442]

Superstudio thus created an alternative to functionalist design. While the oversized, cumbersome dimensions of evasion design might recall Archizoom Associati's Trojan horses, as Roberto Gargiani and Beatrice Lampariello have suggested, there is nonetheless a significant difference between the groups' respective outputs:

> Superstudio sought to approach these "big brightly colored cumbersome" objects not as machines of war but rather as things that were "useful and full of surprises," and "to live with them and play with them together." Thanks to their narrative potential, the objects offered a means of inhibiting contradiction and conflict and an alternative to functionalism; they could be positioned in such a way as to become ambassadors of happiness and "make it possible to live with everyday dreariness." They considered that "every project has a practical function and a contemplative one, and it is this latter that evasion design seeks to develop."[443]

442 Ibid.
443 Gargiani and Lampariello, *Superstudio*, 21.

Superstudio's evasion design and the objects in which it took form represented a rejection of Archizoom Associati's chosen terrain—revolution and contamination from within the system—in favor of a more immediate joie de vivre. They thus developed a critique of consumer goods, denouncing the restrictions engendered by the alienation of liberal, contemporary society. In order to counter these restrictions, Superstudio's members turned their attention to users, who they felt had been neglected by design, and sought to enable them to become inventors in their own right: "What we want to do is lay the foundations for an existence that is one long protest: a 'be-in,'" where interior space "may become a genuine space of involvement (a stage for a continuous performance, or in other words, a place for happenings, a place for the be-in) by the agency of the design products we place in it."[444]

In order to make possible this state of "total involvement," Superstudio proposed a scenario that unfolded in two stages: First "you supply multi-significant (ambiguous) products, objects of universal use, and each user puts them to the use he thinks fit." Next "you supply the rules of a game to be played with all kinds of objects, or containers that can be filled with all kinds of things."[445] Design allowed Superstudio to give form to its objectives, and above all to colonize interior space by "introducing foreign bodies into the system,"[446] reflecting the importance they placed upon individuals and their role in society. Their approach went beyond the conception of design as being associated with either the production of consumer goods or, conversely, protests responding directly to

444 Superstudio, "Evasion Design and Invention Design," in Lang and Menking, *Life without Objects*, 117.
445 Ibid.
446 Ibid.

consumerism; they extended their exploration beyond objects and their qualities to encompass the potential behaviors of their users in a given space. Drawing inspiration from Happenings, Superstudio organized exhibitions filled with consumer goods, including food and appliances, and invited visitors to wander through the space guided only by their instincts.

Superstudio's approach represented an important step away from the object and toward the environment:

> Slowly the project-behavior took the place of the project-object, as the proposition for the Triennale di Milano of 1968 shows. [...] The structure of the pavilion—a large washing machine—induces the visitor to participate as they become part of this same spatial distribution of objects; they must complete an arduous and obligatory journey through optical, tactical, and sonic experiences bombard them with slogans and symbols in a parody of the daily bombardment of the mass media. The messages, between irony and paroxysm, are presented in the seductive guise of archicomics [*archifumetti*]. Here the behavioralist project is not a proposition but simply a reduction of designers' critical reading of reality presented in a language that can be understood by the user, one that uses codes that they are familiar with from their daily experience.[447]

The theoretical aspect of radical architecture—its promotion of unreal, utopian, and poetic models as a source of creativity—clearly entailed a paradox. On the one hand,

447 Navone and Orlandoni, *Architettura "radicale"*, 31.

as the radicals developed models denouncing existing systems and facilitating the conception of a new architecture through purely speculative means, they were fated to create abstract hypotheses; on the other, many of their items of furniture were produced by manufacturers who were also responsible for functionalist furniture destined for general consumption. The radicals could thus be criticized for having failed to extend the benefits of conceptual architecture and the utopia they envisaged beyond a single domain, and for never having addressed this contradiction inherent in their work. Ultimately, the radicals' project was to a large extent reliant on design—or at least their own conception of design.

Around this time, designers went about devising furniture and spaces, boldly taking on roles that had traditionally been the preserve of architects. In theory, they shared a great deal in terms of their approaches and goals. But in reality, neither their intentions nor the results of their work could be considered interchangeable. Where, then, is it possible to draw a line between architecture and design? For Banham, this distinction was to be found in each discipline's relationship to obsolescence; he argues in "Design by Choice" that while obsolescence is a concept alien to architecture, it has been fundamental for design.[448] Obsolescence is inherent to consumerism and market capitalism, and can in fact only exist in a wealthy, industrial society. After establishing this, Banham goes on to underline that it now appears more logical in economic terms to replace a dated or defective product with a new purchase than to have it repaired. Over a short period, this principle creates need while gaining the loyalty of the user-turned-consumer.

448 See Banham, "Design by Choice," in *Design by Choice*, 97–107.

In order to better understand the implications of the idea of obsolescence, it is worth returning to the Modern Movement and its approach to design as nothing more than a subdiscipline of architecture. Invoking history to justify this view, he notes that the Modern Movement held that the architect was the sole figure capable of devising, designing, and creating a theory of objects:

> When the Modern Movement was young, there were obvious and valid reasons for giving architects hegemony over the training of designers and the formulation of theory: architects alone of arts men had any technical training even remotely applicable to product design; alone of tech-men they had a sufficiently liberal education to be able to relate their designs to the general environment of human life; they alone had been doing anything consciously to further the practice and theory of Industrial Design.[449]

In the postwar period, architects continued to consider the interior as an indivisible unity. In the 1960s, the question returned to the fore as architects began to appropriate design. Banham demonstrates how the downfall of modernist architecture can be explained in terms of the differences between the two disciplines. He believes architects lacked the necessary skills and education to engage with the technology and processes essential to the designer's work, and thus architecture's usurpation of design could only be a partial one. Banham further develops his analysis around the fundamentally different conceptions of space and time held by each discipline.

449 Ibid., 97.

The life expectancy of the objects produced by designers differs significantly from those created by architects, who are "habituated to think in terms of a timescale whose basic unit is about half a century."[450] In a highly original analysis, Banham uses these different timescales as a means of explaining architecture's refusal of any division of tasks between disciplines. Architects, he suggests, seek to maximize the aesthetic value of their work, if possible above and beyond the delivery of the project. So while the interior decoration of a building offers both the possibility of adding further value—"Indeed, the prestige inherent in knowing that the chairs are by one of the world's greatest industrial designers and the radios by another adds a peculiar lustre to the whole operation"[451]—it also threatens to compromise the architect's work by introducing extraneous elements. What becomes of an architect-designed home once it is occupied by a working class family rather than a bourgeois one? What happens if they fill the living room with rustic or antique furniture? Such a prospect was unbearable for some modern architects, as we have already seen with Mies and Farnsworth. According to Banham's analysis, they sought to extend and sustain their control over their work for as long as possible in order to avoid this kind of emasculation.

Le Corbusier approached the question of the subsequent life of his work in a more subtle fashion, but one that seems to all the same confirm Banham's analysis. The architect deployed two complementary tactics: furniture was either present in the form of standardized pieces built into the structure itself, or ordered from catalogues such as *Manufrance*, allowing Le Corbusier to furnish his buildings

450 Ibid., 98.
451 Ibid., 100.

with relatively inexpensive and standardized furniture of quality.[452] Since he did not always systematically design the furniture for his buildings, Le Corbusier might appear to be an exception to his profession's controlling tendencies. But a closer analysis of the approach I have just discussed reveals that quite the reverse is true, albeit subtly. Le Corbusier precluded any dialogue between his architecture and its inhabitants by painstakingly planning every element, leaving no room for addition or subtraction of any kind, with submission being the only possible course of action. Banham's conclusion extended an (ironic) invitation to architects to reassess their role and share their power with others.

The analysis of obsolescence that Banham developed allowed him to raise a key distinction between architecture and design. The term "obsolescence" was drawn from the vocabulary of consumption, and referred to a given product's preprogrammed lifespan. Banham set out to define the three different types of obsolescence that had come to exist through a combination of pragmatism and cynicism: one linked to wear and tear, another to constant technical innovation, and another to arbitrarily evolving tastes. The first, obsolescence through wear, deals with a product's flawed manufacture and the choice of poor quality materials that inevitably lead to its malfunction or degradation after a certain period of time, and forces the user to replace it. The second type, technical obsolescence, relies on the incremental improvement of products; similar items are manufactured that are marginally faster, more reliable, or more effective than their predecessors. The third and final type of obsolescence defined by Banham involves

452 See Arthur Rüegg, "Les contributions de Le Corbusier à l'art d'habiter, 1912–1937: De la décoration intérieure à l'équipement," in *Le Corbusier: Une encyclopédie*, ed. Jacques Lucan (Paris: Éditions du Centre Georges Pompidou, 1985), 124–35.

the creation of products that offer users entirely new possibilities or capabilities and thus modify their preexisting needs or tastes; perhaps the most subtle and effective of the three, this is the obsolescence of taste. Such innovations, no longer technological but simply aesthetic, rely on the consumer's sense that they are represented by the products they own in order to elicit desire. This kind of obsolescence is linked to innovation, but more importantly to fashion. Existing products that are in no way defective or dysfunctional are here replaced, and not by ones that are somehow better suited to users' needs: new products simply correspond to an ever-changing idea of what a given product ought to be like. Technical obsolescence depends not only on innovation and discovery, but also on commercial decisions to manufacture and sell replacement products while existing ones are still perfectly capable of fulfilling their assigned functions. Obsolescence through wear, meanwhile, is at once the simplest and the most significant and dictates that defective products are to be replaced rather than repaired. This cycle of replacement resonated with the spirit of the 1960s and ensured the smooth functioning of consumer society and mass production. The three types of obsolescence outlined by Banham—linked to wear, technical progress, and the cycles of fashion—demonstrate that it was a complex notion, with the last two linked to psychological factors as much as material ones. Banham concluded that obsolescence was an integral part of design.

It bears considering whether or not Banham's distinction between architecture and design in terms of the lifespan of their creations remains valid through the end of the 1960s, when the inflatable architecture of Archigram, the Utopie group, and Walter Pichler first appeared, along with the self-supporting structures of Antti Lovag and

Buckminster Fuller. On the whole, Banham's distinction does indeed hold: while renewal was a fundamental notion for this architectural "software," the economic dimension of obsolescence was merely incidental and could not really be said to be a factor in their conception of architectural projects. In obsolescence, Banham had therefore found a reliable means of distinguishing his twin passions of architecture and design from one another; this provided him with firm ground from which to argue for a critical distinction between the two disciplines:

> The aesthetics of serial production must be the aesthetics of the popular arts, not of fine arts.
> To apply durable and time-bound aesthetic procedures to consumable and non-traditional products can only cheapen those procedures and—as in so much Victorian design—debases the fine arts without benefiting the expendable arts.[453]

In this context, it is clear that Banham places architecture among the fine arts. While Banham shows that obsolescence provides one means of differentiating architecture and design, others are clearly possible, such as the relationship of each field to industry. For example, in structural terms, radical Italian design relied on small- to medium-scale firms that were flexible enough to put projects into production faster than larger industrial operations. This was why Colombo integrated distribution networks as a key consideration in his projects.

Though some architects sought to maintain the home and all its constituent elements as the exclusive preserve of their profession, others were ready to accept the division

453 Reyner Banham, "Space for Decoration: A Rejoinder," *Design*, no. 79 (July 1955): 24.

of responsibilities. Colombo's assertion of design's autonomy created a break that could only come at the expense of architecture. The philosopher Henri Van Lier, who was invited to write the preface of *Qu'est-ce que le design?* in 1969, had attempted ten years earlier to explain the new situation faced by the two disciplines in his book *Les arts de l'espace*:

> The mechanistic character of the decorative arts is so great and so linked to their ancillary role, that it has sometimes come to define them. In truth, we had to take the precaution [...] of silencing architecture, as this discipline, too, accords a significant place to mechanized work, with all the intermediaries that this implies. So mechanization cannot serve as our criteria for distinguishing decoration from major art—instead we must think in terms of subordination and non-subordination. However, if we were to insist on defining the decorative in terms of the machine, we could avoid the confusion introduced by architecture by limiting our discussion to small-scale mechanization, the kind that consists of a minute attention to detail and which is sometimes called "industry."[454]

Long considered a constitutive element of architecture at the service of its parent discipline, design now turned its close ties with industry to its own advantage, in context of the failure of architecture to take into account the ongoing industrialization of society. Design's newfound legitimacy

454 Henri Van Lier, *Les arts de l'espace: Peinture – Sculpture – Architecture – Arts Décoratifs* (Paris: Casterman, 1959), 330–31.

made it possible to consider its contribution to changes that had taken place simultaneously in other disciplines, as Branzi argues:

> The Italian object, which lies at the bottom of the material culture pyramid in a perpetually interrupted continuity which ought to lead to never realized global systems [...]. Long before the advent of industrialization, the object was the protagonist of an environmental (rather than a general) revolution in Italian culture, one which did not always refer to architecture but in fact often preceded or straddled it.[455]

But this was a contentious reading shared by few; Claude Parent, for example, argued that design ought to be grateful to architecture for its increased visibility:

> Much later, design (or *l'esthétique industrielle*, as M. [Jacques] Viénot called it in France) stepped out of the shadows and its decorative obsession thanks to the creative and theoretical action of architects [...]. Architects carry the heavy responsibility and the tragic glory to have fought for and promoted design, they have mounted this warhorse with it, in order to win architecture's right to modernity; for this, they would lose for many years the Ariadne's thread of the architectural endeavor.[456]

It is worth remembering at this point that the close relationship between design and the economy has been a sensitive

455 Branzi, *Introduzione al design italiano*, 13.
456 Parent, "Face à face," in "Le design," 19 (see note 49).

issue throughout the history of design; after all, the key purpose of Morris's initial definition, which drew on Ruskin's moral, economic, and political critique of design, and relied on an abstract, communal notion of production, was to challenge the capitalist economic system that was in the process of establishing its hegemony. By revisiting Ruskin's ideas, Morris continued to protest against the harmful consequences of industry, in particular the exacerbation of the very inequalities and poor working conditions that it had promised to abolish, and the promotion of profit over quality. Workers and craftsmen alike urgently needed to win back the dignity they had lost as they were reduced to mere instruments of industrialization. This deeply political conception of design, which accorded it a redemptive dimension, can be found not only in the work of the hygienist movement and Art Nouveau, but also in the propositions of Van de Velde and the Deutscher Werkbund. It can be seen in the enlightened pedagogy of Charles L'Eplattenier, and would later provide fertile terrain for the Bauhaus. The rise of the Modern Movement marked a radical turning point: its conception of design was based on a rejection of historicism and tradition, and an embrace of technology and the machine. Its proponents envisioned the creation of a new and better world as the absolute end goal of all aesthetic endeavor. The difficulties faced by the designers of the 1960s can be traced back to this highly ambivalent relationship toward technology within the discipline. For the first time, designers had the means to produce on a massive scale, but, as I have attempted to show above, this newfound capability was a double-edged sword: the same economic considerations such as production and obsolescence that made it possible to distinguish architecture from design also showed the limits of the latter field. Yet they nonetheless demonstrated that by the 1960s design was unquestionably emerging from the shadows.

At the same time, the relationship between architecture and design became clearer and more mundane throughout this period. It was in this context that, in 1954, the ADI signaled its opposition to the architectural training of designers and insisted on the necessity of a specific program that would allow designers to acquire what Marco Zanuso called a "professional culture."[457] This may have been a response to calls from the likes of Giulio Castelli, then director of the plastic-furniture company Kartell, for designers to occupy key posts in industry to ensure that their vision was reproduced precisely at all stages of manufacture. What is certain is that design was moving away from decoration, which Franco Momigliano, cofounder of the Scuola italiana di Economia Industriale, dismissively referred to as "industrial makeup."[458]

The 1960s were a key period in the battle for design's disciplinary status. Colombo supported its total autonomy, for which he developed a theoretical basis through antidesign, and to which he gave material and visual form through his capsules. The radicals, on the other hand, issued their declaration that "everything is architecture."[459] As Colombo staked design's claim to the entire home environment, the radical architects attempted to redefine the same domestic space as the best expression of an architecture that had shrugged off the last vestiges of a failed modernity; the radicals approached design in terms of decorative and everyday objects by way of controdesign, while Colombo insisted that the designer was the figure best placed to shape contemporary social space, up to and

457 Pansera and Grassi, *L'Italia del design*, 39.
458 Ibid., 41.
459 Hollein, "Alles ist Architektur," 138–39 (see note 75).

including the city as a whole. These opposing positions can be seen part of a process described by Parent, who believed that "a healthy (and extremely necessary) questioning of the environment must involve the appropriate division of territories between the different disciplines."[460] Similarly, they can also be treated as evidence of a recalibration of the relationships of power between disciplines that Branzi evokes; I have previously alluded to his statement on this point, but it is worth reproducing it here in full:

> We were fully aware that the traditional hierarchies that saw town planning as a means of introducing order into the territory had been overturned. The progressive abandonment of the traditional limits of design, now seen as a form of territorial planning, fostered an understanding of the new reality of the metropolis, which could now be defined as a market for consumer goods, and of an architecture caught up in the new dimensions of design but still unable to come up with a renewed image of itself, i.e. a credible role of its own.[461]

In a strange intersection of two very different approaches, the radicals looked to design as an appropriate terrain for the experimentation necessary for their discipline's overhaul, while antidesign abandoned the creation of objects in favor of architecture in the hope of renewing design. As the struggle between the two disciplines continued, it was design that gained the upper hand and gradually became, according to Branzi, "the only discipline that [got] its hands

460 Parent, "Face à face," 20.
461 Branzi, *Hot House*, 66.

dirty in this hybrid, compromised, but terribly real universe. It works with objects and commodities, and therefore at the heart of the true problems of this age."[462] That the 1960s came to be a turning point for both disciplines was largely down to design. The emancipation of design as a discipline, and the threat that this represented to architecture's monopoly over the home, drew strength from design's newfound visibility. However, the transition was far from a smooth one, with architects continuing to perpetuate the modernist conception of design as a concentrated expression of their discipline.

At the same time as all of this, however, the leader of the Movimento d'Arte Concreta (MAC), Bruno Munari, was forging a new image of the designer. Along with the other members of the group, Munari—himself an artist and designer—embarked upon an intensive study of the "experience of artistic synthesis" in 1953.[463] Fellow members of MAC, the architects Bobi Brunori, Gigi Radice, and Mario Ravegnani Morosini called for a "systematic research method" between architectural work and "the formal and compositional work [...] of artists."[464] Their work encouraged Munari to articulate the relationship between art and industry. The group's theorists Franco Passoni and Gillo Dorfles articulated in their 1953 manifestos, "Linea e scopi del mac," and "Manifesto del MAC," respectively, to outline the reasons for the validity of a synthesis of the arts—by no means a new theory—explaining that it allowed for a "direct cooperation between technicians and artists by way of a close collaboration whose ultimate goal would be to achieve something concrete

462 Branzi, *Learning from Milan*, 15.
463 Bandini, *L'esthétique, le politique*, 52 (see note 259).
464 Ibid.

that accounts for function and creates a harmonious link between the worlds of form, space, and practical application of the collective work."[465] It was in this spirit that the MAC participated in Max Bill's project at the Ulm School: their collaboration came with the condition that design be considered an independent discipline, comprising the design of objects and visual and information design alongside planning and urbanism. The significance of design increased again: Munari went as far as to reconsider the designer as an artist, and suggest that design might be a terrain that could revitalize art and compensate for a poverty of artistic thought. His *Useless Machines*, geometric mobiles that produced nothing, were an early expression of this reflection. Having announced the end of the figure of the artist—who he dismissed as a "romantic diva"—he published the "Manifesto del Macchinismo" in 1938. In the manifesto, he declared his firm desire to produce nothing beyond the realm of the spiritual. With the manifesto as his starting point, Munari set about breaking down divisions between different categories of artistic expression, and replacing the tired figure of the artist with that of the designer. According to Munari, it fell to the designer to add a sense of grandeur to everyday life, no matter the object that they were tasked with producing. Once he had assumed his position at the head of the MAC, Munari turned his attention to the relationship between art and industry, and coined the term *artista industriale designer* to reflect his belief that the designer was "the artist of our times."[466] In an interview with Vittorio Fagone shortly before his death, Munari discussed his frequent exchanges with Colombo, and recalled how the notion

465 Ibid.
466 Bruno Munari, *L'arte come mestiere* [1966] (Rome: Laterza, 1997), 19–28.

of the "artist industrial designer" had helped to shape the principles of antidesign.[467]

Munari's project represented a radical shift in the relationships between the different arts. Colombo's career saw him move from one discipline to another: from painting to architecture to design and finally to antidesign. However, while antidesign was unequivocal in its demand to be recognized as a discipline apart, the very notion of the discipline remains a delicate issue: "When wholly true, design is without limits. If it is distorted or falsified, one cannot speak of design. There are no rules, but a very precise discipline."[468] The dynamics between the different disciplines cannot entirely be elided through the notion of the total work of art: this discourse of unity fails to entirely mask architecture's tendency to seek domination over other disciplines, antidesign included. Colombo developed antidesign in a relatively similar fashion, and while he never acknowledged such an intention, it is difficult to avoid the notion that his project was at least partially motivated by a desire to assert control over other disciplines. Antidesign was not the only factor in design's move from the industrial manufacture of objects toward the home as a whole: the crisis of modern architecture was at least as responsible. The ambition to regroup all aesthetic expressions within a single unity ultimately revealed itself to be a prescriptive idea, perhaps even a utopian one. Although it had proved to be a productive notion, it could not account for the

467 Very little evidence attests to the relationship of Joe Colombo and Bruno Munari with the exception of one interview: "When we knew each other, Joe was an artist with the nuclear group [...] at the time in Italy, there was a large movement of artists looking for new ways to communicate [...]. Joe was also interested in design and together we discussed the problems and perils of what was then a new activity. Even today design and art are often blurred and many artists believe they are capable of design when in reality their way of working is highly individual and revolves around the creation of unique pieces [...]. These arguments and other similar ones were those that we discussed with Gianni and Joe." Bruno Munari, "I fratelli Colombo," in *I Colombo*, ed. Vittorio Fagone (Milan: Mazzotta, 1995), 31.

468 Colombo, *Qu'est-ce que le design?*, n.p. (see note 43).

new expressions that came with the hierarchical changes between minor and major arts that were the result of Colombo's vision of design and the radicals' approach to architecture. Design was central to the radicals' conceptual critique that shifted the focus from production to use and went beyond previous utopian models through fiction, as in the case of Superstudio's "Twelve Cautionary Tales"; it thus proved that it had passed a key milestone toward asserting its place as an equal among all other disciplines.

For a New Culture of Design

The situation remained largely unchanged throughout the 1970s. Designers identified with the emerging postmodern movement by invoking their immediate past—controdesign—and linking it to the debate that followed Robert Venturi's landmark 1966 work, *Complexity and Contradiction in Architecture*. Venturi argued that ambiguity and uncertainty were fundamental to individual creativity:

> I like complexity and contradiction in architecture. I do not like the incoherence or arbitrariness of incompetent architecture nor the precious intricacies of picturesqueness or expressionism. Instead, I speak of a complex and contradictory architecture based on the richness and ambiguity of modern experience, including that experience which is inherent in art.[469]

Following on from their adoption of pop culture and aesthetics to distance themselves from modernity and its terminal decline, and in order to contest a Modern Movement that had become more rationalist than functionalist, designers readily adhered to Venturi's example. They began to develop and promote a language that was complex and equivocal, and that would allow design's cultural aspects to come to the fore. Eclecticism and a profusion of references became the order of the day, with bad taste, kitsch, and banality marking a new current of opposition to the rational aesthetic.

469 Robert Venturi, *Complexity and Contradiction in Architecture* [1966] (New York: Museum of Modern Art, 1977), 16.

But this dynamism was soon beset by what could be described as a "thermal" controversy: Branzi's history of Italian design contrasted "cold" design, industrially produced and destined for the mass market, with "hot" design, produced using craft techniques and in small batches for a select circle of collectors. The title of his history, *The Hot House*, was a direct allusion to this idea of a "hot" architecture that was distinct from the "cold" vision promoted by rationalism. But this distinction raised the hackles of Tomás Maldonado, who accused Branzi of using the thermal metaphor to establish a disingenuous binary: "The value judgment implicit in the terms of 'hot' and 'cold' is blatant: on the one hand, we have a cold and therefore inhuman design, and the other a hot, and therefore human, design."[470] He further denounced this approach as derivative, saying it brought nothing new to the debate:

> While these thermal metaphors are quite arbitrary, it is worth noting that the notion of hot design is far from being new. All preindustrial design, upon reflection, was hot design (that is to say an artisanal design requiring few resources and addressing a small number of people). The establishment of an opposition between cold and hot design represents an attempt to pass off as new (and even "radically" new) themes which were in fact largely debated at the end of the 19th and beginning of the 20th century.[471]

Maldonado's objection was not only to the opposition that Branzi sought to establish between the Modern Movement and its detractors; he also rejected Branzi's assertion that

470 Maldonado, "Design caldo vs. design freddo," in *Disegno industriale*, 77–79 (see note 17).
471 Ibid., 77.

the characteristics of hot design were somehow the exclusive preserve of postmodernists. For Maldonado, these qualities were present throughout the history of design and resisted any simplistic binary distinction.

Branzi's dialectical approach can be considered primarily the result of designers' difficulty in situating themselves within the economic system in which they worked. They remained unable to extricate themselves from the contradictions posed by quality design and mass production, despite hopes for a resolution having been raised in the 1960s. With characteristic elegance, Banham analyzes the advent of mass-produced design of quality as follows:

> Both designer and critic must be in close touch with the dynamics of mass-communication. The critic, especially, must have the ability to sell the public to the manufacturer, the courage to speak out in the face of academic hostility, the knowledge to decide where, when and to what extent the standards of the popular arts are preferable to those of the fine arts. He must project the future dreams and desires of people as one who speaks from within their ranks. It is only thus that he can participate in the extraordinary adventure of mass-production, which counters the old aristocratic and defeatist 19th-century slogan, "Few, but roses," and its implied corollary, "Multitudes are weeds," with a new slogan that cuts across all academic categories: "Many, because orchids."[472]

472 Through a comparison of the motor of a Bugatti and that of a Buick V8, Reyner Banham defines two distinct modes of organization, before calling for a serially produced yet quality aesthetic. See Reyner Banham, "A Throw-Away Aesthetic," in *Design by Choice*, 90–93.

But in reality, the issue was far from being settled: even though some designers rejected Branzi's thermal classification, exclusive production runs and private gallery exhibitions remained the profession's staple outlet.

Given the similarities between the two, it is not surprising that this new generation of postmodern designers should have adopted the same strategies as their radical predecessors, nor that they ultimately faced the same dilemma. The limited visibility provided by exclusive exhibition spaces meant that their critique, no matter how biting, failed to find an audience beyond an already receptive and informed circle of visitors. As such, designers looking for a way out of the dominant market system had no choice but to account for and integrate this seemingly inescapable predicament as a positive and constructive element within their work. This rarely mentioned dilemma is discussed frankly by Sottsass in an account of his involvement in the Alchimia and Memphis groups:

> At the beginning of the 1960s, the beat and hippy movements alerted me more and more to these kinds of questions. My reaction to this movement was not a purely intellectual one: it was also physical and emotional. Within the group I gradually became aware of the political significance of the question. We had begun to distance ourselves, to separate the possibilities of design from institutional imperatives. We had reached a point where we had almost stopped designing altogether [...] because we would not accept the rules imposed by producers, we no longer had the opportunity to work as designers.[473]

473 Ettore Sottsass, "Sottsass Explains Memphis," *Designer*, no. 2 (February 1982): 6–8.

This resistance to the creative impulse and acceptance of defeat as part of the designer's creative process seems to confirm the tactics identified by Sparke in her aforementioned 1986 book, *An Introduction to Design and Culture*. She describes how, following a break with the Modern Movement, designers finally attained the long sought-after mass audience, only to move away from it throughout the 1980s. Even if the critiques of Tafuri and Baudrillard could be offset by the enthusiasm of Banham, a growing awareness among designers of their limited scope to effect change in society led them to abandon the discipline's long-held ideal of a democratic design of quality as unfeasible. At the juncture where industrial infrastructure and manufacturers were at long last both able and willing to produce work by designers on a massive scale, designers had left behind their discipline's initial innocence and idealism. Sparke shows that postmodern designers, rejecting the gallery-based critique and the manifestos of the previous generation, were essentially interested in questions of style, self-image, and mass-media culture:

> The power of the process of commodification, and of the postmodern condition that prioritised the importance of material goods in the context of consumption, inevitably imbued Memphis products with a level of "added" value. While, at one level, it remained an elite, gallery oriented phenomenon—the Memphis designers producing an annual show of handmade pieces—it also penetrated the mass market as its images were "pillaged" and endlessly reproduced.[474]

474 Sparke, *Introduction to Design and Culture*, 195 (see note 13).

Design's search for autonomy, meanwhile, now focused on exchanges with adjacent territories, with fashion in particular offering an appealing terrain for postindustrial design to revive its expansionist tendencies. The relationship between design and fashion had sporadically come to the fore throughout history: in 1860, Gottfried Semper reevaluated architecture by locating its origins in textiles and sewing and considering it in terms of material, while in 1920 Le Corbusier suggested with "L'aventure du mobilier" that fashion was the "spirit of the machine age" and the preferable model for the creation of furniture.[475] However, when fashion was invoked by later generations, it was as a means of accentuating a break with the past rather than as an example to follow:

> In general when architects have been concerned with the planning of clothing items they have applied a methodology that has already been tested in the field of classical design. They have designed "objects" possessing a personal figuration. When the individual wears them he carries out an act which reduces his own form to that of the garment, in other words to forms that are generally rational and geometrical.[476]

Dario and Lucia Bartolini's "dress design" continued a trend initiated by Archizoom Associati by establishing a "creative field with its own independent foundation" through their use of a simple and accessible mode of production.[477] Designers were convinced of the relevance of

475 Le Corbusier, "L'aventure du mobilier," in *Précisions*, 107–22 (see note 242).
476 Cristiano Toraldo di Francia, "Superstudio & Radicals," in Migayrou, *Architecture radicale*, 339 (see note 31).
477 Branzi, *Hot House*, 87.

such an approach, and began to define their work in terms of totality, echoing Colombo's ideas:

> The word design ultimately covers everything: the opportunity of producing what one is drawing at the moment, the study of machines, materials and production, for example. If we need a clearer definition we have to use the English word design, which can also mean plan, drawing, etc.[478]

478 Joe Colombo, quoted in Ignazia Favata, "Remembering Joe Colombo," in *Joe Colombo: Inventing the Future*, ed. Alexander von Vegesack and Mateo Kries (Weil-am-Rhein: Vitra, 2005), 45.

The Environment: A Disciplinary Crossroads

The proliferation of the notion of environments in art, architecture, and design attested to the rising prominence of experiences designed to expand perception and consciousness. By the same token, it signaled the waning importance of the object and of materiality that came with architecture's move away from the frustrations of reality toward the possibilities of imagination. Through various mental distortions and intensified physical sensations, environments induced individuals to engage physically with the city renewed by their altered perception. Through the principle of expansion—from the individual to the collective, from the particular to the general—antidesign sought to simultaneously modify the home environment and the city. In place of existing models, such as Branzi's conception of the chair as an ideological model and "ideological copula,"[479] Colombo advanced the notion of a movement from the "microcosm" to the "macrocosm." However, these two terms and the relationship they implied would take on a new meaning, beyond that envisaged by Colombo in the context of the struggle between design and architecture throughout the 1970s to control the psychological and physiological environment. This phenomenon can be explained partly through the rising prominence of the notion of the environment: formerly the preserve of engineers in the nineteenth century, it would gradually be

479 Branzi, "La sedia come modello ideologico," in *Scritti teoretici*, 66–67 (see note 30).
480 Banham discusses the way in which "architects held [the notion of the environment] beneath contempt" and considered it to be the preserve of plumbers and engineers. He goes on to propose to redefine architecture as the production of environments. See Reyner Banham, *The Architecture of the Well-Tempered Environment*, 2nd ed. (London: Architectural Press, 1984), 11.

appropriated in the 1970s by experimental artists, architects, and designers.[480]

The concept of the environment was particularly present in the projects featured in the 1972 MoMA exhibition "Italy: The New Domestic Landscape." It was visible across the different sections defined by Emilio Ambasz, the exhibition's curator: in Mario Bellini's "mobile human space," the *Kar-a-Sutra*, in Gae Aulenti's untitled project involving modular plastic elements, and in Superstudio's *Microevent/Microenvironment*. The environment became yet another territory where architecture and design proposed new ways of operating based on a principle of unity that was, once again, a pretext disguising hegemonic aspirations. These new environments were to form a central part of the Italian domestic landscape as well as the basis for a number of conflicting discourses.

The series of "Visiona" exhibitions, which consisted of environments created by designers, is typical of this phenomenon: here objects and furniture were subsumed into a broader global and environmental project. The "Visiona" exhibitions appeared in annual installments over a period of four years, beginning with Colombo's project in 1969.[481] The following year saw Verner Panton present *Fantasy Landscape*, an environment made up of multicolored jersey forms installed inside a boat, while for the third edition Olivier Mourgue created an apartment consisting of mobile screens. The fourth and final "Visiona" featured the work of textile designer Jack Lenor Larsen, shortly before the 1973 oil crisis forced Bayer, the project's commissioner, to close its prospective research division. Over the course of the four exhibitions, Bayer's textiles served as a pretext

481 The company also curated a 1968 exhibit retroactively titled *Visiona 0*, a slightly different concept that was overseen by Verner Panton and laid the groundwork for the more ambitious installations to come.

for ambitious spatial experiments, with the four designers creating not just items of furniture but psychological and physiological environments.

For architects, the notion of the environment played a different role: it allowed them to develop psychic, perceptual, and sensory spaces that existed entirely outside the mechanisms of capitalism. These environments were to be experienced individually or in pairs; they were defined solely by users and their experience, or by way of devices such as the *Mind Expander* series (1967–69) devised by Haus-Rucker-Co, who refused to classify their work as either architecture or art.[482] This understanding of the environment was influenced by the art of the 1960s, in which the notion of ambience emerged as a central concern and spectators were invited to physically participate in the creative act. As boundaries between artistic categories rapidly blurred, the concept of the environment was simultaneously present in the fields of design (the "Visiona" exhibitions), art (in the work of Robert Rauschenberg, and in Land art), and architecture (Haus-Rucker-Co). The term *ambiente* was also used,[483] as in the title of Germano Celant's exhibition "Ambiente/arte: Dal futurismo alla body art," which regrouped all three disciplines in the Italian Pavilion at the 1976 Venice Biennale.[484] Inspired by everything from kinetic art to Situationist psychogeography, from Constant's "artificial environment" to Happenings, the environment was often used to describe the intersections between experimental music and visual art.

482 See Dieter Bogner, "Haus-Rucker-Co: Architectures provisoires," *Exposé*, no. 4 (2003): 176–83.

483 Branzi uses the term "ambient" in his discussion of Fisiolight, a system of "controlled-light curtains": "With Fisiolight the curtain ceased to be the mere supplement to decoration that it had always been considered [...] and became an active filter, capable of exerting a qualitative control over the natural lighting of the ambient." Branzi, "Design 'Primario,'" in *Hot House*, 96–101.

484 Germano Celant, *Ambiente/arte: Dal futurismo alla body art* (Venice: Edizioni della Biennale di Venezia, 1976).

The environment was a means of engaging the individual in a dynamic relationship through direct experience. With Haus-Rucker-Co's *Mind Expander II* chair, which featured audiovisual devices that forced the body to develop new ways of apprehending reality, the environment acquired a more pronounced exploratory dimension. Designed to be used by two people, one seated in the other's lap, the *Mind Expander II* featured an oversized plastic helmet, embellished with various marks and forms at eye level. This plastic psychoarchitecture altered users' mental states by offering them a distorted view of their surrounding environment while exposing them to various sounds. It acted as a catalyst for multiple stimuli, offering users a journey through psychic and physical perception.

Environments were voids, experiments in dematerialization that sometimes went to extremes, as in the case of Archizoom Associati's project for "Italy: The New Domestic Landscape," entitled *Abitare è facile* (Living is easy). Visitors entered a completely empty room, whose walls were a uniform gray;[485] inside a recording of the voice of a young girl reading the following text was played:

> Listen, I really think it's going to be something quite extraordinary. Very spacious, bright, really well arranged, with no hidden corners, you know. There will be fine lighting, really brilliant, that will clearly show up all those disordered objects.
>
> The fact is, everything will be simple, with no mysteries and nothing soul-disturbing, you know. Wonderful! Really very beautiful—very beautiful,

485 The empty space can be linked both to Superstudio's suppression of objects and the tendency toward dematerialization in the work of Conceptual artists.

> and very large. Quite extraordinary! It will be cool in there too, with an immense silence.
>
> My God, how can I describe to you the wonderful colors! You see many things are quite hard to describe, especially because they'll be used in such a new way. And then, there'll be glass, wood, linoleum, water, plants, vases, and many of those boxes they used to use, in wood or plastic, and all empty...
>
> What's really extraordinary about all this is that many of these things will be handmade, especially the largest ones. Of course, others will obviously be machine-made. The household equipment will be just perfect, in wonderful colors, neutral colors, I should say... All the rest will be bright, and there'll be a big swing with room for two.
>
> You see, there'll be lots of marvelous things, and yet it will look almost empty, it will be so big and so beautiful... How fine it will be... just spending the whole day doing nothing, without working or anything... You know, just great.[486]

Archizoom Associati used the recording as a means of colonizing the architectural tradition from within, and exploring the void as an experimental space in which individual perceptions could be amplified and distorted. Tafuri questioned the apparently liberating qualities of an all-encompassing space like the environment on both political and aesthetic grounds in his critical essay for the exhibition's catalogue.[487] He accused the radicals of cultivating a faux naivety in order to hide the manipulative aspect of

486 Reproduced in Ambasz, *Italy*, 234 (see note 283).
487 Tafuri, "Design and Technological Utopia," in Ambasz, *Italy*, 388–404.

their assault on all forms of expression, including domesticity and the void. He further denounced their development, by way of design, of a fashionable kind of formalism that was altogether compatible with the economy, even as they critiqued the market friendly ideology developed by the Modern Movement. Tafuri saw their work as a cynical echo of capitalism's extension toward every aspect of existence. He believed the group's incorrect reading of Marx had led them to do even more damage than their modernist predecessors, whose political aesthetic they had betrayed and replaced with a social one. Their position was all the more questionable, Tafuri argued, given that their critical production was situated within the comfortable and bourgeois space of the museum and therefore clearly at odds with their stated desire to effect concrete change. Tafuri echoed the criticism directed by architecture students at Archizoom's *Centro di Cospirazione Eclettica* at the 1968 Triennale di Milano: they believed that by positioning this ostensibly radical project within a museum space that was at a safe remove from the market, Archizoom Associati had not only reneged on its promises to intervene in the real world but, worse, neutralized its critical discourse and transformed it into little more than a hollow aesthetic.

To understand the significance of this criticism, it is worth discussing here the trajectory of Archizoom and its members. Over the course of the 1970s, they would leave their hometown of Florence to establish themselves in Milan, a move that coincided with a political and economic shift in their avant-garde activity. In Milan, while financial viability did not become an end in itself, the radicals did enter the design market, partaking in a professionalism long despised among the radicals. Paolo Deganello and Gilberto Corretti became advisors for the design firm Cassina, while Massimo Morozzi worked with Montefibre.

This integration into commercial design, one of the "accessories of capitalism," represented a contradictory conclusion for "terrorist design" and the "destruction of the object."[488] However, it is difficult to determine whether the radicals' professionalization is to be read as a naive gesture, the mellowing of age, an admission of failure, or a cynical move motivated by financial gain.

488 Binazzi, "Non-design," in Migayrou, *Architecture radicale*, 16 (see note 31).

Protesting Design and Design as Protest at the Dawn of Postmodernity

At the start of the postmodern era, designers began to reject the notions of efficiency and effectiveness along with the demands of production and distribution that had historically constrained their discipline. They refused the Modern Movement's definition of their work as providing a service, and a few designers, following the example of the radical architects and artists, chose instead to be their own commissioners; among them was Enzo Mari. He had experienced a commercial failure with his *Day-Night*, a well thought out and high quality sofabed. Following this disappointment, in 1973 Mari drew up nineteen models and plans for various items of furniture, and exhibited them the following year at Galleria Milano under the title *Proposta per un'autoprogettazione*.[489] Although at first glance, Mari's project may appear similar to the do-it-yourself furniture of 1950s America,[490] this was far from the case: by offering blueprints for an entire suite of furniture (bed, chairs, wardrobes, tables) that could easily be created using nothing but wood, nails, and a hammer, Mari circumvented the entire system of furniture production and distribution at the heart of the Italian design industry:

> A project for making easy-to-assemble furniture using rough boards and nails. An elementary technique to teach anyone to look at the present production with a critical eye. (Anyone, apart

489 *Progettazione* meant "design" in the 1960s and '70s, while *autoprogettazione* could be translated as an individual, independent from the market do-it-yourself furniture project.

490 Carolyn M. Goldstein, *Do-It-Yourself: Home Improvement in 20th-Century America* (New York: Princeton Architectural Press, 1998).

> from factories and traders, can use these designs to make them by themselves. The author hopes the idea will last into the future and asks those who build the furniture, and in particular, variations of it, to send photos to his studio at 10 piazzale Baracca, 10-20123 Milan.)[491]

Autoprogettazione rejected the modern industrial aspect of design in favor of the individual craftsmanship that was its origin. However, Mari's project did not signal a nostalgia for some kind of preindustrial noble savage or a belief in the division between nature and culture; he is better understood, as Giulio Carlo Argan suggests, as a Robinson Crusoe figure who had no choice but to construct the necessary items with his bare hands.[492]

The virtues of Mari's project were undeniable; it eluded the commercial and industrial framework as well as the demands of production, released design from the yoke of technology, removed the distributor from the equation, and above all empowered the individual, who was free to modify plans as they saw fit. However, it drew criticism from Italian workers, who attacked Mari for rendering them superfluous and threatening their jobs.

This kind of shift in agency was a characteristic feature of postmodern design, and was embodied by the short existence of Global Tools, a "system of laboratories" that was presented as a continuation of the work of radical architecture. At the XV Triennale di Milano in 1973, the industrial design section paid tribute to the work of the radical architects and controdesign with an exhibition of documents on utopias and avant-gardes. Shortly before the

491 Enzo Mari, *Autoprogettazione*, 2nd ed. (Mantua: Edizioni Corraini, 2008).
492 See Giulio Carlo Argan, *L'espresso* (May 5, 1974); in François Burkhardt et al., *Why Write a Book on Enzo Mari* (Milan: Motta Editore, 1997), 205.

opening of the Triennale, a meeting was convened at the *Casabella* offices; there, Superstudio, Archizoom Associati, Gruppo 9999, Zziggurat, Remo Buti, Riccardo Dalisi, Ugo La Pietra, Gaetano Pesce, Gianni Pettena, Ettore Sottsass, Alessandro Mendini, and Adalberto Dal Lago founded Global Tools. This "system of laboratories" was to conduct research and experiments using traditional, "poor" approaches and techniques, modeled on the innate and vernacular wisdom and skills of the peasant.

Global Tools took the form of a cooperative but presented itself as a school, or rather a "counter-school" or "non-school," that aimed to stimulate individual, creative development through teaching methods that included lessons and workshops. Influenced by Arte Povera, Superstudio developed *design povero* within the group, a design of the subaltern to be realized with "poor technology."[493] By emphasizing bricolage and what Natalini referred to as non-alienated, therapeutic approaches they sought to draw a line under the failures of modernity once and for all. The first projects carried out under the banner of Global Tools left behind the more overtly political dimension of previous work in favor of an anthropological approach. They drew on Dalisi's ongoing project with street children in Naples as well as *Project Zeno*, a series of photos and plans that described in great detail the ingenious tools, methods, and spatial organization devised by an elderly peasant working the land in the countryside surrounding Florence.

493 If the use of handicrafts by Global Tools is linked to Arte Povera, the craft dimension has often served to question design and provide a source of alternatives. Branzi sums up this raison d'être: "Interest in handicrafts is a phenomenon that crops up regularly in the history of design and modern architecture, as a sort of confrontation with a production system that is seen as 'lost innocence.' Throughout the twentieth century, the fact that industrial work has been continually spurned has led to a perception of often non-existent values in handicrafts. People nostalgic for pre-industrial society, for example, are now looking to the values of craftsmanship for a new pattern of organization based on the rediscovery of the individual and on the myths of humanism." Branzi, *Hot House*, 136.

The stated goal of Global Tools was the renewal of design through a "yellow pages for culture,"[494] the development of publications and a program that would foster new and democratic forms of production and individual experimentation and creativity. This significant shift away from the radicals' earlier program was due, in part, to the compromising academic nature of earlier debates. To truly alter design, it became clear that the disappearance of the object they had previously advocated as a liberating act needed to be accompanied by a process of learning and experimentation that could combine theory and practice to stimulate nonintellectual creativity and individual development. They aimed to achieve this through close observation of the work carried out by craftsmen and peasants, who they viewed as offering the only viable alternatives to industrial production.

Global Tools operated according to what Branzi termed a "wider long-term strategy,"[495] though the project would peter out by 1975. By rejecting short-term gains, the project developed around "theses of vital importance which enable us to draw up the premises for more incisive work, work which addresses itself directly to reality and does not avoid it."[496] The group represented a link between radical architecture and the graphic design studio Alchimia, founded in 1976 in Milan by Alessandro and Adriana Guerriero, Bruno and Giorgio Gregori, and Alessandro Mendini. Studio Alchimia positioned itself as the successor to Global Tools, and was to be an experimental laboratory for avant-garde design and an epicenter of international postmodern design. The group, whose members were largely former

494 Ibid., 83.
495 Andrea Branzi, "Radical Notes: Strategia dei tempi lunghi," *Casabella*, no. 370 (October 1972): 245; published in English as "Global Tools," in Migayrou, *Architecture radicale*, 346.
496 Ibid.

practicioners of radical architecture, initiated a new phase of debate in which design held a somewhat ambiguous position. Mendini's "Manifesto di Alchimia" set the tone and goals of the group, affirming that it aimed for neither a total work of art, nor a total art, nor a synthesis of the arts; instead, it would work toward a kind of assemblage of the different arts that would erase distinctions between art, architecture, and design.[497] A clear contradiction emerges in these architects' continued recourse to design and their treatment of it as a playground rather than a discipline in and of itself, as Mendini notes:

> And why—I asked at the outset—are there so many architect designers, but practically no designer architects? I believe this to be due to a question of differences in training: someone who is capable of tracking complex problems can easily devote himself to simpler matters, while the opposite is only rarely true.[498]

Mendini's statement attests to architecture's continued hegemony, despite the vastly different ideological context and his ostensible rejection of the hierarchy established by the Modern Movement. In its place, he argued for a more fragile and more negative "new morality" that would be embodied by Alchimia.

The winter of 1980–81 saw the split of Studio Alchimia and the establishment of the Memphis group, whose name was a reference to Bob Dylan's song "Stuck Inside of Mobile with the Memphis Blues Again." Its founder, Ettore Sottsass, believed that "doing design doesn't mean giving

497 Alessandro Mendini, "Manifesto di Alchimia" (1984), http://www.ateliermendini.it.
498 Alessandro Mendini, quoted in Peter Weiß, "Mendini and Postmodern Culture," in *Alessandro Mendini: Design and Architecture*, ed. Peter Weiß (Milan: Electa, 2001), 44.

form to a more or less stupid product for a more or less sophisticated industry. Design [...] is a way of discussing life, sociality, politics, food, and even design."[499] In many ways close to the radical movement, Memphis rejected outright the values of utopia, progress, and functionalism of the Modern Movement. At the same time, postmodern design would utilize many of its operating principles, but without calling for revolution or a tabula rasa. By seeking to mass produce their creations, rejecting limited editions, and readily defining their work as merchandise, postmodern designers—whom Mendini described as "hotblooded animals"[500]—sought to combine the experiments of the avant-garde with the demands of the market, and to offer individuals not things they needed, but rather things they wanted. They envisaged design as a playful activity in which the supposedly sacred values of the past were gleefully and irreverently recycled.

This context helps to explain the limited success of postmodern designers in developing an independent language distinct from architectural theory, despite their stated intention to "turn its focus upon itself, towards the detail of the mind."[501] This was all the more worrying since the basis for theoretical and disciplinary autonomy that Colombo had defined for design had disappeared following his death in July 1971. As we have already seen, the years that followed saw widespread misuse of the terms anti-design and controdesign as they were recuperated by the radicals. The process was later described by Cristiano Toraldo di Francia:

499 Ettore Sottsass, interview by Barbara Radice, in *Memphis: Research, Experiences, Results, Failures and Successes of New Design* (New York: Rizzoli, 1984), 173.
500 Alessandro Mendini, "Per un'architettura banale" (1978), in *Progetto infelice*, ed. Rosamaria Rinaldied (Milan: Alchimia, 1983), 106–7.
501 Mendini, "Manifesto di Alchimia."

> Definitions such as Conceptual Architecture, Antidesign, Counterdesign, Radical Architecture followed one after the other via articles, and exhibitions until the show "Italy: The New Domestic Landscape" demonstrated the power of the system to integrate its critics, finally historicizing as "counter design" the activity of the avant-garde.[502]

This confusion of terms and concepts continued throughout the years of Studio Alchimia's activity until its official closure in 1991. Mendini's contradictory statements evidence the dynamism of design in redefining the conditions for its disciplinary autonomy. The postmodern movement followed in the footsteps of the radicals, using design as an attempt to infiltrate the market system, albeit in a form that was far less revolutionary and assertive than Colombo's antidesign. Making virtues of banality and popular taste, as Archizoom Associati had done in the past, the postmodern architect-designers promoted a kind of quality-free design: "There is no longer any originality. The place of the invention of new forms has been taken by the variation of decorations, models and surfaces. Design is redesign. Design means decorating."[503]

The group counted Michele De Lucchi, Martine Bedin, Aldo Cibic, Nathalie du Pasquier, George J. Snowden, Matteo Thun, and Marco Zanini among its members, and its foundation would come to mark a break with previous avant-garde movements that had formed in the decades following the Second World War. Confirmed anti-ideologues, the members of Memphis paradoxically developed what might be described as a form of ideology, building on

502 Toraldo di Francia, "Superstudio & Radicals," in Migayrou, *Architecture radicale*, 339.
503 Weiß, "Mendini and Postmodern Culture," in Weiß, *Alessandro Mendini*, 61.

principles of uncertainty borrowed from quantum physics and molecular chemistry:[504]

> Memphis is one of the mutations. It is born of the age of data processing, within the system, not against it. It utilizes the most advanced structures and strategies, it grows and spreads by working directly on the connective tissue of the environment, working on the senses, on details, on microstructures, on speed. Its products are chips of extraordinarily high expressive density, unstable genetic hybrids that strike the planet like a new wind, bearers of new barbarities perhaps, or of another civilization.[505]

Memphis's *nuovo design*, or New Design, was closely linked to cyberspace and its aesthetics, genetic science, and the advanced technologies that were then spurring on new ways of looking at the world. The group's approach evidenced not only its belief in the salvation offered by all-powerful technology, but also its determination to envisage design as a specific cultural discipline and reconstruct "a system of expressive and emotional relations between man and the objects of his domestic habitat."[506] Despite this somewhat facile marketing discourse, Memphis set out a genuine vision for a linguistically controlled re-semanticization of the "absolute object" described by Baudrillard in *Fatal Strategies* through a dual critique that sought to strip away the "aura of usefulness and the more arcane aura of art."[507]

504 See Keith M. Booker, *Monsters, Mushroom Clouds, and the Cold War: American Science Fiction and the Roots of Postmodernism, 1946–1964* (Westport, CT: Greenwood Press, 2001); Barbara Radice and Franco Raggi, "Activities of Studio Alchimia," *Japan Interior Design*, no. 249 (December 1977); Barbara Radice, *Memphis: The New International Style* (Milan: Electa, 1981); *Memphis: Research, Experiences, Results, Failures and Successes*; and Weiß, "Mendini and Postmodern Culture."
505 Radice, *Memphis: Research, Experiences, Results, Failures and Successes*, 144.
506 Ibid., 141.
507 Ibid., 186.

Design was shaped by the unique and often paradoxical conditions of its development: a product of both modernity and the laws of the market, it was also influenced by fine art, industry, and architecture, with each field bringing to bear its own conception of what design was and should be. In light of this, design's invention can be read as a filiation between different arts, which can in turn allow for an understanding of how design was co-opted by the history of architecture and the history of art and reduced to an extension of modern thought. Architecture considered the theory of design to be nothing more than an episode in its own history, while for the fine arts, design was considered in strictly progressive and technical terms. These approximations demonstrate the importance of adjacent disciplines in the definition and articulation of design. However, design was to take on an important role all its own, particularly with the rising prominence of interdisciplinary discourse.

Throughout the 1980s, designers would abandon their political engagement and leave the theoretical dimension of their discipline—of which they had only recently taken control—to others. Drawing on the sociology of Baudrillard, the anthropology of Marcel Mauss, and the semiotics of Barthes, among others, designers working in the 1970s and '80s—the Memphis group in particular—would struggle to define the object of their work. In fact, designers would even lose interest in the question altogether; instead they flirted with the human sciences to expand their scope, as Sottsass had announced, and to encompass "a broader horizon, as if [they] had emerged from design's town center to head for new, uncertain peripheries."[508] At the same time, in the name of the transdisciplinarity that had

508 Sottsass, "Tel père, Memphis," interview by Févre (see note 40).

become the order of the day, designers invited the social sciences to consider their work as an object of study. The critical attention of other disciplines would leave a durable mark on design. Design theorists had been historians of art, architects, and designers themselves, though they had been divided by a somewhat simplistic distinction between theory and practice; now, they had abandoned the critical terrain to other disciplines, with sociologists, semiologists, and psychiatrists stepping in to take their place. Though these adjacent fields each enriched design in their own way, by delegating responsibility for its historical and theoretical dimensions, design put itself in a vulnerable position. Notions of transdisciplinarity and interdisciplinarity would ultimately undermine its independence, even if, as Louis Martin would argue in his essay on transdisciplinarity, the establishment of any discipline necessarily incorporates elements from adjacent territories.[509]

This situation contains a number of parallels with the current state of affairs. In a 1998 interview, Hal Foster remarked that:

> To be interdisciplinary you need to be disciplinary first—to be grounded in one discipline, preferably two, to know the historicity of these discourses before you test them against each other. Many young people now come to interdisciplinary work before they come to disciplinary work. As a result they often fall into an eclecticism that does little work on any discipline; it is more entropic than transgressive.[510]

509 This is the conclusion that Louis Martin reaches in "Interdisciplinarity Transpositions: Bernard Tschumi," in *De-, Dis-, Ex-: The Anxiety of Interdisciplinarity*, ed. Alex Coles and Alexia Deffert (London: Black Dog, 1998), 60–88.

510 Hal Foster, interview by Alex Coles, in Coles and Deffert, *Anxiety of Interdisciplinarity*, 162.

Foster directs his criticism at the diluting effects of interdisciplinarity rather than interdisciplinarity itself, but he exhorts its proponents to exercise caution. Interdisciplinarity requires an expertise in both or all of the disciplines in question—something that is impossible if a discipline does not benefit from full and durable recognition, as has consistently been the case for design. It was in this context that Margolin observed,

> To think of design history as a discipline based on firm assumptions of what design is and how we might study its past is to ignore the dynamic crossings of intellectual boundaries that are occurring elsewhere. For example, researchers outside design history have discovered design to be a rich topic of historical investigation.[511]

I have already discussed Guidot's use of the notion of the "crossroads of the arts" to describe design, and Sparke's concept of "unity in diversity." More recently, in the introduction to the catalogue published alongside the "Design etc: Open Borders" exhibition at Tripostal in Lille in 2004, Droog Design cofounder Renny Ramakers wrote, "This exhibition shows that each practitioner possesses their own discipline but can also integrate others into their work."[512]

The search for artistic freedom through the transgression of disciplinary frontiers has accelerated the shifts in the topography of their relationships between different fields. This widespread approach may explain why the territories of art, design, and architecture are so readily blurred in the work of those operating in each discipline. More

511 Margolin, "Design History and Design Studies," in *Essays*, 220 (see note 6).
512 Renny Ramakers, *Design etc: Open Borders* (Amsterdam: Droog, 2004), n.p.

specifically, the dynamics between different disciplines are now more than ever characterized by porosity and exchange, and are celebrated through the practice of "sampling" that is used by a new generation to cross disciplinary boundaries. However, it is unclear whether the popularity of such an approach signals the disappearance of specialization or rather an ongoing rise in the power of transdisciplinarity at the expense of disciplinary autonomy.

To return once more to the 1980s, the Memphis group announced a "new design," antithetical to the "good taste" of the Modern Movement and Kaufmann's Good Design. Barbara Radice, Memphis's resident critic, aligned these earlier movements with the kind of "expressive poverty" that could be found in Arte Povera. This approach was presented as an antibourgeois stance, and resulted from the refusal to submit to any exterior forces that underpinned their conception of design. In order to counter functionalism and the moralism of the Modern Movement, Memphis made use of decoration, which they believed embodied emotion and feeling. They thus exploited the opposition between decoration and function that had previously been explored at the turn of the twentieth century by Thorstein Veblen in "The Pecuniary Canons of Taste," a chapter of *The Theory of the Leisure Class*. Veblen explained that contrary to received wisdom, utility was actually inversely proportional to appeal, and therefore the less functional an object was, the more attractive it was to the consumer. Memphis revisited decoration and developed a productive critique that celebrated its potential. Branzi explained that "over the last twenty years there has been a progressive expansion of the theoretical and operative limits of design: light, color, fashion, materials, decoration and sounds have become the instruments of a new kind of design aimed at the creation of a more habitable modern metropolis," and added that this was one step toward the "transformation of the world."[513] In 1975, he published *Decorattivo*, a volume on the subject of decoration:

> *Decorattivo* was essentially a sort of working handbook, a compendium of graphic information chosen to provide a basis and stimulus for the creative work of other professionals [...]. Themes were selected not on the basis of seasonal market forecasts but rather on the basis of constancy over historical periods. The first edition of *Decorattivo* dealt with "amorphous" decorations, i.e. textures without organization, and with "tie designs," i.e. geometric decorations that conveyed a strong impression of three dimensionality. [...] New attention from the critics and publication of the decorative manuals resulted in a strong re-awakening of interest in this kind of design: between 1977 and 1980 a series of experiments created new applications for decoration.[514]

Branzi envisaged an annual edition of this collection of "advanced aesthetic production," in which he presented a series of cultural, linguistic, and visual codes. Clearly, it is reductive and inaccurate to consider the work of post-modern designers purely in terms of decoration. However, the example of *Decorattivo* shows how a generation would seek to redefine design according to a romantic way of thinking in which the fragment could contain the whole. Theirs was a vision of the discipline as an amoral vortex that

513 Branzi, *Hot House*, 10.
514 Ibid., 119–20.

would submit the entire domestic sphere to its laws; design here became inseparable from the totality of existence, of which it was simultaneously the most fundamental and the most developed expression.

At a number of points throughout its history, though particularly in the 1920s and the late 1960s, design developed strategies to gain greater recognition as a discipline. Architects would sometimes insist that they had a parallel design practice; they thus conflated (sometimes to the point of caricature) their production of industrially manufactured products with the discipline of design. In turn, this reductive vision gave designers little incentive to recognize the work of architects; in fact, designers and historians of design alike would envisage their discipline in expansionist terms that extended to social, urban, and political questions. Explored through Walter Gropius's *Scope of Total Architecture* (1943),[515] Sybil Moholy-Nagy's *Experiment in Totality* (1950),[516] and Colombo's antidesign (1969), the notion of the totality provided further proof if any were needed that design and architecture often shared common ground, and that each discipline sought to claim this shared territory as its own.

They went about this process using different strategies: modern architects disingenuously promoted a union between the arts in order to better dissimulate their attempts to establish and maintain their authority, while designers opted for a more surreptitious expansionist movement. Though design's ever-closer association with consumerism in the 1980s might appear to have settled the affair, it nonetheless continued to push for its independence from architecture and art, though this was largely in

515 Walter Gropius, *Scope of Total Architecture* (New York: Collier Books, 1962).
516 Sibyl Moholy-Nagy, *Experiment in Totality* (Cambridge, MA: MIT Press, 1969).

vain. In 1987, in a special issue of *Culture Technique*, Mark Brutton attempted to identify a potential path that would allow design a smooth passage from modernity to postmodernity by offering an alternative definition of function—beyond the one established by functionalism at the end of the nineteenth century. He aimed to reconcile design and postmodernity while maintaining the pairing of form and function; to this end he carried out a "desecularization" of function that proposed to expand its definition to include nonquantifiable parameters such as identity, feeling, symbolism, and complexity.[517] Sottsass would later reflect on anti-design and the expansion of design in the following terms:

> [Design] starts when it enters our homes, enters our streets, towns, skies, bodies, and souls. Design starts when it becomes the visual, physical, sensorial representation of the existential metaphor on which we are laying down our lives. This means that design starts when you design the metaphor of life. This means that design starts when you design the metaphor of life, which also means that so-called anti-design in fact was "anti" nothing at all, it was just all for enlarging and deepening the design event.[518]

But despite the designer's remarks, the question was far from being settled, as Branzi unintentionally demonstrates in the closing pages of *The Hot House*. Having opened his work with a discussion of design's difficulty in attaining the status of a discipline, he closes by observing that "the range

517 Mark Brutton, "Après le modernisme," *Culture Technique*, no. 5 (April 1981): 68–71.
518 Ettore Sottsass, "Design and Theory: Two Points of View," in *Design since 1945* (Philadelphia: Philadelphia Museum of Art, 1983), 2–4.

of research work covered by New Design thus places it in a fundamental position as far as the redefinition of architecture itself is concerned."[519] In doing so, Branzi seems to contradict his own original premise and bolster Pevsner's argument that the decorative arts gave rise to modern architecture. The designer concludes that it fell to design to support and respond to the "historical schizophrenia" that was responsible for "the inability of latter-day architecture to fit in with the modern world":[520]

> It is too advanced to form an autonomous domestic civilization of its own, and too backward with respect to the development of production and territorial communication. This incapacity is deep, painful and heroic as well. It is the outcome of a whole-hearted adoption of an atypical role, one of step with history. And architecture was always convinced of being history's favourite child. [...] New Design is thus interested in putting together a different domestic culture, in recovering a system of ties and functions that cannot be explained in purely ergonomic or functional terms, that involve man in his relationship to his domestic habitat from a wider cultural and expressive point of view. The system of living thus conceived represents the threshold of a whole system of environmental and territorial design. There is no way modern architectural culture can carry on without having re-established a proper relationship with the user. The unliveableness of modern cities has usually been dealt with in collective terms by playing around

519 Branzi, *Hot House*, 144.
520 Ibid., 148.

> with public spaces, when in fact it is the direct outcome of the crisis in the relationship between man and his own home.[521]

To these remarks he adds,

> However, the focal point of this as we see it is not the recomposition of a unitary formal and linguistic code that sets out from the home and spreads across the city and territory as a whole; cultural or technical unity in contemporary design not what we are after. As Mario Tronti puts it: "Let's leave big systems to little improvisors."[522]

So while hesitating to consider design as an end in itself, as a means of renewing a faltering architecture, or as a terrain for the exploration and modification of the real, Branzi attempts to evaluate the delicate position of the designer. According to the radicals, the duplicity of the designer, and his central position in the liberal economy, should force him to take into account his responsibility. Branzi believed that the situation that led architecture to look to *design* for its renewal resulted from a typology of functionalism and efficiency. And this, he suggests, must be abandoned in favor of something akin to Hölderlin's poetic dwelling.

521 Ibid.
522 Ibid., 150.

Existenzmaximum: A Design for the World

Design has long sought to expand beyond the territory assigned to it by its artistic and architectural stewards, and today has a far greater reach than ever before. It is fair to say that its repeated incursions into neighboring disciplines are the source of much of the criticism directed at design, particularly the accusations of ubiquity and colonization that are regularly leveled by its detractors. It remains to be seen whether or not this criticism is merely a response to a new and greater independence for design.

The writer Karl Kraus was renowned for his denunciation of society's generalized hypocrisy and artifice in the early twentieth century; he was a confidant of his godfather Adolf Loos and admired by Walter Benjamin. He expressed his concern at the growing prevalence of design and its ramifications, and his anxiety over what he perceived to be a confusion between use value and the value of art.[523] Hal Foster returned to this critique, which was originally directed at Art Nouveau, in his 2002 book *Design and Crime*.[524] While Foster has convincingly argued for the singularity of art as a discipline elsewhere, in *Design and Crime* he treats design, marketing, and graphic design as a single entity, and rejects the notion of design as a discipline. In a sign of the times, Foster's work condemns design for having hollowed out the twentieth century by cultivating confusion between the utilitarian and the aesthetic that extended from "jeans to genes."[525] Foster believes that no aspect of life has been spared by design, which has

523 Karl Kraus, *Die Fackel* (December 1912); in *Werke*, vol. 3 (Munich: Kösel, 1952), 341.
524 Foster, *Design and Crime*, 13–27 (see note 50).
525 Ibid., 17.

become ubiquitous to the point of extending its reach to the human body itself:

> Today you don't have to be filthy rich to be projected not only as designer but as designed—whether the product in question is your home or your business, your sagging face (designer surgery) or your lagging personality (designer drugs), your historical memory (designer museums) or your DNA future (designer children).[526]

His critique focuses in particular on design's commercial dimension, with reference to Loos's 1908 text "Ornament and Crime." In this essay the Viennese architect staunchly condemned the use of ornament, which he considered to be the worst form of barbarism, and one with untold nefarious consequences for culture: "The stragglers slow down the cultural evolution of the nations and of mankind; not only is ornament produced by criminals but also a crime is committed through the fact that ornament inflicts serious injury on people's health, on the national budget and hence on cultural evolution."[527] A crime against society and a crime against culture, ornament was to be eradicated at all cost. Loos's attack was directed above all at the eclectic historicism then in vogue among the Viennese aristocracy. Referring to Loos's text, Foster redeploys the same violent tone to denounce a new criminal: no longer ornament, but the discipline of design itself. While Loos exhorted modern man to embrace the present, Foster references Kraus's remarks on the artistic and functional value of objects to denounce the contamination of art by consumerism. He is

526 Ibid.
527 Adolf Loos, "Ornament and Crime," in *Ornament and Crime: Selected Essays*, ed. Adolf Opel, trans. Michael Mitchell (Riverside, CA: Ariadne Press, 1998), 167.

scathing in his criticism of marketing culture as embodied by the intrusion of design—and therefore commerce—into every aspect of life, and even into art, which had until now escaped the consumerist plague. The designer is, for Foster, consumer civilization's most effective agent.

Foster constructs his argument along two axes: the first deals with the collapse of culture and the inexorable rise of marketing, and the second with the intrusion of design into all aspects of everyday life. He condemns the criminal designer, and despairs for the figure of the artist, who at the beginning of the century appeared capable of resisting industry and the market only to become subjugated by them at its end. He concludes that "there is no such resistance in contemporary design: it delights in postindustrial technologies, and it is happy to sacrifice the semi-autonomy of architecture and art to the manipulations of design."[528] This is a somewhat surprising position given Foster's previous work in which he masterfully demonstrated the uniqueness and value of each individual discipline while taking care to underline the negative consequences of interdisciplinarity.[529] Mendini had previously discussed disciplinary shifts in different terms: for him it was a question of "phenomenology of the project on a complex terrain of infradisciplinary imbrication."[530] In light of the total work of art promoted by architects, the metaphor of the Trojan horse used by Flusser reminds us that "design" is etymologically associated with "ruse" and "subterfuge." The same metaphor has been used to describe the role of design in the radical architects' program. More generally, design has employed a strategy of embedding and infiltrating to attain a measure of equality with architecture and conquer supposedly impenetrable territory.

528 Foster, *Design and Crime*, 18.
529 Hal Foster, interview, in Coles and Deffert, *Anxiety of Interdisciplinarity*, 162.
530 Mendini, "Existenz Maximum," in *Scritti*, 96 (see note 77).

It is possible to gain a greater understanding of design's expansionist tendencies by investigating this strategy through the lens of its architectural counterpart: the total work as it was variously conceived by the different architects of the Modern Movement. In the 1930s, Germany's modern architects coined the neologism Existenzminimum to promote new norms of construction based around a set of clearly defined, rational, metric rules.[531] These rules were supposedly based on "the average man, the universal man, as a module, as an aesthetic unit of measure [...] in other words, we should first consider the building in relation to man as a living being in need of air, light, peace, and warmth."[532] This term would later provide the basis for Existenzmaximum, a form of camouflage through which design could set about redefining the notion of the environment and the psychological perimeter in a process that was central to the neo-avant-garde, from Haus-Rucker-Co to Superstudio, and from Archizoom Associati to Ugo La Pietra or Frei Otto.

The term "Existenzmaximum" first appeared as the title of a 1990 exhibition of the work of young designers in Florence, and was immediately critiqued by Mendini in his review of the show. He expressed his concern that "with its particular attitude, design loses its way, escapes from one set of rules to find itself subject to another: today it offers a vague expression of its desire for dilution."[533] However, Mendini recognized that Existenzmaximum

531 May et al., *Die Wohnung für das Existenzminimum*, 30–34 (see note 66).
532 Ibid. The idea of the "average man" is controversial and political: It originates in the geometric ideals of Leonardo da Vinci's Vitruvian Man, and passes through to the measurements of, for example, Cesare Lombroso and Alphonse Berthillon's categorizations of criminals, the modern advent of ergonomics with Frank and Lilian Gilbreth, Ernst Neufert's "Man as Measure as Goal," Le Corbusier's Modulor scale, and Otto Neurath's Isotype system. See also the eugenic classification by American industrial designers with Raymond Loewy's Evolution Chart and Henry Dreyfuss's *Measure of Man* (1960).
533 Mendini, "Existenz Maximum," in *Scritti*, 95.

was a highly significant concept. In place of the creation of micro-environments that had occupied the radicals, Existenzmaximum proposed an expansion of the environment that would serve as the modus operandi for a design that was ready to definitively mark out its territory and its disciplinary autonomy.

The term was also employed in the 2008 MoMA exhibition "Design and the Elastic Mind," which explored the diversity of design at micro, meso, and macro levels. The exhibition's curator Paola Antonelli had previously explored the idea of Existenzmaximum in a 2001 article.[534] In the MoMA exhibition, she used it to describe an extracorporeal perception of space. This psychic expansion represented an ironic response to the notions of efficacy and functionalist precision that gave rise to Existenzminimum. For Antonelli, Existenzmaximum begins with the miniaturization of an object, such as the Walkman, that in turn allows its user to create, at the touch of a button, a customizable, private environment that extends outward from their body. Existenzmaximum is thus capable of redefining the surrounding world, and serves as a metaphor for design's amplifying movement. Thanks to this "small, yet extraordinarily comfortable spatial device [...] the physical boundaries are protective, rather than oppressive, thus letting the senses and the spirit roam free," whose "most revelatory designs, though, were devoted to apparently innocent objects that could unwillingly create spatial fields."[535] Existenzmaximum enables design to extricate itself from the relationship of scale that had seen it yoked to architecture.

The miniaturized or even immaterial departure point of Existenzmaximum relates not only to design's expansionist

534 Paola Antonelli, "Existenzmaximum," *Big Magazine*, no. 24 (Spring–Summer 2001): 32–35.
535 Ibid.

tendencies but also to its forms, iterations, content, and specific references, and its ability to generate changes and turning points within its own discourse. The affirmation of design's independence and status as a discipline is not a naive demand for recognition, but rather a means of ensuring that design is studied on its own terms and not those of architecture. It is easy to conflate design's autonomy with its ubiquity, since, as Flusser explains, design by its very nature "demonstrates the close relationship between technology and art. This is why today, design can be said to correspond approximately to the point where art and technology (and, by extension, scientific thought, which defines the scale of values) converge to open the path towards a new culture."[536] Here design is interrogated from within and insists upon its independence. While Flusser appears at first to contradict this point of view by equating design, culture, and artifice with one another, through a semantic shift the philosopher ultimately demonstrates that design's apparent trickery is ultimately a means of dispelling other forms of artifice:

> If the word design has taken on such a central importance in today's discourse, it is because we are beginning to lose our faith—and probably with good reason—in art and technology as sources of values, and instead shed light upon the design which underlies them.[537]

Proposing to read design's history according to a principle of expansion does not equate to an interpretation along the lines of the total work of art, which architects used to

536 Flusser, *Shape of Things*, 9 (see note 24).
537 Ibid., 11.

reinforce their hegemony under the cover of a discourse of equality and harmony. For example, it would be inaccurate to interpret the amplification of design to encompass other arts in terms of the Wagnerian Gesamtkunstwerk, as design was at the time uninterested in establishing an ideal model for the totalization of the arts and their integration into a superior, unified whole. Nor can it be likened to the concept promoted by Art Nouveau, whose protest against mechanized, technological society entailed the creation of an interior world that was organized according to psychological categories wherein each detail of the home was elevated to the level of a work of art and placed at the summit of the hierarchy of the arts.[538] Less accurate still would be to suggest that design's expansion is comparable to the "total design" of the Modern Movement, which called for the arts to work in spatial and aesthetic harmony at the service of architecture. It is tempting to imagine that the present-day expansionism of design is but the most recent incarnation of the notion of the totality as it exists in the Gesamtkunstwerk, that this idea has crossed the ages from total design to the synthesis of arts, and that design has finally internalized the principle long promoted by the visual arts and architecture; the idea of a totality that was a historical constant and that favored each discipline in turn, to eventually be inherited by design in the present day, is perhaps an appealing one. However, although design deployed the notion of the totality, unlike architecture and the total work, it did not pretend to aspire to a unification of the arts; it did, however, involve the same aspiration to hegemonic power, which developed as design was strengthened and emboldened by a clear sense of autonomy. Through a process of spatial expansion, design maximized

538 See Silverman, *Art Nouveau in Fin-de-Siècle France*.

its scope and redefined its own axiology. Design's history was one of expansionism from its very origins.

For evidence of this, we need look only to Benjamin's description of the transformation of the home in "Paris, Capital of the Nineteenth Century." Benjamin first analyzes the bourgeois interior, which "was not only the private citizen's universe [but] his étui [casing],"[539] and notes the obsession of its inhabitants for leaving traces of their presence. Benjamin then turns his attention to the "shattering" of the interior with the emergence of the Modern Style,[540] or Jugendstil, the German branch of the Art Nouveau movement. What does Benjamin's exploration of the nineteenth century reveal about design's expansionism? First and foremost, his highly original reading of the ornamental Jugendstil presents it not as an avant-garde movement, but rather as a continuation of the nineteenth century bourgeois interior tradition. Benjamin analyzes this first of design's expansionist *élans* at the turn of the century in terms of a somewhat physiognomist and amnesic total work of art, constructed through a partial exchange with its inhabitants. To demonstrate this thesis, he focuses on the vegetal motifs that were central to Jugendstil: Benjamin considers them to be a mundane attempt to offset industrialization through floral imagery, evidence of a desire to reconcile the home environment with nature in a futile attempt to avoid the transformation of the interior into an "asylum,"[541] and a means of constructing an idealistic fantasy in which the "fictional framework for the individual's life is constituted in the private home."[542] From this

539 Walter Benjamin, "Paris, Capital of the Nineteenth Century: Exposé of 1939," in *The Arcades Project*, trans. Howard Eiland and Kevin McLaughlin (Cambridge, MA: Belknap Press of Harvard University Press, 2002), 20.
540 Benjamin, "Paris, Capital of the Nineteenth Century: Exposé of 1935," in *Arcades*, 9.
541 Ibid.
542 Benjamin, "Exposé of 1939," in *Arcades*, 20.

first example of design's expansion, Benjamin constructs a model for the expansion of the interior outward, from the home into the streets, with the Parisian arcades as an in-between space akin to a "windowless house"[543] or "houses or passages having no outside."[544] In her text on Benjamin, Hannah Arendt links this expansion of the interior in Paris to the fortified towns of the Middle Ages: whereas the latter offered a form of interior that was "severely walled off and protected against the outside," Paris benefited from a "a generously built and planned open-air *intérieur* with the arch of the sky like a majestic ceiling above it."[545] Modern architecture's total work insisted on the alliance and unity of arts; by contrast, and as as Benjamin shows, design expanded inexorably into the territory of different arts, here affecting a change in which "the street becomes the room and the room becomes street."[546]

Yet this process is more complex than it appears at first sight. In his article "Whatever Happened to Total Design?" Mark Wigley examines the double movement undertaken by design and architecture to conquer the world over the course of the twentieth century.[547] On the one hand, it was a question of implosion: a concentration of details and surfaces into a single point according to the author's vision and the prevalent model of the enclosed, protected, and coherent interior. On the other hand, it was an explosion: a broad, all encompassing deployment of the continuous surface whose most complete expression could be found in Gropius's total architecture, with which he sought to maximize the architect's power. Wigley underlines the rising prominence of design as it was applied across all

543 Benjamin, *Arcades*, 532.
544 Ibid., 432.
545 Hannah Arendt, *Men in Dark Times* (New York: Harcourt, Brace & World, 1969), 173.
546 Benjamin, *Arcades*, 406.
547 Wigley, "Whatever Happened to Total Design?," 1–8.

areas of life; he observes that the apparently contradictory dynamics of implosion and explosion often merge with one another, as he revisits the modernist total work of art, a notion characterized by the dissolution of the interior and the exterior, a kind of dematerialization that was proper to modernist architecture. For Wigley, the intersection and fusion of these two opposing dynamics results in a "hyper-interior"—a hypertrophied interior at the point of explosion. Yet this detonation signals not destruction of the interior but its expansion—and by extension that of design—to the street, the city, and the planet. These "pulsating rhythms" of explosion and implosion give rise to a new conception of the cross-contamination between skills and disciplines that the total work of art both invited and feared as it sought to unify arts and space. Design offers an alternative resolution to the explosive model of total architecture, implementing its own strategy of expansion that does away with the pretence of unity and overtly pursues domination. However, the expansionist model of design shares little with "total architecture" or "total design" as they were conceived by Gropius: the fantasy of control and omnipotence implied by these ideas bears little resemblance to the fragmentary and protean nature of design. While the total work of art was succeeded by the total work tout court, and later, total architecture and the synthesis of the arts, design has continued its dynamic evolution, and has regularly sought to place itself at the head of a new hierarchical order.

Conclusion

Design—An Offensive Discipline or a Discipline on the Offensive?

This book attempts to confront head-on the fundamental ambiguity in the unintentional creation of the history of design. The titular accident refers to the process through which 1936 (*Pioneers of the Modern Movement*) and 1948 (*Mechanization Takes Command*) came to be the founding years for the history of design, despite the fact that neither Nikolaus Pevsner nor Sigfried Giedion had such an undertaking in mind. As a result, the history of design found itself in a singular situation: not only was it linked to the history of architecture, it was created by historians who, unaware of the foundational role of their texts for design, had no intention of shaping it. Under such circumstances, is it possible to discuss the history of design, or even a discipline of design? As I have attempted to show, this origin, although accidental, had a decisive effect on design and its history that saw both defined according to modernist principles of functionalism and morality that had been put forward by Pevsner and Giedion. However, these perspectives—partial, biased, and, perhaps most importantly, originating not from design itself but from adjacent disciplines—cannot on their own offer a sufficient basis for the history of design.

Examining the texts of Pevsner and Giedion together in order to study them in a new light therefore represents an unprecedented undertaking in the field of design historiography. My analysis reveals that, despite their many differences, these two texts ultimately both promoted architecture and the values of the Modern Movement. Beyond this somewhat obvious fact, reconsidering history through these two works makes possible a dual portrait of design's origins, one that shows the extent to which functionalism was an aspect of design used to political ends: first by American women such as Catharine Beecher, who used domestic engineering to promote the abolition of slavery, and later in Britain by William Morris in his tireless combat against the more nefarious consequences of industrialization—though his target was by no means industrialization tout court, as I discuss in part 2, "Design Histories."

Having established this political dimension—and without seeking to align my inquiry with either Giedion or Pevsner—I then looked for contradictions in historical events that have gone unnoticed or unchallenged in order to enrich the present analysis. For example, Morris's status as a pioneer was regularly questioned, not least by Pevsner, because of his rejection of the machine; a closer examination of his writings, however, shows that he proposed not to abolish the machine but rather to ensure that it was wholly subject to man and his needs. A similar conclusion can be drawn from a reexamination of the Bauhaus: the agreement of Henry van de Velde and Walter Gropius as to the role of the artist and the famous 1914 rift between Van de Velde and Hermann Muthesius—an episode well known to architecture historians but consistently absent from histories of design—demonstrate an equally nuanced attitude toward the machine. Returning to this event also makes possible an alternative definition of the designer, and furthermore reveals a number of contradictions present in the Bauhaus. Far from being a purely functionalist entity, in its early years the school was in fact the site of an ongoing exchange between expressionism, experimentation, and industrialization. While acknowledging the important exchange between modern architecture and modern design in their creation of a common aesthetic language, by returning to the origins of the history of design and its pivotal moments, I have sought to achieve a vital critical distance from conventional histories.

Associated with architecture to the point of dependence until the end of the 1950s, design continued to be seen in modernist terms; this was largely due to Edgar Kaufmann Jr.'s activity around Good Design in the United States and the notion of *formes utiles* promoted by the Union des Artistes Modernes in France. However, with the crisis of the Modern Movement and the rise of mass consumption, the history of design began to deviate from its founding models and move toward the anti-functionalist position of Asger Jorn and the MIBI, which opposed the Ulmian "neo-Bauhaus." In Reyner Banham, and particularly his *Theory and Design in the First Machine Age*, Pevsner's historical project found a mediator able to skillfully contextualize the history of architecture by identifying its various "zones of silence"; the history of design, which was of little interest to historians until the 1980s, has yet to find its Banham. While designers' manifestos abound, there are few essays that question the foundations of design without repeating theories that echo its modernist origins.

The young Joe Colombo, who at this point was still a painter, met Jorn in what was to be a decisive encounter not only for his career as a designer, but for design as a discipline. This meeting encouraged him to dismantle the modernist interdependence between form and function and to challenge functionalism's reductive view of individual needs and the normative industrial means it offered to satisfy them. The seminal moment in the transformation of design came in 1969 with Colombo's antidesign manifesto; on paper at least, antidesign was nothing less than revolutionary. In the following years, an opposition developed between Colombo's antidesign and radical architecture's controdesign: Colombo rejected the production of objects in favor of the production of space, while the radicals sought to resuscitate what they saw as their dead or dying discipline through unique or limited-edition furniture.

It was a peculiar situation that consisted of two parallel yet opposite movements: as designers attempted to annex territory that had historically belonged to architecture, architects sought to appropriate that of design. The radicals defined themselves in opposition to the ideologies of their modern predecessors; yet their incursion into the field of design unwittingly reinforced the decidedly modernist notion that design was merely a component part of architecture. Antidesign meanwhile adopted the unique vocabulary of the capsule in order to give form to the autonomy it sought to establish. The capsule, whose production was made possible through the homogeneity of plastic materials, represented much more than an aesthetic choice. With the worldwide television broadcast of the moon landing in July 1969, the space capsule loomed large in the global imagination. Colombo used the capsule as both a metaphor and a model to assert design's autonomy and supremacy. It was a form well suited to embody and incorporate the diverse possibilities offered by antidesign. Above all, antidesign effected a break that made a reevaluation of design possible. Colombo's living capsule held a symbolic content and an ideological charge that would prove to be decisive for the history of design; it can be considered a manifesto, and an expression of the disciplinary autonomy to which he aspired. Reconsidering design in all its diversity through the metaphor of the capsule realizes the break that Colombo sought to achieve, particularly as it makes possible a historiographical and territorial reevaluation of the history of design.

The capsule facilitates a rereading of the history of design and its often conflicting relationships to other disciplines, with regard to domestic space. Colombo aimed to monopolize a number of territories and to extend design's reach to include urbanism through an expansionist dynamic that was at once an affirmation of design's status as a discipline and a response to the crisis of architecture. Although Colombo never referenced the notion of the total work, it is impossible to avoid considering its ramifications for antidesign. Starting with Novalis, the idea of the total work developed according to a double principle of expansion and contraction, to borrow Mark Wigley's terms. It relied on the inseparability of the detail and the totality, in other words the inseparability of the everyday object and the environment. By reducing the relationship between disciplines to one of scale, the total work provided a useful model for architecture, wherein the object assumed the role occupied by the fragment in literature. This approach allowed modern architects to treat furniture as a "concentrate of architecture" and the radicals to consider it in terms of an "architectural copula."[548]

Yet thanks to the complexity of its origins, antidesign was able to escape from the constraints imposed by architecture and art to provide a new axis for the history of design. Antidesign's characteristic expansionism means that it is apt to shed light on previous events and episodes in design history and facilitate the study of their consequences through to the present day. But more than simply offering a means of rereading history, design's expansionist movements actively influenced the course of the history of modern architecture, as design sought to prove that it too was capable of acting as a paradigm for the home.

Starting in 1849, with its first appearance in Sir Henry Cole and Richard Redgrave's *Journal of Design and Manufactures*, design's propagation of its own discourse has been of central importance for the discipline. Morris, in turn, believed that the environment could be transformed

548 Branzi, "La sedia come modello ideologico," in *Scritti teoretici*, 67 (see note 30).

through everyday objects; while in the twentieth century, Raymond Loewy later expanded to the industrial designer's terrain to include everything from lipstick to locomotives,[549] which later reappeared in the 1950s as the now ubiquitous refrain—sometimes attributed to Ernesto Nathan Rogers—calling for an expansion from the spoon to the city. Together, these instances form a set of precedents for antidesign, and constitute a history of design articulated around the question of expansion and a spatialization of design that sought to assert its disciplinary autonomy.

It is of course possible to object that antidesign would fall short of its aspirations, like Streamline before it, yet its failure was far from total: despite the ongoing struggle for disciplinary recognition, design's history shows that it often favored a strategy of dissimulation in order to pursue its expansionist program through a "hyper-interior" that dismantled and circumvented the supposed unity of the total work of art and its various formulations. Recalling Vilém Flusser's Trojan horse, antidesign, and by extension design itself, used subterfuge to storm the strongholds of architecture and fine art. Design's invasive dimension had already been alluded to by Morris and the designers of the Streamline movement, and so can offer a lens through which to reconsider the history design even before Colombo would theorize and formalize this expansionism through antidesign.

The objectives entailed by the pursuit of the totality vary according to the different movements and actors. Architects would evoke notions of unity and collaboration while making reference to the total work of art, the total work, and the synthesis of the arts in order to legitimize their action; designers, meanwhile, would hide their expansionist

549 Loewy, "Designer of Locomotives and Lipsticks," 144 (see note 426).

program behind functionalist discourses. Ultimately, both disciplines would attempt to hide an equally ardent desire for supremacy.

Design's expansionism, which differs in the ways outlined above from the total architecture and total design advanced by Gropius, is motivated by a desire for control and omnipotence belied by its fragmented and protean nature. While the total work of art gave way to its successive variants, design continued to develop and extend its conquest to encompass new territories; Norman Bel Geddes's "Futurama" offers a particularly telling example of this dynamic. By deploying the Trojan horse strategy discussed above, design managed to impose itself at the head of a new hierarchical order and to transform the relationship between knowledge and skills and the different disciplines, a shift architecture had previously attempted by looking to unify the arts of space. Yet design succeeded where architecture had failed, thanks to its ability to expand from the interior to the street and beyond, as Walter Benjamin described, to pursue a continuous and limitless expansion. In the turbulent environment of the 1960s, which saw dramatic shifts in the relationship between architecture and design, Colombo's antidesign became the singular embodiment of this tendency.

The 1980s saw the rise of the neo-avant-garde and the pragmatism that was characteristic of postmodern design, with the critical territory of the design field coming to be occupied by the human sciences. Yet designers never relinquished their total control over the home environment, which was further reinforced with the advent of Existenzmaximum. Combining Pevsner and Giedion's narratives allows for a better understand the richness, the diversity, and the importance of their model, despite the flaws linked to the disciplinary positions of the two authors.

This exercise necessarily leads to an analysis of the ways in which design's history has been written, as well as an interrogation of the legitimacy of the historiography of design as it exists today. However, I am less concerned here with challenging the construction and transmission of design history than with the detection of its potentially productive flaws and contradictions. Design and its history are more often associated with the history of architecture than the history of art—even despite the dialogue that has seen design seek to expand and renew art by reconnecting it with humanity since the time of Morris. However, with the emergence of a new generation working under the banners of "design art" and "critical design," the simplistic relation between art and design, and between function and content, has begun to shift.

British critic Alex Coles had discussed design art as an emergent movement following from twentieth-century Pop and Minimalism.[550] As a hybrid practice that places it at the frontier between art and design, design art interrogates the principles of form and function and the relationship between art and everyday life. A number of artists, including Angela Bulloch, Jorge Pardo, Liam Gillick, Andrea Zittel, and Joe Scanlan have used design as a starting point for the development of critical tools and perspectives that form part of the contemporary art landscape. While the exploitation of various disciplinary fields is certainly nothing new—it was in 1986 that Dan Graham remarked that "the relationship between art and architecture is a cliché"[551]—these exchanges have resulted in a significant interest in design among contemporary artists. The origin

550 See Alex Coles, *DesignArt: On Art's Romance with Design* (London: Tate Publishing, 2005); and Alex Coles, ed., *Design and Art*, Documents of Contemporary Art (Cambridge, MA: MIT Press, 2007).

551 Dan Graham, "Kunst als Design/Design als Kunst," *Museumjournaal*, nos. 3–4 (1986): 183–95.

of design and its potential disciplinary autonomy remain delicate subjects, while almost all attempts to consider the relationship between art and architecture have tended so far to degenerate into the rejection of certain codes as functionalist and therefore incompatible with art, and others as decorative and therefore incompatible with architecture.[552] This duality demonstrates the importance and the influence of the two disciplines that have historically been involved in the formation and articulation of design. A veritable maelstrom, this situation has given rise to countless simplistic, reductive, and inaccurate definitions of design. It is still regularly presented through the prism of the respective visions of artists or architects, with each discipline deploying the terms as it sees fit. Though design draws on these strange exchanges between architecture and fine art, it has been able to produce its own discourses and lines of inquiry and to define the conditions for its own existence. However, it has yet to fully extricate itself from the authoritarian grasp of art and architecture, fields that remain in some respects highly averse to admitting that it might be capable of existing as an independent discipline. To fully appreciate the difficulties faced by design as it seeks to gain recognition for the uniqueness of the designer's oeuvre and earn its place in museum exhibitions and collections, an important distinction must be made between design and design art. Design art employs the functional symbolism of industrial design, while its practitioners seek to blur the lines between art and design by incorporating functionality and use value into their work. "Against Design," a 2001 exhibition held at the Institute of

552 See Donald Judd, *Möbel/Furniture* (Zurich: Arche, 1985); republished as "On Furniture," in *Donald Judd: Complete Writings 1975–1986* (Eindhoven: Van Abbemuseum, 1987), 107–8. See also Judd's essay "It's Hard to Find a Good Lamp" (1993), in Coles, *Design and Art*; and *Parachute*, nos. 117 and 118 (2005).

Contemporary Art in Philadelphia, marked the beginning of the design art movement, with the curators explaining the current in the following terms:

> Mid-century designers believed standardized design constituted a utopian ideal, providing affordable, accessible, and functional objects that were also based on principles of good design [...] the artists in "Against Design" are different: they seek to establish individual responses to an environment, rejecting the notion that a utopia must mean the same perfect world for everyone.[553]

This affirmation seems to suggest that the consequences of the collapse of the Modern Movement were not harnessed by designers but rather by the artists of the 2000s, and other proponents of design art would go on to make similar claims. Yet in doing so, they betrayed the limitations of their knowledge of design and its history. Here it is worth considering Angela Bulloch's response to Donald Judd's famous 1986 text "On Furniture." Judd insisted on the gap separating art and design:

> Eighteen years ago someone asked me to design a coffee table. I thought that a work of mine which was essentially a rectangular volume with the upper surface recessed could be altered. This debased the work and produced a bad coffee table which I later threw away. The configuration and the scale of art cannot be transposed into furniture and architecture.[554]

553 Steven Beyer, ed., *Against Design* (Philadelphia: Institute of Contemporary Art, 2001), 9.
554 Judd, "On Furniture," in *Complete Writings*, 107.

In the name of total artistic freedom, Bulloch responded by insisting on the validity of transposition:

> When Donald Judd was making furniture he would always say something like, a chair is not a sculpture, because you cannot see it when you sit in it.
> So its functional value stops it from being an art object—but I think that is nonsense![555]

Similarly, Atelier Van Lieshout plays upon a refusal to differentiate between design and artwork by appropriating elements that have historically characterized the former, such as the multiple, the anonymous work, price, use, function, the catalogue, and the range. Some artists continue to play with or stake a claim to functionality, while others explore the industrial production and diffusion of their work or seek to renew the links between art and everyday life. Designers such as Noam Toran, Auger-Loizeau, the duo Dunne & Raby, or even "ex-designer" Martí Guixé, insist on the uniqueness of their individual oeuvres, their rightful place in museum exhibitions and collections, at the same time as they celebrate the nonfunctionality of their work and its ability to initiate speculative or critical discourse. In this sense, they continue to push for the maximal amplification and expansion of design.

With the multiplication of such crossovers and the accelerating cultural legitimacy of design, it is important to oppose unilateral and reductive definitions of design by emphasizing the dialectical tensions raised within the field: between functionalism and the objective neutrality of function on one hand, and decorative function and subjective, emotional, and imaginative function on the other;

555 Angela Bulloch, *Satellite* (Zurich: Museum für Gegenwartskunst, 1998), 12.

between use value and symbolic and poetic function. Design's recent rise in prominence cannot mask its often piecemeal and paradoxical nature, nor the fact that it remains limited for the most part to the production of objects, and furniture in particular. However, as I have outlined, if we are to offer a characterization of design, we must do so in terms of its expansionist, protean nature and its continuous extension of its field of operation.

As the cartography of art and design has been redrawn in recent years, some have seen in the practice of sampling the end of disciplinary boundaries.[556] Design, which has long been presented through the prism of art or architecture, upended the hierarchy to assert its position as the discipline capable of accommodating all others. A buoyant design has continued to expand the limits of its territory and sought to annex art and architecture. By reversing the long-term process of appropriation in order to absorb other disciplines, it has attempted to assert its autonomy and its ability to reconfigure everything from the culture of the object to that of urbanism. The production of consumer goods that was long its territory has been subsumed into an infinitely larger spatial configuration whose reach extends everywhere and to everything.

556 Ramakers, *Design etc*, n.p. (see note 512).

A

B

C

N

O

P

R

S

T

Acknowledgments

I would like to express my gratitude to Caroline Schneider and her fantastic team, and especially to Tatjana Günthner and Zoë Harris.

For their kind support, I would like to thank Jean-Pierre Greff, director of HEAD – Genève, Professor Pascal Rousseau at Université Paris I Panthéon-Sorbonne, as well as Mathieu Bassée and Cristina Ricupero.

And not least, I am dearly endebted for their kind words and sisterhood to both Paola Antonelli and Michelle Millar Fisher. And lastly, to the always supportive Dan Graham.

Alexandra Midal
Design by Accident:
For a New History of Design

This translation of Alexandra Midal's doctoral thesis "Design par accident: Pour une nouvelle histoire du design" was supported by HEAD – Genève, with additional support from Histoire d'art at University of Paris 1 Panthéon-Sorbonne.

—HEAD
Genève

UNIVERSITÉ PARIS 1
PANTHÉON SORBONNE

Published by Sternberg Press

Translation: James Horton
Copyeditor: Hannah Gregory
Proofreading: Zoë Harris
Design: Haller Brun
Printing: Tallinn Book Printers

ISBN 978-3-95679-143-7

First published 2019, reprinted 2023

Distributed by The MIT Press, Art Data, Idea Books and Les presses du réel

Sternberg Press
71–75 Shelton Street
London WC2H 9JQ
sternberg-press.com